FLIES

for the

Greater Yellowstone Area

FLIES
for the Greater Yellowstone Area

BRUCE STAPLES

HeadWater
Books

STACKPOLE
BOOKS

Published by
STACKPOLE BOOKS
5067 Ritter Road
Mechanicsburg, PA 17055
www.stackpolebooks.com

Printed in the United States of America

First edition

10 9 8 7 6 5 4 3 2 1

Library of Congress Cataloging-in-Publication Data

Staples, Bruce.
    Flies for greater Yellowstone area / Bruce Staples. — First
edition.
        pages cm
    Includes bibliographical references and index.
    ISBN 978-0-8117-0188-4 (pbk.) — ISBN 0-8117-0188-3
(pbk.) 1. Flies, Artificial—Yellowstone National Park
Region. I. Title.
SH451.S667 2014
799.12'40978   2013027745

To Carol,
who has endured my fly-fishing obsession for many years.

Contents

Preface

I appreciate the fly tiers contributing to this book. Each is recognized within the drafts of the patterns they offered. Many exhibited unusual generosity, especially Doug Andres, Kelly Galloup, Bob Jacklin, Buddy Knight, Bucky McCormick, Doug McKnight, Dean Reiner, Al Ritt, Mike Snody, Rick Takahashi, Walter Weise, and Chris Williams.

I must give special thanks to those tiers who sent flies from afar: Doug Andres, Al and Gretchen Beatty, Ken Burkholder, Ben Byng, Jerry Criss, Ron English, Russ Forney, Don Heyden, John Hudgens, Misako Ishimura, Bob Jacklin, Frank Johnson, Merne Judson, Doug Korn, Wayne Luallen, Kuni Masuda, John Newbury, Marvin Nolte, Steve Potter, Al Ritt, Michael Snody, Rick Takahashi, Tim Tollett, Joni Tomich, Scott Urbanski, Tim Wade, John Way, Hans Weilenmann, and Chris Williams.

Thanks go to Boots Allen, Johnny Boyd, Dave Brackett, Paul Bruun, Howard Cole, Jack Dennis, Jimmy Gabettas, Mike Lawson, Criag Mathews, and Gerry "Randy" Randolph for suggesting tiers to contact.

Not being completely knowledgeable about all technical aspects that result in a quality fishery, I must thank Jay Buchner and Dr. Harley Reno for filling in the voids.

Working with Jay Nichols to produce this book was a pleasure. Jay knows what literature will be well received in the fly-fishing industry like very few persons I have encountered. His perfectionism gave me a few trying times, but I know that through his guidance, my efforts were refined into an excellent product. Amy Lerner and Brittany Stoner polished the draft to a finished book.

I offer thanks here, as I should have done in one of my earlier books, to those persons who brought me along the fly-fishing road and on to being a fly-fishing author. I have a debt of gratitude to these folks.

Satoshi "Stan" Yamamura shamed me away from bait fishing and into fly fishing in the early 1970s. A few years later Stan convinced me that fly tying would make me a better fly fisher. I never looked back. First came the obsession to catch the most and the biggest fish on my flies, and to find the best waters in which to do it. Enjoying discovery, I explored Yellowstone Park waters mostly on my own. Bud Lilly and Pat Barnes revealed to me the vast southwestern Montana fishery. Rulon Davis directed me to Yellowstone Park's Fall River Basin. Harry Brinkley took me to the South Fork reach of the Snake River. René Harrop and Mike Lawson directed me to the then Railroad Ranch reach and other choice locations on the Henry's Fork. Udell Leavitt revealed the best in western Wyoming borderland waters. Doug Gibson revealed hidden gems of the Henry's Fork drainage.

Red Rock Pass separates the Henry's Fork drainage from Red Rock–Beaverhead drainage.

Yellowstone Park's Obsidian Creek offers fast light tackle fishing.

Through all these introductions, I became aware that these waters should be protected. Doctor Jim McCue nurtured that through founding the Snake River Cutthroats. So I explored the Greater Yellowstone waters with enthusiasm and growing reverence. Yes, I came to have favorite waters, but I wanted to see and fish in as many places as possible. In doing so, I began to want the most and biggest fish less, and to appreciate the Yellowstone locations more. That appreciation, nurtured by Bob Jacklin's reverence for the history of regional fly fishing, remains with me to this day. Certainly, Bob and I are not alone. For Boots Allen, Mike Lawson, and many others, the same appreciation runs deep. By the mid-1980s, I had fished a good portion of Greater Yellowstone waters.

I began attending various fly-fishing events at the urging of Dennis Bitton, Buck Goodrich, and Ralph Moon. Darwin Atkin convinced me to share my fly-tying skills with others. Doing so, I met renowned persons, including Gary Borger and Gary LaFontaine. After discussing my fly-fishing experiences with them, both suggested I write about them. So by the 1980s I began with magazine articles. Gary Borger revealed to me how to approach publishers when book ideas came. Frank Amato accepted my first three book offerings, and I take satisfaction that

the first, *Snake River Country Flies and Waters,* began the revelation of eastern Idaho waters to the fly-fishing world. After it came several publications on these waters from other authors. Next from Amato Publications came the *Yellowstone Park (River Journal)* and finally *Trout Country Flies.*

Friends—including Boots Allen, Al and Gretchen Beatty, Charlie Hune, Ken Retallic, Nate Schweber, Rick Talkahashi and Jerry Hubka, Tony Lolli, and Greg Thomas—asked me to contribute to books they were authoring. These activities opened another fly-fishing door for me. I came to increasingly enjoy meeting and discussing fly-fishing and fly-tying techniques with other enthusiasts. From Jimmy Gabettas came the opportunity to sustain this by being part of his superb full-service fly shop, All Seasons Angler in Idaho Falls. So doing much of this book was more fun than work. Through these encounters, I saw that so many enthusiasts wish to give back to fly fishing. I honor them for such. I hope having these folks as part of *Flies for the Greater Yellowstone Area* gives them some recognition. My only regret is that I did not have time to meet more fly tiers who could have had a place in this book.

A Word to Tiers

All fly patterns within this book have proven effective in the Greater Yellowstone Area, some at certain places, others for certain events or specific times of the season. Some are effective under all these conditions. There are countless other fly patterns that are useful, but it is beyond the scope of this or any work to capture them all. Doing so would be impossible because new patterns roll off the vises of area tiers continuously, and some tiers remain secretive about their successful patterns. With respect to each pattern discussed, either the originator or the tier recommends the materials given. In many cases a certain product is identified. This is particularly so with hooks and with tying threads. There are equivalents by other manufacturers that are just as effective. There may be situations where only an alternative product is available, so go with that product. Some tying technique descriptions given here could be given in greater detail, but space does not allow more. In some cases it is possible to contact the contributing tier for more details. You can also find more information online. Use your Internet search engine to find sites associated with tier names or with the pattern of interest.

As you read the fly recipes in this book, note the term "color to match natural." The tier that recommends this is observant, has broad experience in presenting the subject pattern, and understands that its effectiveness is best when this change is made. "Polychromatic" is the term that describes this property, and such is the case with many mayfly and midge species. The Pale Morning Dun color variation in adults from drainage to drainage comes to mind. Some terrestrial insects, particularly grasshoppers, seasonably change color to match that of hosting habitat.

There are cases within this book where the tier gives no recommendation for a specific product. Instead, he or she might suggest "olive dubbing" or "yellow yarn." This opens the door for variation, the action all fly tiers enjoy. Come to mention it, isn't this a reason why we have so many patterns? Think of how much less interesting fly tying would be if there were a standard by which we would have to adhere. Of course a standard is necessary in keeping certain types of flies alive. Dressing traditional Catskill patterns, Rangeley streamers, Atlantic salmon flies, or woven Pott or Grant flies are examples. Thus if you believe that fishing success comes from tying a fly to the letter of the law, tie them as given, but then apply

Chesterfield Reservoir offers a bleak countryside but hefty rainbows. PHOTO COURTESY OF DAVE PACE.

Yellowstone cutts in Henry's Lake can become large and robust.

your ideas to make variations. That brings another joy in fly tying: seeing your variations catch fish. Fly tiers have been varying their fly patterns for centuries, and the fish don't seem to care. All you have to do is present the products of your efforts in the right manner. That remains the most important aspect in achieving fly-fishing success.

Here's a word of caution to fly fishers venturing to waters in Yellowstone National Park. Only single barbless hooked flies are legal here. Any use of lead on flies (and leaders and lines) is also illegal. A barbless hook regulation applies on many waters within other parts of the Greater Yellowstone Area. Nonlead regulations are also increasing. Check current Idaho, Montana, and Wyoming fishing regulations to determine these. Tungsten has nearly 90 percent the density of lead, and tying components fashioned from it are a legal way around the lead restriction. I note that fly fishers, myself included, have caught fish for decades on single-hooked and lead-free flies. So if any of the patterns discussed here fashioned with lead and/or more than one hook take your fancy, make alterations on them for use in the park or other so restricted regional waters.

Introduction

The presence of a high-quality sport fishery is the basis for an extensive fly-fishing culture. Within any such culture a fly-tying tradition develops. The more extensive the culture, the more detailed and creative its fly-tying tradition becomes. Such is the case in the Greater Yellowstone Area, where this synergism began in the late nineteenth century.

How does one define the region known as the Greater Yellowstone Area, at least from an angling standpoint? Certainly many opinions exist on its extent, but no one disputes that Yellowstone National Park is the center of the region. No need here to review the quality of coldwater fisheries within the park, but adjacent fisheries and waters have, in many cases, equivalent quality. Some

The Salt Fork reach of the Snake River in Swan Valley, Idaho.

Big Lost River below MacKay, Idaho.

have sources within the park that then, like spokes in a wheel, radiate outward. In fact, the further you travel from the park boundaries down these drainages, the more you can observe man-made alterations that make these coldwater fisheries less productive. So here is my definition of the Greater Yellowstone Area for the purpose of this book: included is eastern Idaho above the Bear River drainage, the Montana counties bordering the park, plus Beaverhead and Madison Counties, and northwestern Wyoming. Demographically that includes about fifty thousand square miles hosting a human population of less than half a million. Half of that population resides in eastern Idaho's portion of the area, but that portion hosts a fly-tying tradition second to none with respect to the number of adherents and renowned personalities.

Significant degradation of waters came later in time to the Greater Yellowstone Area than to other coldwater fisheries in this country. In the beginning, these degradations were not as extensive as those that came earlier to the waters of the Northeast, West Coast states, and Upper

Midwest. Nevertheless, the growth of some metropolitan areas, agriculture, logging, mining, and animal husbandry combined with scant rainfall ensured that water degradation would occur in all parts west of the Rocky Mountains. For example, the fisheries along Utah's Wasatch Front, Colorado's Front Range of the Rocky Mountains, and across the Continental Divide in the Colorado River drainage and the West Coast states were impacted. The degradation did not extend in depth to the Greater Yellowstone Area because the human population there remained relatively sparse and fewer profitable natural resources were present. Thus the coldwater habitat here is far less degraded than in other places in the country, and through growing conservation efforts and responsible husbandry, a natural coldwater fishery exists here that has no equal in the United States. Arguably it never has had an equal, although major changes have taken place within it.

Though the degradation of these waters continues through irrigation, grazing, and forestry practices, in recent decades the regional sustenance subculture has declined and multiple use of waters has included the value of sport fisheries as part of the regional economic mix. For example, fly fishing on Idaho's South Fork reach of the Snake River (the reach below Palisades Dam to the Henry's Fork confluence) brings tens of millions of dollars each year to the local economy. Knowing its economic value, Montana protects the Madison River fishery as if it were a dependent child.

Increasingly, efforts to protect water quality and habitat are coming from state and local government agencies as well as the sportfishing community, as the realization emerges that the area's most valuable natural resource is the high-quality water so much in demand in metropolitan areas across the country. Such actions and attitudes help ensure that the regional fly-fishing and fly-tying tradition will be preserved.

Because of degradation and also the introduction of exotic salmonids, populations of native salmonids—grayling, whitefish, and various strains of cutthroat trout—have diminished. But now a flourishing and naturally reproducing population of brook, brown, lake, and

rainbow trout exists. These were introduced late in the nineteenth century through the political influence of eastern states fly fishers.

Efforts to revive the native salmonid populations are increasing throughout the area. Westslope cutthroat and grayling are being reintroduced into several Montana waters. In eastern Idaho, anglers are encouraged to kill rainbow trout in the South Fork reach of the Snake River in an effort to limit hybridization with cutthroat trout. This policy, although not entirely socially accepted, is meant to preserve Yellowstone and Snake River fine-spotted cutthroat in one of their remaining strongholds.

The fly-tying tradition built because of the Greater Yellowstone salmonid population and quality waters is mainly a twentieth-century phenomenon. Certainly there were nineteenth-century tiers here, but little documentation remains of their activity. One account, George Grant's identification of "Tamarack," describes an obscure character from the eastern states thought to have tied flies while visiting area waters late in the nineteenth century. In the early years of the twentieth century came the rudiments of an emerging fly-tying culture, including

A large Yellowstone cutt foraging the bank.

Carter Harrison's Trude patterns from eastern Idaho's Island Park region and those of Wilbur "Bugs" Beatty, Montana's Jack Boehme, Norman Means, and Franz Pott. As the century progressed, influence came from other tying cultures such as the eastern states and the British Isles. But fly tiers living within the Greater Yellowstone Area would create patterns using materials from native wildlife, inspired by resident aquatic and terrestrial life-forms consumed by salmonids, and dictated by regional stream and stillwater characteristics. Today, with a human population closing in on five hundred thousand, a disproportionate number of accomplished fly tiers reside within the Greater Yellowstone Area. Increasingly, enthusiasts from around the world look to these tiers for creativity in technique or material usages.

With the Greater Yellowstone Area native tying culture in relative infancy, creations from renowned tiers visiting from other regions gained media attention by the fourth decade of the twentieth century. The contributions of Dan Bailey, Ray Bergman, Joe Brooks, and Don Martinez were among the first of these. Don is widely credited with bringing a dry fly-tying and -fishing philosophy to the region. Ray's book *Trout* was the first to describe in detail experiences fishing in Yellowstone National Park and nearby waters in an age when fishing these waters first became affordable for the middle-class angler. E. R. Hewitt's earlier book described fishing in

The author with a spring creek rainbow that is close to thirty inches.

these waters only when it was affordable, because of the cost of travel, for the well-heeled angler.

Dan and Ray could credit much of their experience to the generosity and knowledge of Scotty Chapman, Yellowstone Park's premier fly-fishing and fly-tying ranger. Almost lost through the passage of time and the whims of the fly-fishing public is the fact that Scotty Chapman was the first prolific tier of flies specifically meant for Yellowstone Park waters. Both Dan and Don would stay in the region. So would Bob Carmichael and Leonard "Boots" Allen, whose son Joe and grandson Joseph "Boots" would be numbered among the native tiers. Later came such as Roy Donnelly, Merton Parks, Ernie Schwiebert, Al Troth, Dave Whitlock, and Stan Yamamura. All would promote waters of the region in the media and create fly patterns for fishing it.

As the century progressed into its last quarter, these fly tiers were followed by Jay and Kathy Buchner, Howard Cole, Bob Jacklin, John Juracek, Gary LaFontaine, Craig Mathews, and Scott Sanchez. Most recently Joseph "Boots" Allen, Kelly Galloup, Bucky McCormick, Rowan Nyman, and Arrick Swanson have become part of the culture. True, many of these tiers made or make their living from these waters, but all are their stalwart protectors. Around midcentury, native tiers began gaining media recognition. Pat and Sig Barnes and Marcella Oswald were among the first. Later came Joe Allen, Jack Dennis, and Bing Lempke. But the revolution generated by Doug Swisher and Carl Richards's *Selective Trout* did the most to bring native tiers to the forefront as well as focus attention on producing fly patterns for specific life-cycle stages of aquatic insects. This work, so complete and specific, brought capabilities of such native tiers as Doug Gibson, the Harrops, Mike Lawson, and Doug and Maryanne Siepert into national attention.

From many of these tiers came the use of materials in unique and elegant ways. Examples include the introduction of the House of Harrop (HOH) method in forming wings on no-hackle flies as well as creative uses of cul de canard (CDC), biots from various sources, and turkey flats. Weaving techniques introduced by George Grant, Franz Pott, and Della Sivey would be modified by other regional tiers. Joe Ayre, for example, showed that materials other than yarn, monofilament, chenille, and floss could be woven. Joe demonstrated beautiful weaves with wire and tubing. Charlie Brooks was a pioneer in the use of certain yarns. Gary LaFontaine first featured extensive use of trilobal yarns. John Juracek and Craig Mathews—as well as tiers his Blue Ribbon Flies employed—have made significant contribution to the use of synthetic materials including the immensely popular Z-Lon. Craig also was the first to promote cul de canard to American fly tiers. The international fly-tying community now uses

Yellowstone Park's Duck Creek hosts large brook, brown, and rainbow trout.

many of these materials. Though they are not tiers in the commercial sense, Dan Bailey, Bob Carmichael, Jimmy Gabettas, Will Godfrey, and Bud Lilly became superb judges of tying talent. Many tiers in the region owe their renown to the generosity of men such as these.

All those persons named above make up only the marquee names in the Greater Yellowstone fly-tying tradition. Hundreds of other tiers, not as well known, make significant contributions. Tiers visiting the region become inspired to create flies because of their experiences fishing here. Ray Bergman and his Firehole pattern is a great example of this reaction. Some tie professionally; others, like the bulk of tiers everywhere, tie for the joy of it. You will see examples from the works of native, transplanted, and visiting fly tiers in the following pages. You will also see valuable "where, when, and how to use" information for many of the patterns addressed. That many flies described here come from visiting tiers is

testimony to the quality of regional fishery. Rest assured that economic situations permitting, many of these tiers would relocate to this region in a heartbeat.

Why the above discussion of the waters within the Greater Yellowstone Area and fly tiers, contemporary and historical, in a work devoted to fly tying? Simply because the presence of the extensive and high-quality coldwater fishery and the efforts that support and preserve it are the basis for the rich regional fly-tying culture. If those waters were taken away, or if they never existed, most likely that culture would not be present. Appreciation of these waters is widespread in the area. It has inspired major celebrations including the Henry's Fork Foundation's Henry's Fork Day at Last Chance, Idaho, since 1985; the fabled Jackson Hole One Fly Event taking place each September since 1986; the East Idaho Fly-Tying/Fly-Fishing Expo situated in Idaho Falls, Idaho, since 1994; and the Madison River Festival since 2003 in Ennis, Montana.

Looking southwest from Henry's Lake in October.

Proceeds from each of these go to generate grant funding for the preservation of regional coldwater fisheries and their habitat.

Fly fishers are always seeking new fly patterns having potential or proven effectiveness. With respect to new patterns for inland salmonid fisheries, the fly-fishing world now focuses on what is created in the Greater Yellowstone Area. Over the years there have been several superb books that describe flies originating in this region. But with each passing year, new patterns roll out of the vises of Greater Yellowstone fly tiers. The bulk of these, many eminently worthy because of being effective and/or innovative, have yet to reach fly-fishing media on a broad scale. I therefore believed that a work to update fly fishers about the fly patterns recently created in the Greater Yellowstone Area would have an eager audience. Thus Jay Nichols and I produced this book.

How did I select the flies addressed in the following pages out of surely thousands of worthy candidates originating in the Greater Yellowstone Area? First I concentrated on patterns introduced in the last decade. I knew that fly fishers would want to know which patterns would be the most effective for regional waters. I knew that fly tiers would likewise be interested in effective flies, but also interested in innovative uses and techniques. Thus, I looked for those introduced in the last several years that have proven effective here, meaning that fly fishers coming to the region should consider choosing these for fishing certain waters and certain times of the season.

Included in these effective flies, I offer those that use new as well as proven tying techniques and have effective and innovative use of materials: new and old, native and exotic, familiar and unfamiliar. I chose certain pat-

A misty spring creek morning. PHOTO COURTESY OF KELLY GLISSMEYER.

terns because they represent life-forms unique to the region or to certain waters within. Complexity in fly patterns does not always result in effectiveness, so within this book you will find easily tied patterns as well as those more difficult to tie.

Even though certain fly patterns may be "out of style," they remain effective. Therefore, I chose a few effective patterns of renown from the past created by beloved, famed, or innovative contributors. These older creations still populate the fly bins of regional fly-fishing retailers. Every fly fisher coming to the region should consider these as well as newer patterns for fishing certain waters.

Effective fly patterns coming from commercial, noncommercial, and visiting tiers give evidence of how widespread appreciation for the Greater Yellowstone coldwater fishery is. Note also the broad spectrum of contributing tiers throughout this book with respect to gender, ethnicity (African-American, Asian-American, and Latin-American), and nationality. Let's proceed to look at what this diverse Greater Yellowstone fly-tying culture offers to the worldwide fly-fishing community.

CHAPTER 1

ATTRACTOR PATTERNS

Superbly effective attractor patterns originate in the Greater Yellowstone Region for several reasons: first, the presence of an almost endless number of streams with some to significant amount of gradient where a salmonid must react quickly to an apparent food form passing quickly in the flow, and second, the abundance of food forms. The Humpy, the Renegade, the Wulff series, Donnelly variants, and Scott Sanchez's Everything Emerger are a few of the famed attractors originating here. Attractor patterns are versatile by nature: Renegades are equally effective when fished wet or dry. A beat-up Humpy is a superb emerger. Attractor patterns may be "out of style" in many regions, but that will never be the case here as long as current geologic conditions mean that reaches having gradient are required to bring streams to base levels. In such reaches foraging salmonids have little time to react to what amounts to a glimpse of a potential food form passing by. It's a reaction very much like the person on a windy day when an airborne piece of paper currency flies by. The person wastes no time in pursuing that object regardless of its value.

Attractor patterns can be dry or wet, and some can be fished either way. This is the case with soft-hackle patterns as explained by their contemporary champion Sylvester Nemes. Syl states that "any soft-hackle pattern can be used for a caddisfly, a mayfly, or a midge emerger at any given time." All that is needed is attention paid to natural appearance, color, and size.

Dry attractor patterns are formed from traditional natural materials as well as from synthetic forms. Region-ally and currently, closed-cell foam is chief among synthetic materials used to produce attractor patterns for moving water. The use of this material for tying patterns results in many that double as adult stoneflies, hoppers, moths, or other terrestrial insects. Use of closed-cell foam began in the early 1990s and thus is in relative infancy. New patterns using closed-cell foam therefore literally "roll out of the vises" of regional tiers.

Della (Toni) Sivey's Bar-X nymphs, Wally Eagle's Feather Duster, Gary LaFontaine's Marabou Worm, and the Girdle Bug are but a few of the wet attractors offered in years gone by from famed Greater Yellowstone Area tiers. Then there is the Woolly Worm, the most successful fly pattern of all, made popular with certain reluctance in the region decades ago by Don Martinez.

Why are attractor patterns effective in stillwaters? Foraging salmonids within stillwaters have great opportunities to observe and inspect flies offered. But effectiveness here lies in the ability of a stillwater attractor pattern to resemble a variety of life-forms at one time. In many fishing situations it is not known if a salmonid is keying on, for example, minnows, leeches, damselfly nymphs, or dragonfly nymphs. So a pattern that resembles all of these at one time will give the best chance for being effective.

Because a great quantity of quality still and moving waters remain in the region, effective attractor patterns continue to be created by regional tiers. What follows will give the reader a good sample of effective new patterns from these tiers.

WET PATTERNS

ARF GEN-X SOFT HACKLE

Hook:	#10-20 TMC 3769
Thread:	Olive 8/0 UNI-Thread
Trailing bubbles:	Opal Mirage Flash
Abdomen:	Olive UTC Ultra Wire
Thorax:	Olive holographic Ice Dub
Hackle:	Dyed olive Brahma hen

Al Ritt's Gen-X Soft Hackle is a series of fly tied in several different colors. Some colors, like the olive described above or copper or tan, are imitative, while others, such as hot orange or blue, are attractors. Al conceived this pattern to fill a need for a fly that would penetrate the surface film quickly but not be so heavy as to sink small dry flies he often fishes it behind. The slender wire body helps fill this need. Soft hackles move and pulse in the water and can be dead-drifted, swung, or fished with a lift. Al also uses this pattern effectively in lakes as a dropper off a dry, or cast and retrieved with a swimming motion. The flash off the back imitates gas bubbles coming from an emerger, from a diving egg layer, or they may just act as an attractor. Fish won't say which is the case.

BEADHEAD LA MOUCHE

Hook:	#6-8 Mustad 9672
Bead:	6/0 amethyst or blue iris glass seed bead
Thread:	Black 3/0 Monocord
Tail:	Barbs of red rooster shoulder hackle
Body:	One grizzly saddle hackle and one strand of pearl Krystal Flash

Perhaps the most famous fly for fishing lakes is the Woolly Worm. Its hackle is easily cut and unwinds when a fish strikes but misses the fly. About sixty years ago, Harley Reno experienced destruction of his Woolly Worms in Yellowstone Lake. Many years later, while hosting a summer field trip in alpine ecology, Professor Reno began fishing his successor to the Woolly Worm—La Mouche—in the lakes of Utah's Uinta Mountains and in Greater Yellowstone waters. Since then, Harley has fished La Mouche widely throughout the Northwest, and, a few years ago, added the bead head to the fly. The bead imparts an enticing teetering action to the fly. Now he regularly uses the bead-head version in lakes and streams everywhere and for all kinds of fish.

BEAD HEAD SIDEKICK NYMPH

Hook:	#14 Daiichi 1260
Weight:	0.015-inch-diameter lead-free wire and optional brass bead
Thread:	Black 8/0
Rib:	Fine copper wire
Tail and abdomen:	Jay Fair golden olive marabou
Thorax:	Fine peacock herl
Wing case:	Large opal flash
Legs:	Olive grizzly hen fibers

Ben Byng uses the tip of a marabou feather to form the tail and abdomen. He slightly twists the marabou while rapping forward to form the tapered body. He believes that Jay Fair's golden olive marabou gives the color and fuzzy appearance that makes this fly so effective. Hebgen Lake is one of Ben's favorite places to fish. He uses this fly around the ample weed beds in the lake's arms and bays. A bead can be an option for fast drops along outside edges and channels.

BLM

Hook:	#12-16 Dai-Riki 300
Thread:	White 8/0 UNI-Thread
Tail:	Filoplume feather
Rib:	Brown 8/0
Body:	White tying thread under tan Thin Skin overwrap
Thorax:	Tan dubbing
Wing:	Two light tan CDC feathers tied opposing
Legs:	Two turns of soft brown hackle
Antennae:	Two black bear hairs

Gerry "Randy" Randolph has international renown for creating balsa bugs, but after moving from California to Idaho, he now designs trout flies. This pattern, created in 2005, has proven superbly effective as an all-purpose attractor. Trolled slowly in stillwaters, it can be a midge or mayfly emerger. Drifted just under the surface in moving water, it is a mayfly emerger or caddis pupa. Randy suggests changing colors and size to match specific insects. BLM stands for "Black Like Me."

BOOTY'S QUICK DESCENT NYMPH

Hook:	#16-18 TMC 2487
Bead:	Tungsten
Thread:	Black 12/0 UNI-Thread
Tail:	Brown rooster hackle fibers
Abdomen:	Caddis green Hareline Quick Descent Dubbing
Rib:	Olive fine UNI-Wire
Thorax:	Olive Hareline Quick Descent Dubbing
Wing:	Olive CDC
Wing case:	Brown Z-Lon

The prerunoff season offers some excellent fishing on the Snake River in Jackson Hole. This is one of Boots Allen's prerunoff patterns for the Snake and the South Fork reach of the Snake River during BWO emergences and throughout the season as a caddis pupa. The tungsten bead gets it down quickly. Because of this use, he considers the Quick Descent Nymph to be a general attractor nymph much like the Prince Nymph or Zug Bug. Boots also ties the Quick Descent Nymph in a red/rust hue combo.

BUCK'S BUG

Hook:	#10-14 Mustad 3906B
Bead:	Gold
Thread:	Black 6/0 UNI-Thread
Tail:	Orange Body Fur
Rib:	Gold wire
Body:	Peacock herl
Wing:	Flat silver braid
Hackle:	Brown saddle

Not quite satisfied with construction and effectiveness of other nymph patterns, Buck Goodrich developed this pattern based on the axiom "I take my cream from many cows, but I make my own butter." His pattern is an assemblage of ideas from other patterns, but then what pattern is not? Nevertheless, his easily tied pattern produces well as an attractor pattern throughout Yellowstone National Park's Fall River Basin, Buck's favorite area to fish.

BUFFALO SOLDIER

Hook:	#10-12 TMC 5262
Thread:	Rust brown 8/0 UNI-Thread
Eyes:	Monofilament
Tail:	Buffalo body guard hair
Rib:	Fine red wire
Body:	Buffalo body hair
Wing:	Buffalo body guard hair
Thorax:	Buffalo body hair picked out

Buffalo are becoming numerous in the region. Where they migrate outside Yellowstone National Park boundaries or near private buffalo herds in the region, the hair they shed in springtime is abundant. Durable and workable, this hair is underutilized by fly tiers. Gerry "Randy" Randolph realizes its value and has created a number of wet patterns using buffalo hair. This is his pattern to imitate damselflies or dragonflies, depending on hook size. He also uses it as a leech pattern. In tying it, he secures the eyes first. Then he adds the body and rib, dubs the head around the eyes, and finishes with the guard hair wing.

BURLAP NYMPH

Hook:	#12-16 Dai-Riki 075
Bead (optional):	Gold
Thread:	Black 70-denier UTC

Tail:	Grizzly hackle fibers
Rib:	Fine gold wire
Abdomen:	Burlap fibers
Thorax:	Peacock herl
Collar:	Grizzly hackle

This is an all-purpose pattern by Fred Petersen that can be used to simulate a caddisfly larva or pupa, a cranefly nymph, or an emerging Yellow Sally. Its "buggy" appearance results from burlap that can be further roughed up by using a dubbing rake or picked out with a bodkin. The optional gold bead runs it deeper into runs, pockets, and riffles. Run it deep to simulate larvae or new emergers. Swing it just under the surface to simulate insects climbing through the water column.

COPPER QUILL

Hook:	#10-16 Dai-Riki 060
Bead:	Silver
Thread:	Rusty brown 6/0
Tail:	Guinea hen hackle fibers
Body:	Two strands of different-colored copper wire, i.e., black and copper
Thorax:	Amber or olive dubbing
Wing case:	Black Scud Back or electrician's tape
Legs:	Guinea hen hackle fibers

This pattern by Scott Sanchez is fished much like the Copper John, but is more quickly tied. Place bead on hook shank behind eye with room between to tie in hackle fibers for legs, tips facing forward, and butts extending back beyond bead. Bring thread over top of bead to rear of the bead, tying in butts and back end of wing case. Tie in hackle fibers to form tail. Wrap a wire body, keeping two strands parallel. Trim ends of wire cleanly behind bead and at tail. Dub thorax, bring thread and wing case material over top of bead, tie down, and trim at front of bead. Divide hackle fibers and pull back to form legs extending on either side of bead. Tie these in through finishing head.

DAVE'S REAL SKUNK

Hook:	#10-14 Daiichi 1560
Bead:	Green glass with red center
Weight:	Eight wraps of 0.015-inch-diameter lead or lead-free wire
Thread:	Black 8/0 UNI-Thread
Tail:	Black guard hairs from skunk skin
Rib:	Fine copper wire
Body:	Black guard hairs and undercoat fur from skunk skin
Collar:	Black ostrich herl

Even though that roadkill skunk you found is only "semi-stinky," the Mrs. says: "No way are you bringing that thing in here!" A search on the Internet results in a cured version that the Mrs. will accept. For sure there are not many patterns out there tied with skunk fur, so if you are one who believes fish get used to seeing a much-presented pattern, this one is surely for you. Dave Hamilton's experience is that this fly is a productive attractor pattern. Perhaps if it were tied from an uncured roadkill, that would not be the case!

DELEKTABLE ROOTBEER FLOAT

Hook:	#14-18 Daiichi 1120
Bead:	Silver-lined brown 11/0 Darice Toho round glass
Thread:	Brown 6/0 Danville
Tail:	Ten to twelve wood duck or mallard-dyed wood duck fibers
Rib:	Fine copper wire
Body:	Tying thread
Wing case:	Yellow Beartooth Float Foam strip
Thorax and head:	Peacock Ice Dub
Hackle:	Sparse and oversized Hungarian partridge feather

This is the yellow version of Dan Delekta's Rootbeer Float series of superb attractor patterns. Quickly tied and versatile, it has proven effective on the Madison River near Dan's Cameron, Montana, home and business. Purple, olive, and orange are other versions in this series. The glass bead Dan suggests for the head of this fly and others in the series can be found in craft shops.

EASY SERENDIPITY

Hook:	#16 TMC 3769
Thread:	Black and white Combo thread
Body:	Tying thread
Wing pad:	White Ice Dub

Another simple fly: hook, thread, and one material. Form the body of this pattern created by Craig Mathews and tied by the author with thread wraps on the shank. Tie in the Ice Dub at the head, and double it over to form the wing pad. Cut the result to form a wing pad of desired length. Combo thread is quite new on the fly-tying scene. Its use gives fly tiers a quick and easy way to form segmented bodies. Yes, this pattern looks little like the original Serendipity. However, like its predecessor, it has several uses: midge emerger, midge larva, and caddis emerger. Fred Petersen claims it is a superior Trico emerger.

EL ASCENDER

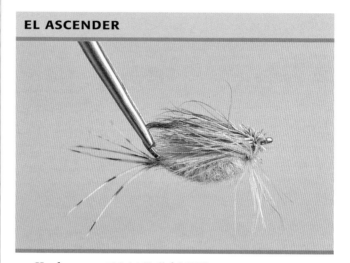

Hook:	#12-14 Daiichi 1170
Thread:	Tan 6/0 UNI-Thread
Tail:	Coq de Leon feather fibers
Body:	Tan Superfine Dubbing
Throat:	Dyed blue dun CDC under deer hair
Wing:	Deer hair
Hackle:	Dyed blue dun

Here is an elegant creation by Federico Prato. In appearance it resembles some European caddis emerger patterns, but for him it can be used for emerging caddisflies and mayflies alike. In many Greater Yellowstone streams, such as the upper Gallatin River, Robinson Creek, the North Fork of the Shoshone River upstream of Cody, Wyoming, and the Cardiac Canyon reach of the Henry's Fork, caddisfly and mayfly emergences can occur simultaneously during early summer afternoons. Federico's pattern would certainly be ideal to use under these conditions.

GB'S PURPLE AVENGER

Hook:	#14-18 Daiichi 1560
Bead:	Black Flymen tungsten
Thread:	Black 70-denier UTC
Tail:	Peacock UNI-Mylar strands $^1/_{32}$-inch wide
Rib:	Blue UTC Ultra Wire (small)
Body:	Dyed purple pheasant tail
Wing case:	Black Nymph Stretch
Thorax:	Purple UV Ice Dub
Legs:	Natural Whiting hen back fibers

Gary Barnes fishes Greater Yellowstone streams throughout the year. This pattern is always in his fly box. He fishes it solo year-round or as a dropper off a rubber-leg nymph during winter outings. During warmer times of the season, he will hang it off a large dry pattern and present it against banks of larger rivers, including the South Fork reach of the Snake River, the Madison River, and the Beaverhead River.

GLITTER NYMPH

Hook:	#12-16 TMC 2457
Thread:	Black 8/0 UNI-Thread
Tail:	Olive Montana Fly Company Glitter Thread strands
Body:	Olive Montana Fly Company Glitter Thread strands
Thorax:	Gray olive (#11) Superfine Dubbing
Wing case:	Olive Montana Fly Company Glitter Thread strands colored with black Sharpie
Legs:	Uncolored butts of Olive Montana Fly Company Glitter Thread strands used to form wing case

Nick Jones designed this pattern as an all-purpose nymph. The recipe above is for his BWO version (pictured). He uses a size 14 hook and brown Glitter Thread to simulate a Mahogany Dun nymph. For tempting rainbow trout in running water during midday, he ties a blue version with an orange thorax "hot spot." Glitter Thread is available in thirty colors.

ICE SOFT HACKLE

Hook:	#8-12 TMC 3761
Thread:	Fire orange 6/0 UNI-Thread
Tail:	Pheasant tail fibers
Rib:	Fine copper wire
Body:	Pheasant tail
Thorax:	Orange Ice Dub
Wing:	UV Krystal Flash
Hackle:	Partridge feather

Arrick Swanson recommends this fly for fishing the Madison River in Yellowstone National Park during autumn. Its body and tail components hint at influence from the pheasant-tail nymph, and its hackle is a standard for soft-hackled flies. In smaller sizes this pattern is used to simulate small caddis emergers while larger ties simulate the emerging October Caddis. It also has successful use as a Mahogany Dun emerger.

JACKLIN'S SOFT HACKLE

Hook:	#12-16 Dai-Riki 60
Thread:	Olive 70-denier or 6/0 Danville
Rib:	Fine gold wire
Body:	Olive dubbing or wool yarn
Hackle:	Folded grouse neck tied in tip first

As with any experienced fly fisher who is also a superb fly tier, Bob Jacklin creates variations of established patterns that better simulate food forms in the waters he enjoys fishing. This soft-hackle variation in the color given above is his favorite for PMD emergences on locations such as the Madison River along Yellowstone Park's West Entrance Road. Recently introduced Danville 70-denier is one of Bob's favorite fly-tying threads.

JIM'S DIP

Hook:	#12-16 TMC 2457
Thread:	Brown 6/0 UNI-Thread
Butt:	Tying thread
Body:	Twisted olive Antron
Wing:	White McFly Foam

Because of its inherent "fuzzyness," Jim Aubrey prefers Antron for tying this all-around attractor pattern over Z-Lon. He also prefers to tie this in olive because that color is so common among aquatic life-forms. After tying in the butt and anchoring the Antron along the hook shank, twist it clockwise. Starting at the butt, take a turn of the twisted Antron, twist it again to tighten, then take another turn. Repeat this action to just behind the hook eye, leaving enough room to tie in the wing. Cut the wing to hook gap length, and leave a stub in front to simulate gills for a midge pupa, head for a caddis pupa, or splitting shuck for a mayfly nymph.

KG'S DEEP PURPLE PERIL

Hook:	#12-14 Dai-Riki 125
Thread:	Black 8/0 UNI-Thread
Rib:	Small holographic purple Mylar
Abdomen:	Black tying thread, optionally coated with epoxy
Thorax:	Black "spectrumized" spiky dubbing
Wing:	White 2-mm-thick closed-cell foam

Taking a tip from steelheaders, trout anglers are making broader use of colors in the ultraviolet end of the visible spectrum to create effective fly patterns. Colors at this far end of the spectrum are the last to disappear. This pattern from Kelly Glissmeyer is an example of this use. Under an indicator pattern, it has proven to be a superbly effective attractor, especially in the early season. See KG's Cased Caddis on page 39 for a description of black "spectrumized" spiky dubbing.

KG'S SOUTH FORK SPECIAL

Hook: #12-14 Dai-Riki 125
Bead: Copper, ³/₃₂-inch
Thread: Olive dun 8/0 UNI-Thread
Tail: Tips of pheasant tail fibers
Back: Pheasant tail fibers (8–10)
Rib: Small chartreuse UNI-Wire
Abdomen: Pearl Ice Dub
Thorax: Olive-brown Ice Dub
Wing case: Pheasant tail fibers
Legs: Olive mottled hen saddle

To extend hen saddle fibers to form legs at a 45-degree angle from the body, snip the tip off the saddle hackle, and brush 20 to 30 fibers on either side of stem forward. Secure the stem with these fibers pointing to the rear to hook just behind the bead with two loose thread wraps. Pull feather segment through thread wraps until tips form legs to desired length at 45-degree angle. Tighten thread and tie off. This attractor pattern has proven effective for Kelly Glissmeyer as a mayfly nymph and caddis pupa on regional waters.

KING OF QUEENS

Hook: #10-14 TMC 3761
Bead: Black
Thread: Black 8/0 UNI-Thread

Tail: Dyed dark dun mallard flank feather fibers
Rib: Fine gold UNI-Wire (BR)
Flashback: Size 12 gold Mylar Tinsel
Abdomen: Olive-brown Antron hare's ear dubbing
Thorax: Peacock black Ice Dub

Michael Snody designed the King of Queens to be an all-around attractor pattern. It imitates clinging, swimming, and drifting mayfly nymphs, as well as various caddis pupae. Mike usually presents this pattern along the river bottom or within a few inches of it. He changes abdomen and thorax colors to imitate colors of insect nymphs inhabiting the waters he fishes. He finds that this pattern works well as a searching fly in off-colored water.

LINDA'S PURPLE WONDER

Hook: #14-16 Dai-Riki 135
Bead: Gold
Thread: Purple 8/0 UNI-Thread
Shuck: Amber crinkled Z-Lon
Rib: Gold wire (extra small)
Body: Purple Wonder Wrap
Thorax: Purple SLF mixed with a small amount of UV callibaetis Ice Dub
Legs: Two or three strands of white Fluoro Fibre
Wing: Tips of white goose biots under a white CDC tuft

This pattern is proving to be a superb dropper fished behind a dry fly in either still or moving water, and its attraction seems not to depend on any ongoing hatch. Effective for Linda Windels and her fishing friends, particularly under low-light conditions, from the early season into September, it appears to simulate an emerger or pupa in both still and moving water and possibly a molting scud in stillwater.

LST

Hook:	#12-16 Dai-Riki 1170
Bead:	Gold
Thread:	Black 8/0 UNI-Thread
Tail:	Hungarian partridge feather fibers
Body:	Gold Mylar tinsel
Thorax:	Peacock herl
Hackle:	Hungarian partridge

Being the consummate stillwater fly fisher, Gerry "Randy" Randolph has many patterns for fishing the gulper activity around the region. This is one of the patterns he created for gulpers, and it has brought him great success on Quake and Ennis Lakes. He fishes it in the shallows and around weed beds early in the day until he observes gulper activity on the surface. He named this fly LST or Lightning Strikes Twice after the number of lightning strikes he sees before getting off the water.

LUCKY CHARMS

Hook:	#8-16 TMC 3769
Bead:	Gold tungsten
Thread:	Orange 3/0 UNI-Thread
Rib:	Fine copper wire
Tail:	Ring-necked pheasant tail fiber tips
Abdomen:	Rainbow Scud dubbing

Wing case:	Ring-necked pheasant tail fiber
Thorax:	Golden brown Ice Dub
Legs:	Copper Wonder Wrap
Hot spot:	Tying thread

Dan Gates ties this pattern with a "buggy" appearance that imitates almost any kind of nymph. Thus it is a great generic mayfly nymph pattern requiring only a size change to simulate a natural. Try fishing it as a dropper off a dry pattern. In tailwaters, such as below Jackson Lake, it works well as a *Mysis* shrimp pattern. When tied in sizes 8 to 12, it doubles as a small stonefly nymph imitation.

MIKE'S DROPPER TWO

Hook:	#14-16 TMC 2487
Bead:	Gold
Thread:	Olive 8/0 UNI-Thread
Tail separator:	Dubbed ball of dark olive Hare's Ear Plus at top of hook bend
Tails:	Turkey biots dyed olive
Abdomen:	Overhand weave with four strands of small-diameter wire, brown and copper-brown on top, copper and chartreuse on bottom
Underbody:	Holographic silver strand
Wing case:	Natural mottled oak Thin Skin strip
Legs:	Wapsi #100 black Spanflex
Thorax:	Dark olive Hare's Ear Plus

This is the second nymph Mike Snody designed as a dropper after observing refracted light below the surface film. This one seems to work best when fished below a large dry fly such as a hopper pattern. Present it where banks have steep drop-offs or around rocks in deep water adjacent to banks.

MINCH'S BEAD, HARE AND COPPER

Hook:	#10-18 Dai-Riki 060
Bead:	Copper
Thread:	Tan 6/0 Flymaster
Rib:	Copper wire
Tail:	Center section of well-mottled brown partridge flank feather
Body:	Hare's mask
Legs:	Remaining section of partridge feather used for legs tied in "V" style
Head:	Natural hare's mask dubbing

Matt Minch's pattern is a most effective fly for fall-run browns. Fish it deep, fish it under a dry, swing it, or trail it behind a streamer. Recently it has been proven effective when used from a drift boat. This was Matt's go-to fly for his many trips to fish New Zealand waters, many of which are like those in the Greater Yellowstone Area.

MISAKO'S TENKARA FLY

Hook:	#12 Gamakatsu S-10B
Threads:	Dark brown and orange-red 6/0
Tag:	Tying thread

Body:	Brown thread for body and head with a few orange-red thread wraps behind head
Head:	Peacock herl
Hackle:	Golden badger, reverse wrapped

Originating centuries ago in Japan, Tenkara-style flies have come into popular use on trout streams in Western America. Enthusiasts have created many versions, but this pattern is Misako Ishimura's. Misako, chairperson of World Fly Fishing of Japan, is a frequent visitor to Greater Yellowstone Area waters. She has proven her pattern to be an effective wet attractor or emerger on such waters as the Madison River, the Henry's Fork, Soda Butte Creek, and the Yellowstone River whether fished with a Tenkara-style rod or a traditional American fly rod.

MOTOR BR

Hook:	#10-16 TMC 2487
Bead:	Gold Cyclops
Thread:	Olive 8/0 UNI-Thread
Underbody:	Peacock black Crystal Mirror Flash
Body:	Twelve-guage electric motor wire
Thorax/Collar:	Olive Ice Dub

This is Mike Snody's go-to pattern to present in faster current where and when fish are feeding on drifting caddis pupae or mayfly nymphs. As it moves quickly past feeding fish, its subtle sparkle attracts them to strike. Mike is a proponent of electric motor wire because of it density, toughness, and malleability. He crimps the end of the wire tied in to help produce a tapered body. He winds it in loose spirals, then wraps the Crystal Mirror Flash between these winds. He recommends 14-gauge wire for smaller versions of this pattern and suggests lightly brushing the thorax toward the rear to obtain life-like movement.

MVP

Hook:	#4-20 TMC 2488H
Bead:	Silver tungsten
Thread:	Olive 6/0 or 8/0 UNI-Thread, light cahill for lighter flies, brown for darker
Tail:	Light cream, white, olive, gray, or brown Antron yarn
Underbody:	Pearl Mylar no. 16 or 18 for small flies, no. 14 for larger
Rib:	Small silver Ultra Wire
Overbody:	McFly Foam strip
Hackle:	Blue dun hen
Head/collar:	Ice Dub

After placing bead and tying in the tail, wrap thread two-thirds up shank. Tie in McFly Foam on top of shank, securing it with thread wraps back to bend over the McFly Foam. Tie in a piece of pearl Mylar and Ultra Wire. Wrap the Mylar Tinsel back and forth to form body. Rib with wire for durability. Pull McFly Foam over body, forming a hump. Tie down at front of body. Wrap two or three turns of hackle and form an Ice Dub collar. This is Tim Tollett's go-to attractor pattern. Color combinations he recommends include (tail, McFly Foam, collar): olive, golden olive; light olive, caddis green, olive-brown; red, McCheese, orange; white, light pink, UV yellow; gray, gray-olive, olive-brown; white, black, orange; and others.

MYSTIC GRAY BEADHEAD

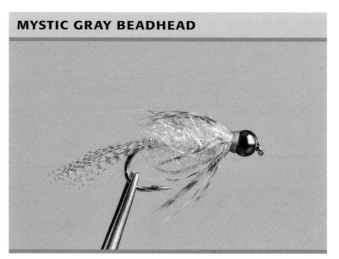

Hook:	#12 Daiichi 1710
Bead:	Charcoal black or silver, 1/8-inch
Weight:	Ten turns at midshank of 0.020-inch-diameter lead-free wire
Thread:	Light gray 8/0 or 6/0 UNI-Thread
Tail:	Natural or dyed gray dun mallard flank feather fibers
Body:	Light gray Wapsi Prism dubbing
Hackle:	One turn of gray Whiting Brahma hen saddle or partridge

This fly, part of Buddy Knight's Mystic series, is also known as the Holy Ghost. As an attractor nymph it makes use of ample UV reflective fibers. It is also effective when tied without a bead. It seems particularly successful in stillwaters when fished around banks and along drop-offs, especially during afternoons.

MYSTIC TAN BEADHEAD

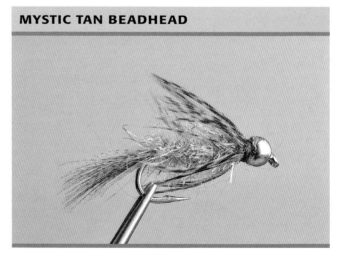

Hook:	#12 Daiichi 1710
Bead:	Gold, 1/8-inch
Weight:	Ten turns at midshank of 0.020-inch-diameter lead-free wire
Thread:	Brown 8/0 or 6/0 UNI-Thread

Tail:	Wood duck flank feather fibers
Body:	Tan Mystic dubbing
Hackle:	One turn of March Brown Whiting Brahma hen saddle or partridge-dyed brown

Another of Buddy Knight's Mystic series, it too can be tied with and without a bead. Primarily a stillwater pattern, Buddy uses it to imitate *Callibaetis* emergers and caddis pupae. He presents it on an intermediate or a sinking-tip line and applies short strips. Buddy's Mystic dubbing is a blend of several materials, with Ice Dub being the main ingredient.

ORANGE FOX NYMPH

Hook:	#16-20 Daiichi 1120
Bead:	Copper or brass
Thread:	Black 8/0 UNI-Thread
Tail:	Black hackle fibers
Rib:	Small silver Ultra Wire
Body:	Fire orange dubbing
Thorax:	Natural fox squirrel dubbing with guard hairs

Spencer Higa prefers a flared tail and guard hairs radiating out of the dubbed thorax to give a "buggier" look to this wet attractor pattern. He uses it with success in autumn in streams at the northeast corner of Yellowstone Park, including Slough Creek, Soda Butte Creek, and Lamar River, where it likely simulates a Mahogany Dun nymph. During summer months one of his favorite streams in which to use it is the Greys River. If you have yet to fish western Wyoming's Greys River, put this most beautiful of freestone streams on your "must visit" list.

OTTER'S EMBRYO EGG

Hook:	#8 TMC 2457
Thread:	Red 6/0 prewaxed Danville
Veil:	Otter's Milking Veil, 1-inch piece
Embryo:	Red 8/0 glass bead
Egg:	Apricot 8 mm Otter's Soft Egg

To create Walt (The Otter) Mueller Jr's fly, use a small darning needle to impale a channel through the center of an Otter's Soft Egg, then force a glass embryo bead into the channel. After wrapping a thread base, tie on veil piece at midpoint. Double the veil with ends pointing rear, leaving bobbin hanging at rear. Superglue thread base. Push egg past eye, while wiggling it (to bypass and push bead above the shank and off-center inside the egg) and over glued thread wraps. Bring thread firmly to front on underside of egg. Take most of veil over top of egg and spread with downward pressure from thumb to cover 120-180 degrees over egg. Tie in, under moderate tension, at front of egg. Take two loose wraps of thread and pull veil tightly to compress and hold egg onto hook. Take two tight wraps and fold remaining veil back to rear marrying fibers there and tie off. Drift Otter's Soft Egg patterns less than six inches above stream bottom.

OTTER'S SOFT SUCKER SPAWN

Hook:	#12 TMC 2457
Thread:	Red 6/0 prewaxed Danville
Veil:	Otter's Milking Veil, 1½-inch piece
Eggs:	Otter's 2 x 2 mm, 6-egg double row section

To create this fly by Walt Mueller Jr, impale hook point into egg on top left, down through the center ribbon, and out through egg on bottom right of the six-egg section. Keep egg string bunched around hook bend, pushing it forward only enough to place bend and barb into vise. The section's flat ribbon should be on the bottom of the fly. Wrap thread base on shank from rear forward and superglue wraps. Gently push egg string onto shank to eye. Take tying thread at eye, then from underneath do two wraps between, over and under first and second egg row, then between these rows. Take two wraps at rear, pass thread back over center of eggs, and tie off two more wraps. Then rewrap over eggs to rear a second time. With thread to rear, tie in a small amount of veil material. Place dab of superglue on top of eggs, spread veil tightly over top toward front. Tie off with excess trailing to rear.

OTTER'S THREE EGG CLUSTER

Hook:	#8 TMC 2457
Thread:	Red 6/0 prewaxed Danville
Veil:	Otter's Milking Veil, 1½-inch piece
Eggs:	Otter's 3-egg (6 mm) cluster

For this fly by Walt Mueller Jr, wrap thread base and tie veil piece midpoint at rear of shank. Double the veil with both ends pointing rear, leaving bobbin hanging there. Superglue the thread base. Push bottom two eggs in the cluster past the hook eye onto the shank over glued thread wraps so that rear egg butts against veil. Bring the tying thread underneath the cluster to hook eye and secure. Take most of two halves of veil and form an "X" behind the cluster. Pull the "X'd" veil over the top of the two lower impaled eggs and to the hook eye. Make another "X" here, lightly tie off the veil, and pull it to the right to compress the eggs. Tie off and pull the veil to the rear on either side to marry with the few veil fibers left behind.

PARTRIDGE AND ORANGE VARIATION

Hook:	#14-20 Daiichi 1140
Thread:	Orange 8/0 UNI-Thread
Rib:	Yellow 8/0 UNI-Thread
Body:	Orange 8/0 UNI-Thread

| Thorax: | Burnt orange dubbing |
| Hackle: | Hungarian partridge |

In communications with me to describe this pattern, Charles Jardine wonders if this one would horrify T. E. Pritt. Nevertheless, it is Charles's variation for fishing in the United States. Fish it upstream and across, on the swing or dead drift. It can also be fished as a dropper under an adult caddisfly pattern. In eastern Idaho, variations, like this one from Charles, are also fished during Yellow Sally emergences. So the Partridge and Orange, whichever variation used, can simulate—in addition to above discussed insects—a diving adult caddisfly or a sunken mayfly spinner.

PAUL BRUUN NYMPH

Hook:	#12-16 Dai-Riki 075
Bead:	Peacock green 8/0 glass, Gick no. 4-175
Thread:	Black 6/0 UNI-Thread
Rib:	Fine copper wire
Tail/shuck:	Orange McFly Foam fibers
Body:	Black rabbit with guard hairs
Collar:	Amber squirrel belly dubbing

Following Gary LaFontaine's "hot spot" theory, Joe Burke uses a brightly colored shuck to attract trout to this pattern. Joe presents this pattern using an "up the leader" technique. Presented in this manner, it is effective as a chironomid emerger suspended in water over stirred-up Jackson Lake mudflats where mackinaw come in to forage. Brook trout in western Wyoming streams fall for it when presented in this technique. So do golden trout in mountain lakes of the region, and cutthroat and whitefish in the Snake River. Joe suggests substituting a tungsten or glass bead to drop this pattern deeper in moving water.

PEACOCK AND BLACK

Hook:	#4-10 Mustad 79580
Thread:	Black 3/0 Monocord
Tail:	Red sparkle yarn or poly yarn
Underbody:	Black yarn
Overbody:	Peacock herl
Hackle:	Black saddle palmered over body
Wing:	Black marabou

Don Heyden's experience is that a yarn underbody seats peacock herl more securely than when wound on a bare or thread-wrapped hook shank. After wrapping the shank with thread, tying in tail, peacock herl tips, hackle tip, and yarn butt at top of the hook bend, he wraps yarn around the hook shank. He forms a peacock herl "rope" around the tying thread, wraps a turn behind the tied-in hackle, then forward, forming the body. Palmering the hackle, tying in the marabou wing, trimming excesses, and forming the head finishes this quickly tied fly. According to Don, this pattern is effective when slowly trolled in stillwaters, or swept along banks or other structure in streams.

PINK AND PURPLE

Hook:	#16 TMC 2488
Thread:	Red 8/0 UNI-Thread
Abdomen/tail:	1 mm purple Ultra Chenille
Wing case and gills:	White Antron
Thorax:	Pink rabbit fur dubbing

This fly by Scott Urbanski is particularly effective during the early season. The reason is that it simulates several different life-forms—all of which can be washed into moving water because of erosion—including crane-fly larvae, earthworms, grubs, and others. It can also simulate an annelid, the aquatic worm that fish seem to crave. All of these forms dead-drift in the current, and so Scott recommends that strategy for presenting it. Because it simulates so many life-forms, it is very effective, especially during the early season.

PLEASANT TAIL NYMPH

Hook:	#12-16 Daiichi 1170
Bead:	Brass, 1/8, 3/32, 5/64-inch
Thread:	Dark brown 8/0
Tail:	Pheasant tail, 7–8 fibers
Rib:	Pearl Flashabou strand and 5X tippet material
Body:	Light cahill synthetic dubbing and peacock herl
Wing case/legs:	Pheasant tail fibers

After mounting bead and tying in tail, tie in Flashabou strand along far side of shank and tippet on near side. Tie in three to four peacock herls at midshank, take thread back to bend, and dub body to herl tie-in point. Bring herl over top of body, tie in, rib with Flashabou stretched to emit blue color, and counterrib with monofilament. Match tips of 18 to 20 pheasant tail fibers of length equal to hook and tail and tie in just behind the bead, tips facing rear. Slide bead over their tie-in point, jump thread to front of bead, and build a cone. Pull fiber butts over top of bead, divide into equal amounts, and tie in to form head and legs on either side. This is a great all-around pattern by Merne Judson.

PRINCESS

Hook:	#10-14 Daiichi 1710
Bead:	Gold, 1/8-inch
Weight:	Ten turns at midshank of 0.020-inch-diameter lead-free wire
Thread:	Black 6/0 or 8/0 UNI-Thread
Tail:	Red Darlon or Antron yarn
Rib:	Fine gold wire or tinsel
Body:	Peacock herl
Wing:	White Darlon or Antron yarn
Hackle:	One turn soft brown hen hackle

After wrapping the lead-free wire, Buddy Knight pushes it forward on the shank into the recess at the rear of the bead. This locks the bead in place and readies the shank for finishing the body. He doubles both the tail and the wing by tying in the material for each at its center, then pulling the top piece over itself and tying it down. This is one of his favorite flies to tie in as a trailer behind another fly.

ROYAL KEBARI

Hook:	#12 Knapek G scud hook
Thread:	Black 8/0 UNI-Thread
Tag:	Red Flymaster Plus
Rib:	Fine gold Mylar
Body:	Peacock herl
Hackle:	Cream and coachman brown saddle

John Kimura prefers the Czech Knapek hook for this pattern because its gaps are generally one size wider for a given size than hooks made in this country. He counterwraps the Mylar rib over the peacock herl body for added durability. He wraps the front (cream) hackle first, then the coachman brown hackle right behind it and ties off the fly. This aids in keeping hackle fibers pointing forward in the Tenkara style. John finds that this pattern is very effective when presented on smaller waters, such as the upper Gibbon River and Grayling Creek in Yellowstone National Park.

ROYAL NYMPH

Hook:	#12-16 Mustad 3906B
Thread:	Dark brown 6/0 Danville Flymaster
Tail:	Dark brown elk hock
Butt:	Single peacock herl
Body:	Single strand of red flat floss

| Thorax: | Dubbed from blended amounts of two-thirds brown fur with guard hairs and one-third dark-brown sparkle yarn |
| Wing case: | Pheasant tail fibers |

Don Heyden makes use of elk hock, one of the most durable natural materials available, for the tail of this pattern. He suggests that the wing case width should be about the same as gap width of the hook. He picks out guard hairs from the finished thorax to simulate legs. Don recommends using this pattern as a wet attractor, particularly when trout seem not to be keying on a particular nymph pattern.

RUBBER LEGGED FLOOSY

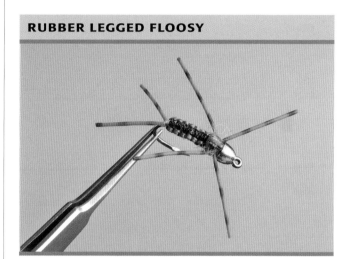

Hook:	#6-12 TMC 2499 SPBL
Weight:	0.020-inch-diameter lead or lead-free wire
Thread:	White Gudebrod GX2
Cone:	Gold
Tail:	Black/orange barred rubber legs
Body:	Overhand weave of black Kreinik fly-tying ribbon (top) and orange embroidery floss (bottom)
Wing case:	Red Flashabou strip centered under clear Scud Back
Legs:	Black/orange barred rubber legs
Thorax:	Tan Superfine Dubbing

Featured above is the golden stone version of Branden Tueller's Rubber Legged Floosy. By changing size and colors, this pattern can simulate several naturals. Try it in size 10 as a damselfly nymph. Change body and thorax colors from orange and tan to olive. Change leg colors to olive and black barred. Tied as a giant stonefly nymph, this pattern should be on a size 6 hook with a body woven from the same components as for the golden stonefly nymph, but with a black cone and black rubber legs.

RUBBER LEG HARE'S EAR

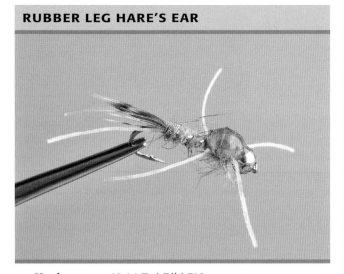

Hook:	#10-14 Dai-Riki 710
Bead:	Silver, brass, or gold
Thread:	Tan 8/0
Rib:	Fine gold nylon tinsel
Tail:	India hen back fibers with one Montana Fly Company Tentacles #3 clear or tan on each side, each slightly longer than the hen back fibers
Body:	Hare's ear Hareline Dubbin
Legs:	Montana Fly Company Tentacles #3 clear or tan
Thorax:	Hare's ear Hareline Dubbin
Wing case:	Z-Poxy

After tying in the bead, securing it, and tying on the ribbing, Vic Loiselle ties in the tail materials next. First the tentacles go on by folding a two-inch length at midlength over tying thread and tying in at top of hook bend. Trim tentacles to hook length, and tie in hen back fibers. Form and rib the body, tie in legs at either side, and dub the thorax. After whip-finishing the head, add a drop of Z-poxy at the top of the thorax to form a wing case.

SPANISH GOLD

Hook:	#15-19 TMC 102Y
Bead:	Gold
Thread:	Fire orange 8/0 UNI-Thread
Tails:	Medium dun mallard flank feather fibers
Abdomen:	Gold Mylar strip
Thorax:	Peacock Ice Dub
Collar (behind bead):	Fire orange UNI-Thread

Michael Snody designed this attractor particularly for discolored, deeper, or dark (in shadows) water. Try it as a trailer behind a larger nymph pattern presented on dead drift, especially in the early morning or evening when shadows are longest. Try it in smaller streams such as Indian, Obsidian, and Solfatara Creeks in Yellowstone National Park. Brook and brown trout in streams such as these seem particularly attracted to this pattern.

STILL WATER WILLIE

Hook:	#2-10 Mustad 79580
Thread:	Black 6/0 Danville Flymaster
Body:	Palmered brown marabou

Collar: Palmered black marabou
Head: Black tying thread

This unpublished pattern is Will Godfrey's favorite for fishing Henry's Lake and the west end of Island Park Reservoir. Henry's Lake has a reputation as one of the best stillwater trout fisheries in existence. Island Park Reservoir blows hot and cold with respect to successful fishing. The exception is the west end of the reservoir where Trude Springs supplies high quality water for the trout population congregating around this quality source. Experienced fly fishers migrate here for chances to catch huge rainbows. Will Godfrey and his fishing friends use this simple pattern here in small sizes to imitate damselfly nymphs and large sizes to imitate leeches.

SUCKER EGG CLUSTER

Hook: #16 Daiichi 1150
Thread: White 6/0 UNI-Thread
Egg cluster (body): White Diamond Braid loops
Tail: Butt end of Diamond Braid

John Taylor covers the hook shank with tying thread before tying in the Diamond Braid loops that simulate an egg cluster. A thread-wrapped shank secures the loops more securely than a bare shank. Each spring suckers migrate to instream spawning areas throughout the Greater Yellowstone Area. The multitude of ripe females releasing a huge number of eggs attracts salmonids to feed on drifting spawn. John created this pattern to present to feeding salmonids during these times. He also ties this pattern using pink or orange Diamond Braid. As another option to get this pattern deeper, he adds a gold or silver tungsten bead before forming the Diamond Braid loops. He fishes this pattern under an indicator and on a sinking-tip line just downstream of spawning suckers.

TAK'S GO2 PRINCE

Hook: #10-16 TMC 9300
Bead: Gold
Thread: Olive dun 8/0 UNI-Thread
Tail: Whiting Farms brown hen hackle fibers
Rib: Pearl Flashabou strand
Body: Peacock herl
Wing: White polyester yarn
Hackle: Whiting Farms brown midge saddle hackle
Collar: Peacock Ice Dub

Rick Takahashi determined that Whiting Farms hen neck feathers are excellent substitutes for the brown goose biots. He selects these over other hen neck producers because of fiber quality of larger feathers from the lower neck. He plucks fluff from the base and preens fibers to stand perpendicular to the stem. He grabs a portion of those fibers, pulls them from the stem, and ties them in at the top of the bend, replacing the brown Prince Nymph goose biots. Rick also observed that pearl Flashabou wrapped around the peacock herl body reflects a greenish tint. He uses Whiting Farms brown midge saddle hackle because of color and ease of application. White polyester yarn is much easier than goose biots to tie in and trim to shape. The gold bead gets the fly down and simulates the gas bubble an emerging caddis forms.

TAK'S GO2 RED

Hook:	#14-18 TMC 9300
Bead:	Gold
Thread:	Olive dun 8/0 UNI-Thread
Tail:	Whiting Farms brown hen hackle fibers
Body:	Red medium UNI-Wire
Wing:	White polyester yarn
Hackle:	Whiting Farms brown midge saddle hackle
Collar:	Peacock Ice Dub

This is one of Rick Takahashi's GO2 series of nymph patterns. He uses it from time to time in place of his GO2 Prince in the combination rig described in the discussion of his GO2 Caddis (see page 43). It is especially effective in smaller sizes for stillwaters when fish are keying on bloodworms. When this occurs, present it under an indicator. Find the taking depth, and this fly will produce.

T EGG

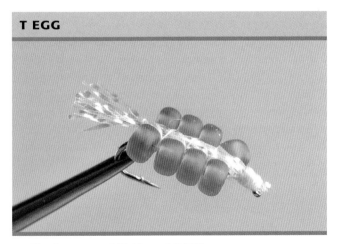

Hook:	#6-10 Mustad 94831
Thread:	Metallic white
Tail:	Pearl Krystal Flash strands
Eggs:	Clear orange hyacinth 10/0 beads
Body:	Tying thread

The lower part of the South Fork reach of the Snake River is primarily a brown trout fishery. Adult browns here begin spawning in late October, with peak activity in November. Streamer patterns rule the popularity roost during these times. However, the use of egg patterns is gaining in popularity. The flows are usually down to around 1500 cfs and the water is absolutely clear, allowing sight-fishing with egg patterns, such as Merrill Tea's highly effective cluster pattern. Securing eggs with monofilament threaded through each, then anchored to the hook with tying thread, results in durability.

TURKEY & BEAD SOFT HACKLE

Hook:	#12 Skalka Wet Nymph
Bead:	Gold tungsten, 2.8 mm
Thread:	Black 6/0
Rib:	Small copper wire
Body:	Turkey wing or tail feather fibers
Hackle:	Blue grouse saddle feather

John Kimura frequently visits Greater Yellowstone waters. Turkey & Bead Soft Hackle is his searching mode pattern for the area. After placing a bead behind the hook eye, he ties in two or three turkey tail or body feather fibers tip first and dull side facing out. Next he attached the copper wire, the butt of which he covers with tying thread and cement. He wraps the turkey fibers forward, shiny side out, then ribs the body in the opposite direction. He ties off body and rib excess and thread, adds some cement to the tie-off point, and slides the bead over it. He reattaches thread in front of the bead, and ties in the tip of a blue grouse feather, two turns of which finishes the fly.

WEISE'S FOUR FEATHER

Hook:	#12-18 Dai-Riki 060
Bead:	Gold
Thread:	Dark brown 8/0 UNI-Thread
Rib:	Gold wire
Tail:	Wood duck flank fibers
Abdomen:	Natural ostrich herl
Wing case:	Pheasant tail fibers over gold or tan Krystal Flash
Thorax:	Peacock herl
Legs:	Tips of pheasant tail fibers and Krystal Flash used to form wing case

Walter Weise named this fly for the four different feathers used, which are all among the most effective feathers used in tying nymphs: peacock herl, ostrich herl, pheasant tail, and wood duck flank. Typically the larger sizes are effective fished deep under an indicator just after runoff and for fall-run browns, while sizes 16-18 work best as dropper nymphs in late summer.

WEISE'S HULA PRINCESS

Hook:	#12-16 Montana Fly Company 7077
Bead:	Gold
Thread:	Dark brown 8/0 UNI-Thread
Rib:	Gold wire

Body:	Peacock herl
Wing:	White Widow's Web
Head:	Natural ostrich herl

This pattern is Walter Weise's answer for a serendipity type fly. When using a scud hook on nymph patterns such as this, Walter prefers a gold bead that is one size smaller than proportional. Note how the ostrich herl effectively hides thread wraps just behind the bead. Present this pattern in sizes 12 and 14 deep during high-flow periods and in size 16 as a dropper under an attractor, dry, or hopper during July and August.

WHO KNOWS FREAKING WHY SOFT HACKLE (AKA "BEATS ME")

Hook:	#6-18 TMC 5262
Thread:	Rusty brown 8/0 UNI-Thread
Abdomen:	For larger sizes, Gudebrod Champion Metallic "Herl Peacock" Braid; for smaller sizes, Gudebrod dyed peacock Mini-Diamond Braid
Thorax:	Three turns of peacock eye fiber, dyed red or pink
Hackle:	Three turns of natural guinea fowl flank feather for larger sizes; gray partridge neck feather for smaller sizes

Doug Andres uses a streamer hook for this pattern to sink it subsurface to swirling fish rather than in the film as an emerger. Its name refers to uncertainty as to why it seems universally effective. Likely it may imitate a Green Rock Worm, a damsel nymph, a small leech, or aquatic insects of similar hues. It is very effective on the fall-run browns up the Madison River inside Yellowstone National Park when tied up to size 6, on the Firehole River during hatches of the White Miller, and as a general searching nymph pattern. Add a bead head for fishing deeper runs and holes.

WOVEN PRINCE NYMPH

Hook:	#10-16 TMC 200R
Bead:	Silver
Weight:	0.015-inch-diameter lead-free wire
Thread:	Black 6/0
Tails:	Black goose biots
Body:	Half-hitch weave of black DMC embroidery floss (top) and Midge Diamond Braid (bottom)
Thorax:	Dubbed Whitlock SLF dragonfly blend
Wing case:	Black Scud Back
Horns:	Natural goose biots

Logan Cutts forms the body and thorax of this nymph in the same manner that he ties his Woven Golden Stonefly Nymph (see page 145). His use of Diamond Braid and embroidery floss to weave the body is unique. Embroidery floss comes in eight strands. He reduces the number of strands (three strands for sizes 10 to 12, two strands for sizes 14 to 16) in his working piece depending on the size of the hook to be used.

YES

Hook:	#8 Mustad 3906B
Thread:	Black 3/0 Monocord
Tail:	Six pheasant tail barbs
Body:	Light brown Polarfleece with thin red Polarfleece ring in front
Hackle/head:	Bronze or brown rooster saddle

The Yes (short for "Yesterday") is another one of Harley Reno's favorite wet flies for brown and rainbow trout inhabiting cascading and fast-flow streams of the Absaroka Mountains and the whole of the Yellowstone uplift. A way to fish this fly is as a dropper tied directly into the leader about 18 inches above any heavily weighted fly (e.g., a stonefly nymph). The fly is supple and, with the red collar under the cone-shaped hood over the body, is clearly visible. Hence, Yes is an effective strike indicator. Many times Harley has caught two large trout at a time. Landing two fish is a real challenge in a strong current or fast-flowing stream.

DRY PATTERNS

ALL AROUND EMERGER

Hook:	#12-20 Mustad R 30
Thread:	Black 6/0 UNI-Thread
Tail:	Dun Antron
Body:	Goose biot, color to match natural
Underwing:	Krinkled Z-Lon
Overwing:	Natural CDC puff
Head:	Three natural ostrich mini plumes

The Harriman State Park reach of the Henry's Fork is a great example of a stream that hosts multiple emergences at once. Here during midseason, caddis and more than one mayfly species can be emerging simultaneously. Kieran Frye's All Around Emerger is an ideal pattern for use during a multiple hatch situation. In different sizes and colors it can be the single pattern in your fly box to match emerging naturals while searching for what the fish are taking. Tie in the goose biot with notch facing hook eye to obtain a furled body.

ANTACID

Hook:	#10-12 Daiichi 1170
Thread:	Tan 8/0 Danville
Body:	Cinnamon Superfine Dubbing

Thorax:	Brown Superfine Dubbing
Underwing:	Gold holographic Krystal Flash
Wing:	Deer hair
Legs:	Black and white barred Centipede Legs
Head:	Cinnamon Superfine Dubbing

Although this pattern has the body shape of an ant, it is a very effective dry attractor pattern. Kelly Galloup uses it throughout the region with great success to imitate not only a flying ant, but also a hopper or an adult caddisfly. This makes it one of his favorite patterns, a fly for all seasons, for all waters, and a hot seller commercially around the country.

BALSA HUMPY

Hook:	#10-16 TMC 100
Thread:	Black 8/0 UNI-Thread
Tail:	Whiting Farms hackle fibers
Body:	Balsa wood carved to shape, primed, airbrushed or marking-penned tan, and lacquered to finish
Hackle:	Whiting Farms saddle

Want a Humpy that will float like a cork and the body of which will not unravel? This is it. Gerry "Randy" Randolph ties the hackle fiber tail on first. After cementing the hook with fast-drying epoxy in a slot along the bottom of the finished balsa body, he uses epoxy wood filler to fill the slot. Next, he hackles this fly. The result is almost unsinkable, but because of its hard body, react quickly to strikes when you fish it.

CIRCUS PEANUT

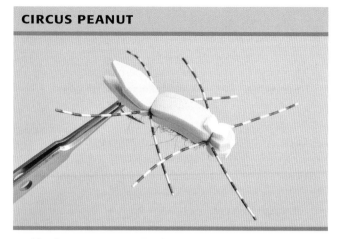

Hook:	#4-10 TMC 300
Thread:	Camel 6/0 UNI-Thread
Underbody:	Golden stone mottled nymph blend
Overbody:	Two pieces of 4-mm closed-cell foam trimmed to shape
Legs:	Tan barred Spirit River legs
Indicator:	White closed-cell foam
Head:	Extension of foam pieces used to form body

Cover entire shank with dubbed underbody. Tie in the overbody pieces and a set of legs on either side above the hook point. Two body pieces should separate and extend to the rear about half the hook shank length. Behind the eye secure the front of the body, a set of legs on each side, and the indicator. Will Dornan's pattern is a real favorite on Jackson Hole streams where it can simulate adult golden stoneflies, giant stoneflies, or hoppers in fast water.

CDC POWER ANT

Hook:	#12-16 Daiichi 1170
Thread:	Fluorescent red 8/0 UNI-Thread
Butt:	Red Superfine Dubbing
Body:	Cinnamon Superfine Dubbing

Wing:	Snow goose CDC feather
Legs:	Fine black rubber legs
Hackle:	Reddish brown saddle

This is another of Joe Burke's patterns having success in the Jackson Hole reach of the Snake River during the Jackson Hole One Fly contest. In small sizes it is effective during Trico emergences in the Snake River just below Jackson Lake Dam into the Oxbow Bend section. Variations of this pattern Joe offers include using black moose mane for legs, amber rubber legs, chocolate brown dubbing for simulating cinnamon ants, black dubbing for black ants. In all variations he uses the same hackle color and trims hackle on bottom to the same plain as the hook bend.

COMPOWER DUN

Hook:	#8-12 TMC 100
Thread:	Black 3/0
Tail:	Dark moose body hair
Wing:	Mule deer hair
Body:	Muskrat dubbing
Hackle:	Dyed brown grizzly saddle
Head:	Muskrat dubbing

Guy Turck offers this as a searching pattern, which I tied. He recommends tying on the tail, then the wing that is a variation of the Compara-dun style. Next he dubs the body, winds the hackle, and dubs the head. Last, hackle and any deer hair on the bottom of the fly is cut away. The Compower Dun can be tied without a hackle, but it will not float as well. On the heavy waters of rivers around Jackson Hole, this fly has proven its worth by being visible, durable, and effective.

CRUEL MAID

Hook:	#10-16 Dai-Riki 300
Thread:	Black 8/0 UNI-Thread
Tail:	Mule deer flank hair
Abdomen:	Brown silk or rayon floss
Rear hackle:	Grizzly saddle
Thorax:	Tan dubbing
Wing:	Teal flank fibers
Front hackle:	Ginger or ginger grizzly saddle slightly oversized

This dry attractor pattern is LeRoy Cook's favorite for the smaller streams he loves to fish. Literally hundreds of small streams spangle the region. Only a few of these have reached the media to become destinations for visiting fly fishers. As with most of LeRoy's patterns, it is easily tied and uses readily available materials.

DADDY LONG LEGS

Hook:	#10 Orvis 1523
Thread:	Camel 8/0 UNI-Thread
Body:	Ginger Angora goat dubbing
Legs:	Knotted 0.006-inch Maxima
Hackle:	Dyed dark brown grizzly hen

This is a multiuse pattern. Dave Brackett fishes it mostly in stillwaters around weed beds. He has used it successfully as a dry attractor and as a terrestrial pattern. He ties in the first set of legs on either side of the shank about two-thirds the way up the hook shank from the rear, then finishes dubbing the body. The other set of legs he ties in just in front of the body and before he hackles the fly.

DANDRUFF

Hook:	#18-24 TMC 206BL
Thread:	Black
Rib:	6X monofilament
Body:	Stripped peacock eye quill
Wing:	Two or three natural CDC plumes

This is Jay Buchner's go-to pattern for midge adults and small mayfly duns. In the Greater Yellowstone Area there are plenty of opportunities to use a double-duty pattern such as this because midge adults and small mayfly adults can be on the water simultaneously. This happens frequently, but in the early and late season these two can be the dominant emerging species on which trout feed. Jay counterwraps the stripped peacock eye quill body with monofilament to add durability, and he extends the CDC wing only to the hook bend.

DELEKTABLE TEASER PURPLE

Hook:	#16-18 Daiichi 1170
Thread:	Purple 6/0 Danville
Shuck:	Rusty brown Z-Yarn
Rib:	Small gold wire
Body:	Purple Antron yarn
Thorax:	Peacock Ice Dub
Underwing:	Blond elk hair
Overwing:	White Widow's Web
Hackle:	Brown and grizzly saddles
Legs:	Brown Sili Legs
Head:	Hare's Ear Plus dubbing

Dan Delekta uses Antron yarn strands to form a slender body. He counterwraps it with the gold wire. He ties the elk-hair underwing in near the front of the body, the tips pointing forward. He trims tips off, resulting in less bulk, and trims the butt ends pointing rear the same length as the underwing rear section. The hackle (grizzly in front of brown) props the overwing front section upright. Sili Legs, tied behind the hackle, act as outriggers. Hare's Ear Plus dubbing completes the head with a drop of superglue on the end of the dubbing; make one full turn around the hook shank. When the superglued dubbing end comes in contact with the dubbing on the hook shank, the fly is completed.

FILM STAR

Hook:	#18-20 Daiichi 1310
Thread:	Brown 8/0 waxed UNI-Thread
Shuck:	Sparse olive Z-Lon
Humped wings:	Pale gray Z-Lon
Body:	Dark olive Superfine Dubbing
Hackle:	Medium dun

Tie in short sparse shuck above hook point, about half shank length. Tie in about 20 to 25 strands of gray Z-Lon at same point as shuck, with long ends pointed toward rear. Tie in hackle at same point as shuck and Z-Lon. Dub sparse body forward to one eye-length behind eye. Spiral four turns of hackle forward over body. Fold gray Z-Lon wing forward over hackled body, and tie down at front of body. Use bodkin or needle to lift wing into a slack hump, allowing material to slide through the two turns of thread. Tie wing down tight, trim excess, and whip-finish. Nelson Ishiyama's Film Star imitates an emerging BWO or midge. Both insects hump their bodies upward when emerging, thus the loose Z-Lon hump imitates emerging wings. It's a deadly fly, especially at times when only midges and BWO emerge, often at the same time.

FORE & AFT BIG HOLE DEMON

Hook:	#13-19 TMC 103BL
Thread:	Hot pink 8/0 UNI-Thread
Tail:	Badger body hair fibers

Rear body segment:	Peacock herl
Rear hackle:	Badger saddle palmered through peacock herl
Body center:	Flat silver tinsel
Front body:	Peacock herl
Hackle:	Badger saddle hackle palmered through peacock herl

Whereas the original Big Hole Demon was a streamer pattern, Tom Harman's pattern is a dry attractor. Its high visibility makes it a great choice for fishing faster water such as the Ruby and Gallatin Rivers and, naturally, the Big Hole River. On larger sizes, Tom applies an oval silver tinsel rib. He also offers a dark version with brown hackle fore and aft, as well as a flat gold tinsel center body.

GFA

Hook:	#8-12 Dai-Riki 280
Thread:	Yellow 6/0 UNI-Thread
Body:	Light gold 2-mm closed-cell foam
Wing:	Natural whitetail deer body
Legs:	Brown barred Sili Legs
Indicator:	Chartreuse Razor Foam

The body has four segments, the last of which acts as an extended body. This leaves an expanse of bare hook hanging down at the rear of the fly acting as a keel to prevent it from flipping over on its back as some foam patterns tend to do. This pattern acts as a hopper, a caddis, an attractor, a stonefly, a moth, or whatever a trout is seeking. Other foam colors Walter Weise suggests for tying this pattern include cocoa, olive, black, peach, pink, purple, lilac, and the various wood-grain foams. GFA stands for "general foam attractor." You can tie an underwing of pearl Krystal Flash.

GUNNILATOR

Hook:	#12-16 TMC 200R
Thread:	Dark brown 8/0 UNI-Thread
Tail:	Bleached coastal deer hair
Abdomen:	Pale yellow Superfine Dubbing
Rib:	Reddish-brown hackle and 5X monofilament
Wing:	UV blue Krystal Flash and bleached coastal deer hair
Thorax:	Pale yellow Superfine Dubbing
Hackle:	Pale yellow grizzly saddle

The stacked deer-hair tail is formed just short of the hook length. The Superfine dubbed body (over a thread-wrapped shank) with its hackle rib is made more durable by counterwrapped monofilament. The strand of Krystal Flash for the underwing is folded twice and tied in at its center, giving four pieces to each side. The loop ends are trimmed in proportion to hook size. The stacked deer-hair wing is set at a 45-degree angle and tied in at the front of the abdomen at the center of the hook. After the hackle is tied in at the front of the wings, the thorax is dubbed, and the hackle is wrapped through it. Merne Judson's use of Superfine Dubbing over brown thread results in a natural coloration. The blue Krystal Flash fibers provide a subtle, attractive glitter.

HARE'S EAR PARACHUTE

Hook:	#12-18 TMC 100
Thread:	Dark olive 8/0 UNI-Thread
Tail:	Brown Whiting (tailing pack)
Body:	Light hare's ear dubbing
Thorax:	Light hare's ear dubbing
Wing post:	Yellow McFlylon with a few midge Krystal Flash fibers
Hackle:	Barred ginger dry-fly saddle

Quickly tied and very visible, this is Brad Befus's go-to pattern, especially for smaller streams and any high country waters. Try it on the upper Gallatin River and tributaries such as Fan Creek. It works very well on Grayling Creek and Soda Butte Creek. Brad has used it as a *Callibaetis* dun imitation as well as for other mayfly duns. He also uses pink or white materials in forming the wing post.

HO CANDY

Hook:	#2-6 TMC 200R
Thread:	Fluorescent orange 6/0 UNI-Thread
Tail:	Golden pheasant tippet fibers
Abdomen:	Yellow Spectrum Ice Dub

Wing:	White poly yarn under pearl Krystal Flash
Overwing:	Tips of deer hair used to form bullet head
Legs:	Black barred tan rubber legs
Head:	Natural deer body hair

Tim Wade created this fly for the abundant freestone streams in the greater Yellowstone Area. He points to its particular success on the North Fork of the Shoshone River and the Clark's Fork of the Yellowstone River, where it is used as an adult stonefly imitation or as a hopper pattern. In addition to the yellow version pictured and discussed above, he offers it in a red (red Orvis Spectrum Ice Dub abdomen), a royal (peacock Orvis Spectrum Ice and red Orvis Spectrum Ice dubbing abdomen), and a Double X version (second set of legs mounted at midabdomen and tan foam strip tied in over abdomen). Tim also suggests trailing any version with his North Fork Special.

HOT BUTT SHARP & BUFF

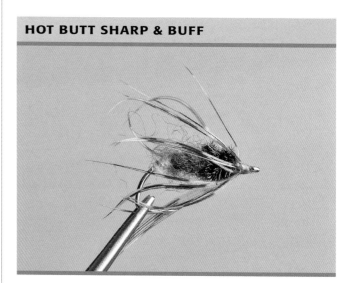

Hook:	#11 Alec Jackson's Crystal Soft Hackle Trout Fly
Thread:	Tan 70-denier UTC Ultra Thread
Tag:	Chartreuse Lagartun French Mini Flat Braid
Abdomen:	Bison undercoat or "bison down"
Thorax:	Tan UV Ice Dub
Hackle:	Sharp-tailed grouse back feather

Bison hair is available in the Greater Yellowstone Area like nowhere else on earth. It is easily collected along bison migration routes in springtime when bison shed their winter coats. The down must be combed from the coarser guard hairs and cleaned of dirt, grass seeds, and other foreign materials. After dubbing the down into an abdomen and Ice Dub into a thorax, Bob Starck uses a Velcro brush to comb out the bison and Ice Dub fibers. This is Bob's favorite searching fly, whether swung like a soft-hackle or dead-drifted. He also substitutes a partridge flank feather for the hackle and a red butt "hot spot" to give the fly a different look.

JIMMY-Z

Hook:	#10-14 Dai-Riki 300
Thread:	Yellow 6/0 UNI-Thread
Tail:	Red calf tail fibers
Rib:	Grizzly saddle hackle
Abdomen:	Chartreuse dubbing
Underwing:	Pearl Angel Hair
Wing:	White calf tail
Legs:	Size small brown and tan Centipede rubber legs
Overwing/collar:	Tips of deer hair used to form head
Head:	Deer hair clipped to shape

Jimmy Gabettas ties in deer hair for the collar/overwing, then the rubber legs on either side. After these, he ties in and spins deer hair. He clips this deer hair to shape the head. This fly won the 2004 Jackson Hole One Fly contest. It is also Jimmy's favorite small stream dry-fly pattern, where it can simulate a caddisfly, Yellow Sally, hopper, or deer fly.

JR GRANDE

Hook:	#10-16 Dai-Riki 300
Thread:	Black 8/0 UNI-Thread
Tail:	Speckled Coq de Leon fibers
Body:	Black Larva Lace Super Floss
Post:	Fluorescent orange Hi-Viz
Thorax:	Black Superfine Dubbing
Hackle:	Coachman brown grizzly saddle

When Jerry Toft visits the Greater Yellowstone Area to fish, this pattern is always in his fly box. It produces on the Harriman State Park reach of the Henry's Fork and on nearby streams, including Warm River. On all these, it effectively imitates insects from ants to Mahogany Duns. Brook trout and cutthroat trout in smaller waters seem to heartily respond to it. Jerry's original version used a golden pheasant tippet post and a dyed-black white quill body. He now uses the Hi-Viz post for added visibility and the Super Floss for improved durability.

MAGIC RENEGADE

Hook:	#6-16 Daiichi 1170
Thread:	Black
Tag:	Touch dubbing, LaFontaine Double Magic (DM) style
Rear hackle:	Brown dry-fly saddle
Body:	Peacock herl
Front hackle:	White dry-fly saddle
Head:	Tying thread

This fly by Gretchen Beatty takes advantage of the LaFontaine DM style (where natural and synthetic fibers are combined in a dubbing loop) in the application of its tag. A detailed description for preparing Double Magic dubbing is given in Al and Gretchen Beatty's book *LaFontaine's Legacy* (Lyons Press, 2008). The Magic Renegade is a real killer for the fish on the Madison and Gallatin Rivers in Yellowstone Park and any other similar cobble-bottom streams. It is the Beatty's go-to pattern for some of Idaho's freestone rivers. By changing the color of the dubbing in the tag, it is equally attractive in many other environments: for example, a yellow DM tag is a real fish-catcher on the Yellowstone River upstream from Livingston, Montana.

RUBBER LEG DOUBLE HUMPY

Hook:	#4-10 Daiichi 1720
Thread:	Yellow or red 3/0 Monocord
Tail:	Deer body hair
Underbodies:	Tying thread
Wings/backs:	Deer body hair with tips forming upright and divided wings
Legs:	Black-and-white banded rubber legs
Hackle:	Grizzly

This fly has been an Allen family tradition for decades. Boots Allen's contribution is the rubber legs that make it more lifelike and therefore more effective. It can be fished dry (dead-drift or skittered along the surface) or wet (sunk at shallow depth close to overhead structure, then pulled away). Add the rubber leg strips to this pattern before winding the hackle. Consider tying more than two Humpies on a long shank hook and see if the result brings even more interest!

SARAH'S BUG

Hook:	#8-16 TMC 100
Thread:	Dark brown 8/0 UNI-Thread
Tail:	Golden pheasant

Body:	Peacock herl
Rib:	Extra limp Flashabou and 5X monofilament
Wing:	UV pearl Krystal Flash and white Para Post
Hackle:	One each grizzly and coachman brown saddle

This is Sarah Judson's favorite dry pattern for fishing the Greater Yellowstone Area waters. She appreciates it visibility and versatility. Sarah's husband, Merne, ties this pattern in various sizes to imitate insects drifting on the surface. The peacock herl body with its Flashabou rib is made more durable by counterwrapped monofilament. The strand of Krystal Flash for the underwing is folded twice and tied in at its center, giving four pieces to each side. The loop ends are trimmed in proportion to hook size. The Para Post wing is set at a 45-degree angle. The two hackles are tied in at the wing base, then wrapped forward three or four turns, each depending on hook size.

SLAMMER

Hook:	#16-20 Dai-Riki 320
Thread:	8/0 UNI-Thread, color to match natural
Tail:	Krystal Flash fibers, color to match natural
Body:	Tying thread over tail fibers secured to hook shank
Thorax:	Base built of tying thread, then Hareline dubbing, color to match natural
Wing:	Post of white Antron
Hackle:	Dry-fly quality white saddle

Fred Sica's Slammer is a superbly versatile attractor pattern in which materials can be varied in color and hooks in sizes to match a wide variety of stoneflies, mayflies, and midges. For example, a yellow body and red egg sac gives a Yellow Sally. A black Slammer becomes a midge and uses a black hackle. An olive theme gives a Blue-Winged Olive (BWO). A pattern imitating the pinkish-tinged Pale Morning Dun (PMD) duns that emerge from the South Fork reach of the Snake River is pictured above. Fred has tried various Slammer versions on the Henry's Fork and the Madison River. All these streams have good riffles and runs where the Slammer is effective. Fred suggests fishing it as a lead fly trailed by an emerger pattern.

SMIDGET

Hook:	#16 Daiichi 1640
Thread:	Light cahill 8/0 UNI-Thread
Shuck:	White Antron or Z-Lon fibers
Body:	Tying thread
Back/head:	Pink McFly Foam
Hackle:	Dry-fly quality grizzly

This is another attractor pattern Tim Tollett created for many occasions along the Beaverhead River drainage, including spring creeks. Some midges there have a pink hue, so the pink Smidget is shown above. The Smidget can also be used to simulate floating ants, beetles, caddisflies, and mayflies. Cut out a light olive, dark olive, black, or lime McFly Foam accordingly to form its shellback, head, and wing case. Tied with light yellow McFly Foam and a red butt, the Smidget can be a small Yellow Sally.

SYNTH DOUBLE WING

Hook:	#8-12 Montana Fly Company 7000
Thread:	Black 8/0 UNI-Thread
Tail:	Caddis amber Z-Lon
Tag:	Fluorescent orange 140-denier thread
Rear wing:	Brown Widow's Web fibers
Body:	Peacock herl
Body hackle:	Golden straw or tan dyed grizzly, trimmed top and bottom
Front wing:	Polar bear Widow's Web fibers
Front hackle:	Brown grizzly saddle

This pattern is a development of Gary LaFontaine's original Double Wing concept that replaces the original's hair wings with synthetic materials to increase durability and floatation and slash overall tying time. Walter Weise coats the fluorescent orange tag of this pattern with superglue to add a subtle sparkle and increase durability. He suggests using it as a dry attractor. It is also very effective during the heavy flows of runoff when trailing a large Salmonfly pattern or when supporting a dropper nymph.

TIM'S ALTERNATOR

Hook:	#8-16 Dai-Riki 270
Thread:	Black 6/0 UNI-Thread
Abdomen:	Fine flat Mylar tinsel
Wing:	Bleached elk
Thorax:	Peacock herl
Hackle:	Brown dry-fly saddle

Tim King offers this pattern as a dry attractor that can be an emerging caddisfly or mayfly. Treated with floatant, the Mylar abdomen rides in the surface film while the treated wing and thorax rides on top of it. Start the Mylar abdomen over the barb and end at the shank midpoint. Tie in the wing with tips just past the hook bend and posted at a 45-degree angle. Tie in the rear of the peacock herl thorax, wrap the hackle, and complete the thorax to behind the hook eye.

TIM'S CARBURATOR

Hook:	#4-12 Dai-Riki 270
Thread:	Black 6/0 UNI-Thread
Abdomen:	Antique gold dubbing
Wing:	Bleached elk hair

Wing case: Black and yellow closed-cell foam
Thorax: Peacock herl
Legs: Tan/black barred rubber legs
Hackle: Brown dry-fly saddle

Tim King's low riding attractor pattern seems successful in bringing fish to the surface on bright days. Dub the body forward to midshank. Tie in the wing with tips just past the hook bend and posted at a 45-degree angle. Tie in the foam wing case butt end ahead of the wing and form the peacock herl thorax halfway to the eye. Tie in the legs, wrap the hackle at legs, and trim away top barbs. Finish the thorax and pull the foam wing case over the top to be secured just behind the eye. Consider different colors for the wing case and brown dubbing for the thorax.

TRASHMASTER

Hook: #14-20 TMC 2488H for nymph or wet fly; #14-20 TMC 921 for dry fly
Thread: Light cahill UNI-Thread
Butt: Red Hareline Dubbin
Body: Pale yellow dubbing and UV Ice Dub mix
Rib: Small gold Ultra Wire
Wing: Dyed white or natural CDC
Head: Red fox squirrel dubbing

Tim Tollett's pattern simulates all dead or drowning insects that fish key on during latter stages of an emergence. He prefers to fish it in the surface film or even as a nymph under a split shot. It can also be fished on the surface. Use it for taking large, elusive trout. A pearl Krystal Flash underwing is optional.

TUTTI FRUTTI BEN FRANKLIN

Hook: #14 Mustad 94840
Thread: Gray 6/0 UNI-Thread
Wing: Gray deer hair with fine tips; fluorescent pink, yellow, chartreuse, and fluorescent orange-dyed hair
Body: Gray closed-cell foam strip

Steven Fernandez devised this pattern for fast water. It can be used to represent caddisflies, stoneflies, crickets, hoppers, etc. He specifies a light wire hook with a turned-down eye in the size to match the natural. It floats high without expensive dry-fly hackle and is easy to see under almost any condition because of multicolor wing.

CHAPTER 2

CADDISFLY LIFE CYCLE

There are more caddisfly species in Rocky Mountain waters than those of mayflies and stoneflies combined in the same region. Within Rocky Mountain habitats, including those in the Greater Yellowstone Area, caddisflies have adapted to a wide range of aqueous systems. They are most widespread in cool streams having some gradient. Streams of this type and in all sizes abound in the region, but caddisflies have also adapted to warmer and slower-moving streams. Some species inhabit stillwaters. Diverse and durable, they can tolerate less dissolved oxygen in waters than mayflies and stoneflies. Warmer water temperatures allow lower dissolved oxygen solubility and thus can be a measure of stream degradation. Although degradation of waters has happened for human reasons already mentioned in the introduction, warmer waters in the Greater Yellowstone Area happen mainly because of geologic conditions, such as found on the Firehole River, or because of temporary drought conditions. It must be remembered that most of the region receives less than 20 inches of precipitation a year, and that most of this is concentrated during winter.

Rhyacophilidae, Hydropsychidae, Glossosomatidae, Hydroptilidae, Brachycentridae, and Lepidostomatidae families of caddisflies are all represented in Greater Yellowstone Area waters. Within these families a large number of species are present, and one wonders why fly tiers have not created more specific patterns for caddisfly species. A good part of the answer to this question is biological as well as historical. Many of our fly-fishing and fly-tying traditions originated in the British Isles, where mayfly species are abundant and widespread. Caddisfly species there number less than fifty.

Caddisflies mature through four metamorphic stages (egg, larva, pupa, adult). The pupal stage is most important as an available food for salmonids; thus this stage is the major subject for fly tiers. Larval forms of caddisfly families can be free living, meaning swimming freely in water, or case building. Case builders make use of all kinds of detritus materials on stream bottoms. Case-building larvae are seldom imitated by fly tiers. Free-living pupal forms are most easily utilized by salmonids as food forms, so they are commonly simulated by tiers. Synthetic materials have done much for simulating larval and free-swimming and cased pupal forms. Adult caddisfly patterns are also a major subject for regional fly tiers.

Through scuba-diving observations, well known fly fisherman Gary LaFontaine saw that tiny air bubbles near the surface of emerging caddis give that insect a subtle sparkle. His subsequent discovery that the synthetic yarn Antron effectively simulates these air bubbles revolutionized the way caddis pupa flies are tied. Antron, a three-sided yarn, not only reflects light in a subtle manner, but it is also translucent. The influence of Gary's discoveries, as explained in his benchmark book *Caddisflies*, has influenced how fly tiers everywhere simulate caddisfly pupae and free-swimming larvae. Thus the use of Antron, Z-Lon, or other yarns with equal reflective properties will be seen in many of the patterns described below.

LARVA, PUPA, AND FREE-SWIMMING LARVA PATTERNS

ARF BOTTOM HUGGER CADDIS

Hook:	#10-14 TMC 2457
Thread:	Olive-green 70-denier UTC Ultra Thread
Head:	Black stonefly Flymen Fishing Company tungsten head bead
Shellback:	Olive Scud Back, 1/8-inch wide caddis green Hare's Ice Dub
Abdomen:	Three caddis green Flymen Fishing Company beads
Thorax:	Peacock Hare's Ice Dub

Al Ritt designed this fly to be bounced along the bottom, so one should carry a good supply of them while fishing. Al's uncommon and clever use of several beads provides a segmented appearance and adds sparkle for this deep-water fly. He dead-drifts it alone or fishes it as an anchor in any two-fly rig.

ATT EMERGER

Hook:	#10-18 TMC 2457
Bead:	Gold
Weight:	Twelve to fifteen wraps of 0.020-inch-diameter lead or lead-free wire

Thread:	Olive 70-denier
Rib:	Gold tinsel
Tail:	Copper Antron yarn
Abdomen:	Peacock Spectra Dubbing
Underwing:	Copper Antron yarn
Wing:	Olive Swiss Straw
Thorax:	Peacock Spectra Dubbing
Hackle:	Partridge flank

Tim Wade designed this pattern (ATT is for "All the Time" Emerger) for the heavy current streams in the Greater Yellowstone Area. These streams abound in caddisflies, a major food item for resident salmonids. The buggy appearance and color are important for these durable patterns. Tim offers the olive (green) version, described and pictured above; and a tan version in which tan dubbing (abdomen and thorax) replaces olive dubbing, brown Antron yarn (tail) replaces copper Antron yarn, and a few white hackle fibers are added to the underwing.

CADDIS EMERGER

Hook:	#8 TMC 2457
Bead:	Gold, 5/32-inch diameter
Thread:	Black 8/0 UNI-Thread
Tails:	Duck biot tips
Body:	Fine red UNI-Wire
Thorax:	Peacock herl
Wing case:	Pearlescent holographic tinsel
Hackle:	Hen pheasant flank feather

During the several years he lived in West Yellowstone during vacations, Jim Fisher experienced the wonderful fishing that surrounded the town. He tied flies to meet each of the many food forms available to resident salmonids. This pattern, his favorite caddis emerger, makes a different use for red wire that is popular in patterns imitating bloodworms. Jim found his pattern to be effective throughout the season during caddis emergences from the Madison River and the Henry's Fork.

CASED CADDIS

Hook:	#8-12 TMC 2499SPBL
Bead:	Gold or black
Thread:	Black or green 3/0 or 6/0
Rib:	4X monofilament
Body:	Pheasant tail fibers
Thorax:	Green Krystal Flash or Flashabou twisted around tying thread for strength

Hundreds of caddisfly species inhabit area streams. According to Rick Hafele and Dave Hughes in *Western Hatches*, there are more caddisflies species in the West than of mayflies and stoneflies combined. They are most diverse in cool, well-oxygenated waters where case builders are a major family in terms of species and numbers. Salmonids feed on these, case and all. Thus it is wise to have patterns such as the Cased Caddis by Jay Buchner in the fly box when visiting area streams.

ERV EMERGER

Hook:	#12-14 Dai-Riki 135
Thread:	Brown 3/0 Danville Monocord
Body:	Dubbed trilobal fibers in either cinnamon, golden olive, cream, or dark brown
Wing case:	Pheasant tail segment
Thorax:	Peacock herl
Hackle:	Hungarian partridge
Hinge:	Staple formed from 38-pound stainless-steel wire
Wing:	Elk mane tied on hinge

John Newbury designed this pattern to simulate a caddis pupa swimming to the surface to emerge. In Greater Yellowstone waters it has proven to be an excellent October Caddis emerger. Tie the fly, except the wing, on the Dai-Riki 135. Form the hinge as described in the discussion of John's Wiggle Damsel (page 65). Tie the elk-hair wing on the front half of the hinge, and pass the other end of the wire through the eye of the Dai-Riki 135 hook. Bend the end back to touch the hinge, thus securing it to the hook. Cover the rear half of the hinge with tying thread.

FREESTONE CASE CADDIS

Hook:	#12-16 Daiichi 1120
Bead:	Black brass
Thread:	Chartreuse 8/0 UNI-Thread

Rib:	Small copper wire
Body:	Ring-necked pheasant tail strands wrapped over peacock herl
Head:	Insect green Superfine Dubbing
Legs:	Black ostrich herl

After sliding the bead onto the hook to the eye and tying in the butt of the wire rib, Nick English ties in, depending on hook size, six to ten pheasant tail strands, then two or three, again depending on hook size, peacock herls. After reinforcing the peacock herls with thread, he spirals them forward, forming the underbody to within a sixteenth of an inch behind the bead. He wraps the pheasant tail fibers over the peacock herl to the same location. Next Nick ribs the body and dubs a small head, leaving room to form legs behind the bead. About five wraps of ostrich herl behind the bead forms legs and a whip-finish completes the fly that he and his parents suggest should be fished close to the bottom of streams having a good caddisfly population.

GRAPE SLUSHIE

Hook:	#16-18 Daiichi 1130
Bead:	Purple glass
Thread:	Purple 8/0 UNI-Thread
Rib:	Fine red copper wire
Body:	Brown UV Ice Dub

Here is a different, but easily tied and very effective caddis pupa pattern by John Arnold. It has also come into use in the Greater Yellowstone Area as a midge pupa pattern. Named after a dessert as was done with the older Ice Cream Cone midge pupa pattern, it is now gaining in popularity through this dual use. And as with any new fly pattern, modifications are being made. When used as a midge pupa, fish it under an indicator at a depth where feeding fish are responding or as a dropper off a dry or emerging midge pattern.

GREEN CADDIS MITE

Hook:	#4-12 Dai-Riki 710
Thread:	Black 6/0 Danville Flymaster
Underbody:	Two strands of light yellow DMC embroidery floss
Body:	Caddis green FisHair
Hackle:	Barred badger guard hair
Head:	Peacock herl

Chuck Collins uses the Pott Mite weave to form the body of this caddis pupa pattern. (Search www.flyanglersonline.com for instructions on this technique.) Rather than using traditional hair for the overbody, he experiments with modern synthetic fibers such as FisHair, his favorite. He minimizes body materials to obtain the slim, tapered shape of a caddis pupa body. Stack the badger guard hair and cleaned-off undercoat before being evenly distributed and tied in by the dark butt end. After the fly is completed, the badger hair hackle is trimmed to be about 20 percent longer than the body.

GREEN CADDIS ROCKWORM

Hook:	#8-16 TMC 2457
Bead:	Black tungsten
Thread:	Fluorescent chartreuse 140-denier Danville
Rib:	Dark green Sparkle Flex or fluorescent chartreuse D-Rib
Body:	Chartreuse rabbit fur
Thorax:	Peacock herl

This was the pattern Bob Jacklin created, then used to take a 10-pound brown trout from the Madison River just below the Cabin Creek confluence on June 16, 2006. This fish was more than likely a Quake Lake fish foraging in the river. Here is another example of a simple pattern placed properly to bring an unforgettable result. As one might expect, sales of this pattern have been up for Bob since he took this fish.

HENRY'S LAKE CADDIS

Hook:	#8 Mustad R74
Thread:	Medium brown and dark brown 70-denier
Body:	Tan seal fur blend with orange undertones

Body bubble/tail:	Wood duck flank wound as a collar, then pulled back over body with tips forming tail
Collar:	Partridge flank feather
Head:	Dark brown seal dubbing

Marvin Nolte covers the hook shank with medium brown thread to the bend, leaving a foot-long tag end there. He dubs a shaggy body on the rear two-thirds of the shank, then ties in the wood duck feather tip first. He whip-finishes and cuts off the thread, then winds a wood duck feather as a wet fly collar. Gathering its fibers at the bend, he gently secures them using the thread tag end, forming a bubble around the body, then whip-finishes the thread. He secures dark brown tying thread in front of the body and winds a partridge feather tip first. He dubs the seal fur head to finish the fly. During midsummer twilights, a large caddisfly emerges from Henry's Lake. Observing that fish prey on this caddisfly, Marvin designed this pattern to imitate it using a sinking line with short, slow pulls.

HOOKER WITH ATTITUDE

Hook:	#10-12 TMC 2487
Weight:	0.015-inch-diameter lead or lead-free wire on entire shank with 0.010-inch-diameter lead or lead-free wire on top of it on middle third of shank
Thread:	Black 6/0 UNI-Thread
Flashback:	Strip of pearlescent Mylar
Rib:	Small copper wire
Body:	Overhand weave of medium dark brown embroidery yarn on top and light tan sparkle yarn on bottom
Legs:	"V" cut brownish partridge feather

Shellback for head: Mottled oak natural Thin Skin
Head: Black peacock Ice Dub

Michael Snody's realistic caddis larva pattern has enough subtle flash to make it attractive at depth as well as higher in the water column. The copper wire adds segmentation to the flashback while securing it to the woven body, and the partridge legs add motion. Fish this pattern on the stream bottom or drifting low in the water column.

KG'S CASED CADDIS

Hook:	#12-14 Dai-Riki 060
Bead:	Black nickel, 3/32-inch
Thread:	Black 8/0 UNI-Thread
Abdomen:	Small diameter light tan Estaz chenille through which sparse, spiky hare's ear is dubbed
Peaking caddis:	Two wraps of chartreuse Fine and Dry Dubbing
Head and legs:	Black "spectrumized" spiky dubbing

After forming body on rear two-thirds of shank and securing Estaz chenille, the tying thread used is spiraled back to rear, touch dubbed with natural hare's ear fibers and wrapped through the chenille. The peaking caddis, head, and legs are formed next behind the bead. Black "spectrumized" dubbing is Kelly Glissmeyer's creation in which he mixes very small amounts of blue, orange, pink, and red fibers to the black material to impart subtle color centers within its mass.

KORN'S GREEN LANTERN

Hook:	#14-16 Daiichi 1550
Bead:	Toho green 11/0 glass
Thread:	Olive 200 Serafil or 8/0 UNI-Thread
Tail/shellback/wing:	Fox squirrel tail
Rib:	28-gauge copper wire
Abdomen:	Bright green dubbing
Collar:	Loose green dubbing

Doug Korn cuts the tips off the stack of squirrel tail hairs he uses to form the tail, shellback, and wing of this pattern. He ties in the ends left from cutting away tips behind the bead, wraps the tying thread back to the bend over the squirrel-hair stack, and splits the stack into one-third for the tail, two-thirds for the shellback and wing. After pulling the portion for the shellback forward over the dubbed and ribbed body and tying it off behind the bead, he then folds the portion to the rear to form the wing and adds the collar. This is a great caddis pupa pattern for use on Soda Butte Creek, Lamar River, and Slough Creek in the northeast corner of Yellowstone National Park.

KORN'S MARABOU CADDIS

LITEBRIGHT SERENDIPITY

Hook:	#14-16 Daiichi 1120
Thread:	Brown 8/0 waxed UNI-Thread
Rib:	Fine copper wire
Body:	Marabou fibers dubbed on waxed thread
Thorax cover #1:	Holographic tinsel silver
Wings/Legs:	Partridge feather
Thorax:	Fox squirrel or hare's ear dubbing
Thorax cover #2:	Partridge feather butt

After forming the ribbed body, tie in the tinsel strip and the "V" cut partridge feather, tips facing rear, forming legs and wings. Fold the partridge feather butt back to the rear, dub the thorax, and pull forward, forming the thorax cover. Pull the tinsel strip forward over the folded partridge feather, forming the top thorax cover. Tie off just behind hook eye. Apply a drop of BUG-BOND on the tinsel thorax cover. Treat with a UV light to harden. Doug Korn designed this caddis fly to have the bubble back of an emerging caddis. He uses BUG-BOND on the top thorax cover to produce this effect. Variations include: bead head, thorax cover of opal tinsel ribbing. This fly in tan or olive is very effective as a dropper in sizes 14 to 16 in waters of Yellowstone National Park where caddisflies are present.

Hook:	#12-18 TMC 2457
Bead:	Silver
Thread:	Tan 8/0 UNI-Thread
Abdomen:	Dark olive twisted Z-Lon
Thorax:	Dubbed pearlescent Lite Brite behind dubbed sparkle hare's mask

Howard Cole recommends that twisting the Z-Lon fibers into a rope after attaching them to the hook shank makes a more durable and segmented appearing body. To keep the Z-Lon rope in proportion to hook size, he removes fiber from it before twisting. Howard also recommends use of a dubbing loop to apply the Lite Brite and sparkle hare's mask dubbing, but offers that a loosely dubbed thorax picked out with a bodkin will also do. He uses this pattern to imitate caddisfly pupae and larvae. Smaller sizes could be used to imitate midge pupae. Howard also ties this pattern with red twisted Z-Lon abdomen.

MALLARD CADDIS

Hook:	#12-16 TMC 2457
Thread:	Olive 8/0
Body:	Peacock herl
Wing:	Tip section from mallard flank feather

Sylvester Nemes introduced this pattern at the 2008 Western Rocky Mountain Council FFF Conclave in West Yellowstone, Montana. This was the last public event in which he demonstrated his fly-tying skills. At the time he offered that this pattern was his favorite caddis emerger pattern. He talked of using it on spring creeks and famed rivers of southwestern Montana. He would dead-drift it just below the surface, then lift his rod tip to raise it in the water column as it approached working fish. Syl authored six books, all addressing the soft-hackled fly. Any work on Greater Yellowstone fly patterns would be incomplete without some of Syl's patterns.

MIKE'S CZECH NYMPH (ORANGE HEART)

Hook:	#10-12 TMC 2487
Weight:	0.010- or 0.015-inch-diameter lead or lead-free wire
Thread:	Camel 6/0 UNI-Thread for abdomen, fire orange 6/0 UNI-Thread for orange heart, and black 6/0 UNI-Thread for thorax
Shell:	Brown Thin Skin
Inner rib:	Gold Flashabou
Outer rib:	0.004-inch-diameter tippet material
Abdomen:	Hare's ear and gold Dubbin dubbing mixed
Orange heart:	LaFontaine golden russet dubbing
Thorax:	UV black Ice Dub

Michael Snody designed this caddis larva pattern specifically for brown trout, thus the use of gold and orange materials. It has proven effective on the South Fork reach of the Snake River and the Madison River. He believes the black UV dubbing gives this fly a lifelike head.

NAKED CADDIS

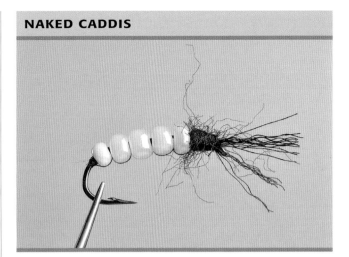

Hook:	#6 Mustad 9672
Thread:	Black 3/0 Danville Monocord
Body:	Four 4/0 opaque pearl glass seed beads and one 6/0 cream-colored glass seed bead
Head:	One strand of black yarn combed and teased
Legs:	Four strands of Bestway Super Hair folded twice

For some unknown reason, larvae of several large caddisflies species (e.g., *Dicosmoecus*) drop their stone cases (thecae) and become free-swimming along the stream bottom. Soon thereafter, they begin rebuilding their thecae. But during the period of nakedness, trout of all kinds and sizes gorge themselves on those succulent morsels. Sadly, most fly fishermen are oblivious to those events, and so miss the chance of a lifetime for some unbelievable fly fishing. Harley Reno, however, has experienced those events many times during the late summer and early fall on large streams and rivers throughout the Greater Yellowstone Area, including in streams and rivers of the Absaroka Mountains. He suggests that, when nothing else seems to work, try casting the Naked Caddis. You likely will be surprised!

POLY TWIST CADDIS LARVA

Hook:	#12-16 Mustad 3906B
Thread:	Black 6/0 Danville Flymaster
Body:	Olive poly yarn
Thorax:	Blended amounts of two-thirds black fur with guard hairs and one-third black Sparkle Yarn

Don Heyden attaches the poly yarn along the rear three-quarters of the hook shank and builds a tapered body with tying thread. After the yarn is secured to a point slightly down the bend, he twists the yarn tightly until just before it begins to kink. He wraps the resulting "rope" forward clockwise, forming a segmented body. He dubs the thorax and finishes it by picking out guard hairs to form legs. Through dead-drifting this pattern at depth from an up and across cast, this pattern has proven effective in many Greater Yellowstone Area streams. Change poly yarn color to match that of any caddis larva encountered.

RHYACOPHILA PUPA

Hook:	#10-14 Mustad 3906
Thread:	Black 6/0
Body:	Olive Ice Dub
Thorax:	Golden brown Ice Dub
Legs:	Brown hen hackle

Rhyacophila caddisflies inhabit all streams of gradient in the Greater Yellowstone Area. They emerge from April to November and are an important food form for salmonids. They inhabit streams of gradient in other salmonid-hosting waters around the country, but not in the same numbers. Although Kieran Frye lives in Mt. Pleasant, Pennsylvania, he makes many visits to Greater Yellowstone waters. This is one of his go-to patterns because he is aware that pupae of this caddisfly are available to salmonids there throughout the season.

RUBY'S CADDIS EMERGER

Hook:	#12-18 Daiichi 1130
Thread:	Orange 6/0 Danville flat-waxed nylon
Shuck:	Five or six strands of cream Antron mixed with three ostrich herl tips
Body:	Twisted bundle of ostrich herl for the rear third; Sow-Scud Dubbing for the front two-thirds
Wing:	Blond or light elk hair
Collar:	Light ginger dry-fly saddle

This pattern is Russ Forney's presentation choice when fish are taking active caddisflies in Greater Yellowstone Area waters and those beyond. Try green, tan, gray, and orange variations or any color to match that of active caddisflies. The hair wing and hackle keep the top of the fly on the surface with the curved body dropping below the surface film.

SPEYED PRINCE

Hook:	#7 Izuo A. H.
Bead:	Black tungsten, $3/16$-inch
Thread:	Red 6/0 UNI-Thread
Tag:	Red tying thread
Rib:	Red wire
Overbody:	Silver or gold Mylar strip
Body:	Light green rabbit fur dubbing
Wings:	White goose biots
Hackle:	Soft black hen saddle
Head:	Light brown dubbing

Scott Urbanski created this pattern for emerging large caddisflies, including the October Caddis. It has an unusual configuration with a long tag and short body ribbed with red wire. The presentation that works best is a deep swing near the bottom while maintaining a tight line. Fish take it as it rises from the bottom.

TAK'S GO2 CADDIS

Hook:	#14-18 TMC 9300
Bead:	Gold
Thread:	Olive dun 8/0 UNI-Thread
Tail:	Brown Whiting Farms hen hackle fibers
Rib:	Pearl Flashabou strand

Body:	Peacock herl
Wing:	White polyester yarn
Hackle:	Brown Whiting Farms midge saddle
Collar:	Peacock Ice Dub

Rick Takahashi fishes his GO2 Prince and GO2 Caddis all year long and in every water condition. He catches fish in both streams and stillwaters wherever he fished this combination. He prepares nymph rigs as follows for all types of stream conditions, but a bit longer when fishing stillwaters. His fundamental component is a $7^{1}/_{2}$-foot 4X tapered leader. He ties on a 16- to 18-inch length of 5X tippet. To that he ties on a 10- to 12-inch section of 6X tippet. To the 6X tippet he attaches his first nymph pattern (GO2 Prince). He then attaches another section of 10 to 12 inches of 6X tippet to the eye of the first nymph and then ties on his dropper nymph (GO2 Caddis).

WEISE'S GLASS HEAD PT SOFT HACKLE

Hook:	#14-16 Dai-Riki 060
Thread:	Dark brown 6/0 MFC
Bead:	Amber 11/0 glass
Hackle:	Speckled brown India hen fibers
Rib:	Fine gold wire
Body:	Pheasant tail fibers
Thorax:	Peacock herl

After mounting the bead on the hook, Walter Weise strips fibers from the hen hackle and ties them in tips forward and evenly distributed behind the bead. After forming the ribbed body and thorax, he brings the thread throught the hackle and behind the bead. Here a few thread wraps orient the hackle tips to the rear of the fly. He suggests this hackling method because of the stem thickness of the hen hackle. He recommends this pattern particularly for the early and late season on the Firehole River.

ADULT PATTERNS

ALIEN EGG LAYING CADDIS

Hook:	#8-14 TMC 2302
Thread:	Dark olive 8/0 UNI-Thread
Egg sac:	Chartreuse closed-cell foam
Rib:	Copper Krystal Flash strand
Abdomen:	Caddis green Hare-Tron dubbing
Underwing:	Tent shape from Web Wing sheet
Overwing:	Deer hair mixed with a few strands of rainbow Krystal Flash
Legs:	Medium speckled olive Centipede Legs
Hackle:	Badger saddle
Thorax:	Tan Ice Dub

Egg-laying caddis occur throughout the season on Yellowstone Area streams. Particularly heavy swarms of egg-laying adults occur in the afternoon on the Madison River and the Henry's Fork in the latter part of June. Timing is important for success during these actions. It is best to be fishing near the beginning of the egg-laying event before responding fish get filled. This is Michael Snody's pattern for success at these times. He also uses it in larger sizes to simulate the October Caddis emerging late in the season.

ARF TRAILING BUBBLE HAREY CADDIS

Hook:	#14-18 TMC 101
Thread:	Olive 8/0 UNI-Thread
Trailing bubbles:	Opal Mirage Flashabou
Abdomen:	Olive Superfine Dubbing
Underwing:	Opal Mirage Flashabou
Wing:	Tan snowshoe hare (from back feet)
Thorax:	Olive Superfine Dubbing
Hackle:	Olive grizzly dyed saddle (V-trimmed in bottom)

Al Ritt's Trailing Bubble Harey Caddis and his Trailing Bubble Harey Yellowstone (see page 147) make use of the same concept and address multiple stages of certain caddis and little yellow stonefly species. The flashes off the back (trailing bubbles) are meant to mimic gas bubbles coming off the back of quickly emerging insects and diving egg layers returning to the surface. This pattern can be dead-drifted with the flash underwing imitating the movement of a fluttering wing or skittered like an emerger or surface egg layer. It can also be sunken and fished with a lift to act as an emerger or egg layer returning to the surface.

BALLOON CADDIS

Hook:	#12-18 Daiichi 1170
Thread:	Cream or light brown 8/0 Montana Fly Company
Body:	Velveteen tan rabbit fur dubbing
Hackle:	Light ginger or medium-barred ginger saddle palmered around body
Wing:	Natural early season elk
Thorax/head:	Yellow 2-mm closed-cell foam or yellow polycelon foam

Chris Helm's pattern is based on one by Austria's Roman Moser. Chris's changes include a palmered midge hackle (size 20 to 22 on a size 12 pattern) and the use of closed-cell foam for the head rather than polycelon. Both Chris and Roman describe this pattern as a caddisfly as it leaves its pupal shuck and begins to spread its wings. It is a superb fast-water pattern that does not sink easily, thus Chris recommends it for such waters as the middle Madison and upper Gallatin Rivers.

BENT CADDIS EMERGER

Hook:	#14 Daiichi 1130
Thread:	Tan 8/0
Shuck:	Amber micro Z-Lon

Rib:	Opal Mirage Flashabou
Abdomen:	Pale olive Hare-Tron dubbing
Wing:	Tan TroutHunter CDC
Overwing:	Six partridge feathers
Hackle:	Cree rooster saddle

Ben Byng ties the body down onto the bend of the hook. He leaves the CDC and partridge waste hanging on the eye of the hook to form the head, much like on an Elk Hair Caddis. Cut this waste to form a head once the fly is whip-finished. Through a twilight fishing experience during a Madison River caddisfly emergence, Ben discovered that this fly having a heavy CDC wing was quite easy to see on the broken surface. The use of a scud hook for this fly helps when the caddisfly is diving back into the water to lay eggs and/or emerging.

BLACK CADDIS

Hook:	#16-20 Daiichi 1170
Thread:	Black-brown 6/0 UNI-Thread
Antennae:	Black Microfibetts
Butt:	Yellow/green Shimmer Skin for egg-laying female
Body:	Black-brown Superfine Dubbing
Wings:	Weedguard fabric
Hackle:	Undersized black saddle

Hugh Huntley bends a length of Microfibett double for antennae. He faces the bend in this piece to the rear and ties it in behind the hook eye, pointing the two ends forward. Weedguard, from which he cuts wings, is a fine-textured, durable fabric placed around plants and flowers to inhibit weed growth. It is offered in home and garden shops and plant nurseries. Weedguard can be used without being colored or given any color desired through using marking pens. During afternoons Hugh experiences success with this pattern on the Yellowstone River and his "home waters," the Bighorn River.

BLACK CADDIS PUPIL

Hook:	#16-18 Dai-Riki 075
Thread:	Olive dun 8/0 UNI-Thread
Tail:	Yellow gold Antron yarn
Wing:	Natural brown TroutHunter CDC
Body:	Olive Superfine Dubbing

Frank Johnson suggests using a wet fly/nymph hook for added strength when tying this pattern. He ties in the tail, five or six fibers, then begins the minimally dubbed body—because caddis have very short, slender bodies under their long wings—at a point on the shank directly above the hook point. Tail length is twice the distance of the hook point to the end of the bend, and the tail should have a slight taper. He mounts at the front of body a medium-sized CDC feather, tips pointing to rear. He adjusts the length of the wing to bend of the hook by pulling butt under thread wraps toward the hook eye, and ties off. This pattern simulates the emerger, stillborn, and cripple stages of hatching caddis. Fish it trailing a full-dress adult caddisfly pattern.

BLUE CADDIS EMERGER

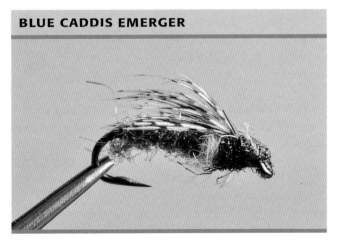

Hook:	#14-16 Daiichi 1530
Thread:	Olive 6/0 UNI-Thread
Body:	Blue Ice Dub

Thorax:	Yellow Fine and Dry Dubbing
Wing:	Hungarian partridge hackle fibers
Head:	Peacock herl

John Taylor designed this pattern for use on southeastern Idaho irrigation reservoirs when caddisflies emerge in early and midsummer. Patterns need be tied on a stout hook because large, strong trout are common inhabitants in these reservoirs. Because of his success with this pattern, John tried it in some of his favorite streams, including Yellowstone National Park's Slough Creek. Dead-drifted below an indicator here in the early season it has proven very effective. This pattern can also be tied with a gold bead of diameter proportional to hook size.

BRACKETT CADDIS EMERGER

Hook:	#16 Daiichi 1270
Thread:	Brown 8/0 UNI-Thread
Shuck:	Tan Z-Lon fibers
Rib:	Very fine gold wire
Body:	Dubbing, color to match natural
Hackle:	Tan saddle
Wing:	Dark dun snowshoe rabbit
Head:	White packing foam

Northwestern Wyoming has an abundance of freestone streams all of which host caddisflies in generous numbers. Dave Brackett visits all these waters, including the much-visited Snake River, the remotely beautiful but accessible Greys River, and a multitude of smaller waters within and nearby to Jackson Hole. This is his go-to caddis pattern for these waters. To help support the wing in a 45-degree upright position, he ties in the hackle behind it.

CDC EGG LAYING CADDIS

Hook: #16 TMC 100
Thread: Tan 8/0 UNI-Thread
Body: Natural brown CDC dubbing
Wing: Natural CDC
Head: Same as body

This pattern by Craig Mathews is much more easily tied than other egg-laying caddis patterns. Other than hook and thread it has only three components: body, wing, and head, all of which are of CDC. Caddisflies in various life-cycle stages are present in streams throughout the season. Peaks of activity are early and late in the season. Fertilized females of several species dive to lay eggs on substrate or submerged structure. Returning to the surface to lay further egg masses, they are vulnerable to foraging salmonids. This new pattern has been tested and has proven effective in simulating females that have returned to or are near the surface.

CLACKA CADDIS

Hook: #12-16 MFC 7000
Thread: Dark brown 8/0 UNI-Thread
Tail: Caddis gold Z-Lon
Body: Peacock herl

Wing: White MFC Widow's Web
Thorax: Chocolate brown Ice Dub
Hackle: Chocolate brown saddle

Described and pictured above is the Coachman version of Walter Weise's Clacka Caddis series. It has proven superbly effective as a high floating and visible caddis adult or even a dry attractor on the Yellowstone River and other area streams of similar gradient. Walter suggests using two peacock herls to form the body on smaller versions and three herls for the body of larger versions. Trim hackle fibers from the bottom of the fly, allowing it to ride lower on the surface. Other body colors in this series include lime, olive, pink, and tan.

DENNIS FLUTTERING CADDIS

Hook: #12-16 Dai-Riki 300
Thread: Brown 8/0 UNI-Thread
Body: Hare's ear dubbing
Underwing: Pearl Krystal Flash
Post: Butt ends of underwing
Wing: Hungarian partridge feather
Hackle: Grizzly saddle

Jack Dennis and his daughter, Amy, saw how effective Krystal Flash is for simulating a fluttering wing on a stonefly pattern, especially in the Amy's Special. They therefore applied this material to the wing of an adult caddisfly pattern. This fly is the result. To make it more delicate than the Amy's Special, the body is dubbed slender, and fewer Krystal Flash fibers are used to form the underwing and post. The bulky wing of light elk hair used in the Amy's Special is replaced in this pattern with a Hungarian grouse feather to give a delicate wing. The result is a highly effective and very visible pattern.

DY CADDIS

Hook:	#14-20 Daiichi 1120
Thread:	Black 8/0 UNI-Thread
Rib:	Tying thread
Extended body:	Closed-cell foam strip
Wing:	Medallion Sheeting
Collar:	Deer hair
Hackle:	Blue dun saddle

Deward Yocum forms an extended body by clamping the head of a sewing needle and the tip of tying thread in his vise with the needle point extending outward. He runs the thread along the shaft to the point, and makes five wraps of thread just at the point. He folds the foam strip around the point to extend along either side of the shaft, tying in the strip with five thread wraps at the point. He makes a diagonal cut from the fold so that its top surface is slightly longer than the bottom. To achieve segmentation, he advances the thread forward and wraps it around the foam repeatedly up the shaft to form segments. He removes the tied-off foam body, rolls it on a flat surface to achieve consistent shape, then attaches it to the hook shank. The strip tie-in area, colored black with a pen, is the thorax over which he wraps wing, collar, and hackle.

ELK CRYSTAL CADDIS

Hook:	#10-16 TMC 9300
Thread:	Black 8/0 UNI-Thread
Rib:	Pearl Krystal Flash
Body:	Peacock Arizona Synthetic Dubbing
Underwing:	Pearl Krystal Flash
Post:	Butt ends of Krystal Flash underwing
Wing:	Stacked light elk hair
Thorax:	Arizona crystal rabbit dubbing
Hackle:	Light olive-dyed grizzly, natural brown, or dun saddle

Jack Dennis's use of Krystal Flash to form the underwing and post of this fly is repeated in others of his patterns to simulate moving wings. After he stands the post up with thread wraps, he dubs a thorax around the base of the post with the hackle butt tied in. Originally he used rainbow thread for the wing and post, but he recommends that more easily obtained Krystal Flash works just as well.

FLUTTERING WHITE MILLER

Hook:	#16-20 TMC 100
Thread:	Light olive 8/0 UNI-Thread
Body:	Caddis green Superfine Dubbing

Wing: Two strands of white Z-Lon divided
Hackle: Oversized light dun saddle

To create this fly orginated by Blue Ribbon Flies and tied by Rowan Nyman, first dub a tapered body on the rear three-quarters of the shank, then form a thread base for securing the wings in front of the body. Tie in the wings on either side of the body and splay them out with thread wraps. Wrap three turns of hackle over the butt ends of the white Z-Lon wings, and clip these ends to a length short enough to form a head.

FOAM CADDIS

Hook: #12-16 TMC 100
Thread: White 6/0
Body: Tan translucent Razor Foam
Wing: Bleached deer body hair
Hackle: Cream saddle

Caddisflies are the major food form in all Greater Yellowstone streams. They begin emerging as early as April and continue to do so through late autumn. In a pinch, this pattern by Arrick Swanson can be used to simulate a spruce moth.

GALLOUP'S ULTRA CADDIS

Hook: #16-20 TMC 101 or 531
Thread: 6/0 or 8/0 UNI-Thread, red for black bodies, olive for all other colors
Abdomen: Short, fine deer hair tied in tip first around shank at hook bend, then pulled forward and secured with segmenting tying thread wraps
Wing: Short, fine natural deer hair
Head: Short, fine deer hair, color to match body, spun and clipped

Evening caddisfly falls are common events on area freestone streams such as the Madison, Gallatin, and Yellowstone Rivers, not to mention the multitude of small streams. Kelly Galloup tied this fly to represent a spent caddisfly during these activities. It is a low rider, making it a bit tough to see when the angler is facing the sun, but it is very effective. Tied in smaller sizes, this fly also double as a midge adult.

GREEN NECTARINE

Hook:	#12-18 TMC 2312
Thread:	Olive 8/0 UNI-Thread
Abdomen:	Caddis green or light olive Antron dubbing
Rib:	Palmered and clipped dun or grizzly hackle
Antennae:	Two stripped dun or grizzly hackle stems
Wings:	Dun-dyed or natural mallard flank feathers, reverse tied and clipped
Thorax:	Caddis green or olive Antron dubbing mix

Doug Andres applies a thread base on hook shank, ties in clipped hackle for rib, tip first, at the hook bend. He waxes thread before touch-dubbing and twisting thread, and dubs abdomen on rear two-thirds of shank and ribs with five turns of hackle. He secures and cements in place a stripped hackle stem to either side of the hook in front of dubbing to form antennae. He ties in horizontally on either side equivalent sized and shaped reverse-wrapped mallard flank feathers in front of abdomen, and trims excess. He dubs a thorax over the base of tied-in wings and forward to rear of the head. Coat wings with head cement for added durability.

ISHIYAMA CADDIS

Hook:	#12-20 Daiichi 1170
Thread:	Tan 6/0 Flymaster waxed
Body:	Superfine Dubbing, color to match natural
Underwing:	CDC feather
Wing:	Hen back feather, backed with Scotch Tape and reinforced with Flexament
Legs:	Deer hair with short black tips
Head:	Brown Superfine Dubbing
Wing case:	Narrow quill slip matching wing color

To create Nelson Ishiyama's fly, prepare wing by laying feather, dull side down, onto tape's sticky side. Ensure stem is straight and feather in full shape. Coat wing with Flexament. Allow to dry. Dub body three-quarter shank length. Tie in CDC feather, tips evened, one-quarter shank length past bend. Fold prepared wing feather in half along stem, tape side underneath, and trim into caddis wing shape. Tie in wing, stem centered on top of hook, sides straddling body, slightly longer than tented CDC fibers. Tie in quill strip centered on top of hook, in front of wing tie-in, and covering top of body. Tie in about 20 deer hairs centered on top of hook at wing tie-in point. Trim butts and dub over them. Pull long end of the wing case strip forward, splitting deer hairs to fan on either side. Tie down wing case and whip-finish.

KG'S HENRY'S FORK EGG-LAYING CADDIS

Hook:	#14 Dai-Riki 125
Thread:	Tan 8/0 UNI-Thread
Egg sac:	Bright pale olive Nature's Spirit Fine and Dry Dubbing
Abdomen:	Brown olive Nature's Spirit Fine and Dry Dubbing
Thorax:	Same as abdomen
Wings:	Bleached deer hair with brown tips
Head:	Tips of deer hair used to form wing clipped to shape

Kelly Glissmeyer's pattern simulates the *Hydropsyche* caddis that fly during early summer evening to lay eggs on the water. Fish lie in wait for their presence just below Ashton Dam on the Henry's Fork. At times they can be numerous enough to be a breathing nuisance. Kelly ties the wings on this pattern to be a quarter of the hook length past the bend. For added durability, he adds a drop of cement on the tying thread in back of the head.

KORN'S CDC SPENT-WING PARACHUTE CADDIS

Hook:	#14 MFC 7000
Thread:	Split tan Serafil 200
Body:	Tan type #1 or #4 CDC feather

Wing:	Two hen pheasant feathers tied flat with cement spread on top
Post:	White CDC type #3 puff
Hackle:	One natural type #1 or #4 CDC feather

Doug Korn takes numeric feather designations from Hans Weilenmann's CDC feather chart. Wrap tan CDC feather forward to form body and tie in wing. Fold #3 CDC puff in half and post. Prepare the CDC feather for hackling using a Marc Petitjean Magic Tool. Insert the prepared CDC feather in the split thread and spin to create CDC hackle. Wind the CDC hackle on hook shank, first behind post, then in front while lifting fibers. Wrap hackle to the eye. Trim parachute post to length and underside of fly flat. Tie off and trim thread. Doug fishes caddisfly imitations as droppers but also wanted a highly visible, floating lead caddisfly for Slough Creek and Soda Butte Creek. Fish this fly and trail a Korn's Green Lantern (see page 39) about 14 inches off the bend of the hook for a dynamic duo.

LEPTO CADDIS EMERGER

Hook:	#14-16 TMC 206BL
Bead:	Clear glass
Thread:	Tan 8/0 UNI-Thread
Tail:	Wood duck flank fibers over amber Z-Lon
Body:	Gray-olive dubbing
Overbody:	Gray CDC
Wing:	Dun snowshoe rabbit hairs inside a few partridge flank fibers
Head:	Gray-olive dubbing

This unique caddisfly emerger offered by Howard Cole features CDC fibers forming a shellbacklike loop over the top half of the dubbed body. Howard is a proponent of using snowshoe rabbit foot hairs in forming wings because of its buoyancy and its durability. Another feature of this fly that Howard uses on others of his creations is wood duck flank fibers over shorter amber Z-Lon fibers in forming the tail.

MIKE'S TAN SPARKLE CADDIS

Hook: #12-16 TMC 2487
Thread: Tan 8/0 UNI-Thread
Abdomen: One strand of tan Sparkle Yarn
Underbody: One holographic silver Flashabou strip
Thorax: Hare's ear dubbing mixed with gold Dubbin
Wing: Pearl Midge Flash and light gray deer hair
Hackle: Barred dun or light brown saddle
Head: Tan UV Ice Dub

When trout are rising to caddisflies on the surface but seem to ignore a high floating pattern, Michael Snody suggests this pattern. It solved this problem for him on the Madison River after he designed it to float in the surface film with the abdomen slightly beneath. To obtain a segmented effect, twist the tan sparkle yarn before winding it for the abdomen. Use this pattern anywhere tan caddis emerge.

MISSOURI RIVER CADDIS

Hook: #14-18 Daiichi 1130
Body: Olive, light caddis green, tan, or orange/rust wool dubbing
Gas bubble: White Z-Lon strands
Antennae: Wood duck flank feather
Head: Peacock herl

Bob Lay wraps a thread base behind the rear two-thirds of the hook, returns thread to starting point, and ties in Z-Lon strands along the shank. He dubs the body on the thread base. He pulls the Z-Lon forward, securing it in front of the body with two loose thread wraps, forming a one-inch Z-Lon loop above it. He divides the loop equally and pulls the loops down over each side of the hook. He places a bodkin through the loops, resting it on the vise where the hook is secured. He pulls the Z-Lon straight up from the hook, secures it, and trims excess. He teases the Z-Lon loops around the hook, completing the gas bubble. He cuts two stem sections holding three or four fibers each from a wood duck feather. With fiber lengths even, he places them up at an angle from beneath the hook and extending past the rear. He secures these to form antennae and trims excess. He forms the head with three peacock herls over the antenna base.

MOTHER'S DAY CADDIS EMERGER

Hook:	#16 TMC 100
Thread:	Black 70-denier UTC Ultra Thread
Trailing shuck:	Amber Antron
Body:	Four peacock herls
Wing:	Blond bear hair
Head:	Black dubbing

The famed Mother's Day caddisfly emergences on the Yellowstone and Madison Rivers usually happen in May. The same emergence can take place in mid-May on the South Fork reach of the Snake River if waters are not high and cold. This is Elden Berrett's pattern for fishing each of these events. He prefers bear hair for the wing of this pattern because of its durability and ability to hold a shape. Changing the body color to black, he uses this pattern for a caddis emergence happening on the lower Henry's Fork in June.

NECTARINE

Hook:	#12-18 TMC 2312
Thread:	Tan 8/0 UNI-Thread
Abdomen:	Cream HOH CEN D32 dubbing blend
Rib:	Brown or other contrasting feather, palmered and clipped
Antennae:	Two brown hackle stems, stripped

Wings:	Reverse-wrapped wood duck or cinnamon-dyed mallard flank feathers
Thorax:	Cream HOH CEN dubbing

Doug Andres designed this pattern to imitate the White Miller and Long-Horned Caddisflies, including *Ocetis* and *Nectopsyche* (from which its name derives). It is very effective on the Firehole River, the Gibbon River, and other area streams hosting these caddis species. See the description of the Green Nectarine on page 50 for tying details. Craig Mathews attests to how effective Doug's Nectarine series can be on area waters during September and October.

PARACHUTE CADDIS

Hook:	#12-16 Dai-Riki 320
Thread:	Tan 8/0 UNI-Thread
Wing post:	White Hi-Viz fibers
Body:	Stripped brown hackle stem
Wing:	Natural CDC feathers
Thorax:	Olive-brown Superfine Dubbing
Hackle:	Slightly oversized grizzly saddle

After wrapping a thread base on the hook shank, Dean Reiner ties in the wing post. He secures the butt end of the post to the rear along the shank. After soaking the stem to minimize splitting during wrapping, he ties it in by the tip, natural curve down, shiny side up, and spirals it forward, forming the body. After supergluing the body, Dean ties in the CDC feathers, convex sides out, just behind the post and extending to the hook bend. He ties in the hackle stem, feather facing to rear, dubs the thorax over the wing and hackle butts, wraps the hackle, and whip-finishes to complete the fly.

PUTERBAUGH CADDIS VARIANT

Hook:	#11-17 TMC 102Y
Thread:	Tan 12/0 Benecchi
Body:	Tying thread
Extended body:	Gray 1.5-mm closed-cell foam
Wing:	Deer hair
Thorax:	Natural cream snowshoe hare

To create a spikier look, Hans Weilenmann prefers to use the split thread dubbing technique to build the thorax of this pattern. He suggests that bleached elk hair can be used as well as deer hair to form the wing. The colors of the pattern pictured above can also be varied to match those of the natural insect. Trim the hackle fibers away at the bottom of the fly to achieve a lower ride in the water.

RIPE NECTARINE

Hook:	#8-10 TMC 2312
Thread:	Rusty brown 8/0 UNI-Thread
Abdomen:	October Caddis Antron dubbing mix
Rib:	Furnace saddle hackle, clipped and palmered
Antennae:	Two stripped dark brown hackle stems

Wings:	Two reverse-wrapped cinnamon-dyed mallard flank feathers
Thorax:	October Caddis Antron dubbing mix

This is Doug Andres's Nectarine pattern for simulating the adult October Caddis so common in the autumn on many regional waters. This is the largest pattern in his Nectarine series. See description of the Green Nectarine on page 50 for tying details, but note the difference in hook size and materials colors. *Limnephilidae* caddis, locally known as "periwinkles," are stillwater dwellers in the area. It is worth considering using this pattern for imitating the adult of this large caddis when gulpers are working. Subsitute half Wapsi burnt orange dubbing (#13) and Wapsi ginger dubbing (#42) for October Caddis Antron dubbing mix.

SHAKEY BEALY

Hook:	#10-12 Dai-Riki 280
Thread:	Brown 6/0 UNI-Thread
Tail:	Mallard flank feather fibers dyed wood duck over Krystal Flash used to form wing
Rib:	Brown cotton thread
Body:	Amber Superfine Dubbing
Thorax:	Orange ostrich herl
Hackle:	Partridge body feather
Wing:	Eight or nine strands of orange Krystal Flash

Shakey Beal was a fly-fishing Yellowstone Park ranger known for his love of the Madison River. Nick Nicklaus intends this pattern to be an October Caddisfly imitation. Its body should be tapered and occupy the rear two-thirds of the shank. Tie in the ostrich herl over the front end of the body, then wrap the thorax. The ends of the Krystal Flash wing should extend to the rear of the body. Nick ties in the partridge hackle by the butt to add bulk. Blue Ribbon Flies personnel have found this fly to also be an effective Yellow Sally pattern. Hats off to versatility!

SYN CADDIS

Hook:	#16 TMC 100
Thread:	Orange 8/0 UNI-Thread
Body:	Tan Superfine Dubbing
Wing:	Tan EP Fibers
Thorax:	Tan Superfine Dubbing
Post:	Orange EP Fibers
Hackle:	Ginger saddle

So many times we answer the "What pattern would you suggest?" with "Pick one you think you can see best in the water you intend to fish." So many times caddis activity is over fast, broken water. With this answer and situation in mind, Paul Stimpson offers this highly visible pattern with its post in a bright color and a light-colored wing. Pictured above is the tan version with an orange post. Other post colors he suggests include fluorescent green or pink. After tying in the post and body, tie in the wing, then dub the thorax over the base of the wing.

TAK'S 12 O'CLOCK CADDIS

Hook:	#14-16 TMC 2302
Thread:	Hopper yellow 70-denier UTC Ultra Thread
Underbody:	Green 8/0 UNI-Thread
Overbody:	Tan 2-mm closed-cell foam
Wing:	Natural deer hair

Legs:	Small yellow Montana Fly Company speckled Centipede Legs

Rick Takahashi uses a River Roads Creation Hopper Wing cutter size 10 or equivalent to form the overbody. He wraps thread on rear two-thirds of the shank and glues the thread wraps. He positions the foam on top of the shank, round end facing rear, and even with bend. He uses thread wraps to secure foam on top of the hook in front of cemented thread wraps and makes snug wraps to form a "waist" here, then trims forward edge even with hook eye. He ties in legs at either side of "waist." He stacks a clump of deer hair half the diameter of a no. 2 pencil and ties the clump in at the "waist" so that the tips extend to the end of the overbody. He tightens the thread while holding the deer hair to flare above the overbody, trims the butts in an even perpendicular cut, and ties off.

X2 CADDIS

Hook:	#16 TMC 900BL
Thread:	Tan 8/0 UNI-Thread
Shuck:	Amber Z-Lon fibers
Rib:	Pearl Krystal Flash, 4–5 turns
Body:	Brachycentrus or tan Z-Lon dubbing
Wing:	Deer hair
Head:	Hydropsyche dubbing over clipped deer-hair butts.

Bucky McCormick dubs a tapered body on the rear three-quarters of the shank and wraps a thread base for the wings. He ties in the deer-hair wing and clips their butts short enough such that the head will be in proportion after dubbing over them. This easily tied emerging caddis pattern by Blue Ribbon Flies is proving to be very effective on regional streams.

CHAPTER 3

DAMSELFLIES AND DRAGONFLIES

To many fly fishers, damselflies and dragonflies are stillwater residents only. Not true! They can be numerous enough in low-gradient streams and in quieter locations in high-gradient streams to be important food forms for salmonids. Both require plentiful submerged vegetation to survive. Nymphs of both are available through the season, but their peak emergence is typically late spring to early summer.

Damselflies are on a single-year life cycle, whereas dragonflies take three or more years to become breeding adults. If you can escape from the early-summer standard of casting mayfly life-cycle patterns on meadow streams such as Slough Creek, Bechler River, the Harriman reach of the Henry's Fork, Boundary Creek, and the upper Blackfoot River in eastern Idaho, you will be surprised how effective a dry damselfly pattern can be.

Damselfly nymph patterns can be fished in stillwaters and slow-moving streams with success throughout the season. Damselfly nymph patterns must be tied with relatively slender bodies. Their proper presentation is a very slow retrieve that simulates the manner in which the natural nymphs swim.

The fly-fishing world is aware of the Henry's Lake damselfly emergence, and crowds come to enjoy trout responding when the emergence peaks during late June and early July. But at the same time, nymphs moving toward shorelines in such waters as the upper end of Elk Lake and the shallows of Wade Lake and Hidden Lake—all part of southwestern Montana's graben lakes—can be just as prolific. Even at smaller, out-of-the-way gems such as southwestern Montana's Smith Lake and Yellowstone Park's Beula Lake and Trout Lake, large fish responding to these nymphs can result in unforgettable fly-fishing experiences.

Dragonflies tend to become active earlier in the season in many waters of the region than damselfly nymphs do, and during their migration peak, patterns for them can be deadly in the early season when fished with an intermittent retrieve along the bottom of stillwaters. When they migrate toward vegetated shorelines en masse, fast fishing results. Patterns tied for them must be bulky and made from supple materials to simulate the robust nymphs in motion. A great example is Charlie Brooks's Assam Dragon, the quintessential dragonfly nymph pattern coming from the Greater Yellowstone Area. Strong and agile fliers, adult dragonflies are much more difficult for salmonids to capture and are not as numerous around Yellowstone waters as in warmer climates. Thus adult dragonflies are less popular as a tying subject than adult damselfly patterns.

NYMPH PATTERNS

ARF SLIMFLASH DAMSEL

Hook:	#12-16 TMC 3761
Thread:	Olive 8/0 UNI-Thread
Eyes:	Black plastic bead chain
Tail:	Damsel olive marabou with opal Mirage Flash strand on either side
Rib:	Single strand opal Mirage Flash
Abdomen:	Damsel olive marabou
Wing case:	Mixed opal Mirage Tinsel and olive Antron yarn

There seems no practical way to retrieve a fly with the undulating tail-whip of the natural damselfly nymph. Therefore Al Ritt focused on the illusion of movement in his SlimFlash Damsel. The marabou tail moves as the fly swims and when wrapped as a body, marabou barbs move the entire length of the fly. The Mirage Flash rib reflects light in all directions and appears similar to a light-reflecting exoskeleton. Al usually ties this fly unweighted to imitate the migrating nymphs swimming high in the water column, but he ties some with small bead-chain eyes to fish deep earlier in the season before they are emerging. His favorite presentation is stripping to imitate the migrating natural. Cast to fish cruising edges of weeds ambushing migrating nymphs or to those flushing bugs out of weeds, then chasing them down.

BALSA DRAGONFLY NYMPH

Hook:	#6-8 Mustad 33903
Thread:	Black 70-denier UTC Ultra Thread
Eyes:	Silver brass dumbbell eyes
Body:	Balsa wood carved to shape, primed, airbrushed brown, and lacquered to finish
Wing case:	Trimmed peacock green body feather
Legs:	Ring-necked pheasant rump feather fibers
Head:	Black rabbit fur dubbing

Gerry "Randy" Randolph ties in the dumbbell eyes for this pattern on the bottom of the shank just behind the hook eye. Off the hook he forms and finishes the body with a mounting slot, then attaches and bonds it to the hook shank with epoxy. He leaves room in front of the body to tie in the wing case and legs after the epoxy has cured. He dubs the head around the dumbbell eyes. The combination of buoyant body and dumbbell eyes gives this fly an attractive bouncing motion on being retrieved.

BLUE DAMSEL SIX PACK

Hook:	#10 TMC 5263
Thread:	Royal blue 8/0 UNI-Thread
Abdomen:	Bright blue ring-necked rooster pheasant rump feather
Rib:	Hot yellow UNI-Wire
Thorax:	Peacock herl
Hackle:	Bright blue ring-necked pheasant rump feather

As with all his soft-hackle patterns, Doug Andres first wraps the shank with tying thread. He uses a streamer hook to sink this pattern under the surface across a stream or at moderate depth in stillwater in front of trout feeding on damselfly nymphs. He forms the body by attaching, tip first at the top of the bend, a large bright blue feather from the top of the pheasant rump. He advances the thread three-quarters the way up the hook shank, then twists the feather, forming a "rope" that he spirals up the shank to the hanging thread. The yellow wire rib secures this body in place. He ties in an ornate pheasant rump ("church window") feather, tip first, and then wraps three or four turns, ties off, trims, and forms a thread head. This pattern has proven effective during Quake Lake and Firehole River damselfly hatches.

BOSTIC DRAGON

Hook:	#12-16 Daiichi 1740
Thread:	Burnt orange 70-denier UTC Ultra Thread
Tail:	Orange chickabou fibers
Body:	Medium orange/olive variegated chenille
Collar:	A few turns of guinea fowl flank feather in back of a few turns of pheasant rump
Eyes:	Black bead chain
Head:	Fluorescent orange-dyed squirrel dubbing

According to Shawn Bostic, fluorescent orange-dyed squirrel dubbing is the correct color for a dragonfly nymph. He likes the same color for crayfish patterns. He fishes this pattern in the shallows using a 12-foot-long leader, floating line, and darting retrieve. This method seems particularly effective in bringing strikes before weeds build up in springtime, and in autumn when the weeds have broken up. To simulate a molting insect, he uses fluorescent blue colors for the body and head.

BUTTAMA MOHAIR DRAGON

Hook:	#6 Dai-Riki 700
Thread:	Olive 6/0 UNI-Thread
Eyes:	Black bead chain
Underbody:	Yarn, any color

Rib:	Medium copper wire
Body:	Brown mohair
Hackle:	Partridge
Wing case:	Lacquered turkey quill segment
Head:	Brown mohair dubbing
Head cover:	Lacquered turkey quill segment

To create Mike Andreasen's fly, build the scrap yarn underbody to shape and coat with cement. Tie in eyes, one eye diameter length in back of hook eye. Tie in rib and mohair at hook bend and tight wrap forward to the two-thirds point on the shank. Counterwrap the rib, then tie in the turkey quill segment wing case with most pointing forward. Tie in and wrap the hackle, then bring the turkey quill back, separating the hackle to either side and doubling the wing case. Tie in another turkey quill strip pointing to rear at this point. Dub the head in proportion to the body. Bring the turkey quill segment forward between the eyes and tie off. Try this pattern anywhere dragonflies inhabit Greater Yellowstone waters.

BY DAMN

Front hook:	#8 Daiichi 1120
Thread:	Black 6/0 UNI-Thread
Eyes:	Silver bead chain
Stinger hook:	#10 Daiichi 1260
Connection:	Power Pro line 40-pound-test
Tail:	Olive marabou fibers
Extended body:	Olive Nymph Rib
Body:	Light olive Spirit River Nymph Blend
Hackle:	Sparse black

Tie in the stinger hook with tail and Nymph Rib mounted to connection, then cut away the bend. Tie in the front part of the connection along the front hook shank and superglue the wraps. Mount bead-chain eyes on the bottom of the front hook shank. Dub the Nymph Blend body to just in front of the eyes. Tie in the hackle

and whip-finish. Remove fly from the vise, and comb out the body. "You are going to catch fish with this fly, by damn!" says Josh Peavler. It is meant to be a damselfly nymph, but he also uses it as a trailer behind a streamer when fishing stillwater.

DAMSELFLY NYMPH

Hook:	#10-12 TMC 5263
Thread:	Olive 70-denier UTC Ultra Thread
Tail:	Golden olive marabou fibers under strip of brown or green spooled Mylar
Rib:	Fine green or copper wire
Body:	Golden olive marabou fibers twisted around shank
Shellback:	Light olive Scud Back, $^1/_8$-inch wide
Thorax:	Golden peacock Arizona Simi Seal dubbing
Eyes:	Dazl Eyes, $^3/_{32}$-inch diameter

Everet Evans presents this pattern mostly under an indicator. He ties in the dumbbell eyes on the bottom of the shank in order to help it ride horizontally under the indicator. Everet is one of the growing number of stillwater fly fishers that fish damselfly nymph, leech, scud, and snail patterns under an indicator. This technique, although very effective, requires constant attention to the indicator. A very occasional twitch or the results of wave action are the only motions this fly receives when fished in this manner.

DRAGON DANCER

Hook:	#4-8 Partridge H3ST Draper
Thread:	Black 6/0 UNI-Thread
Tail:	Ring-necked pheasant cock tail feather fibers
Rib:	Fine gold wire
Body:	Ring-necked pheasant cock tail feather fibers
Gills:	Aftershaft feather from ring-necked pheasant cock tail feather
Legs:	Ring-necked pheasant cock "church window" feather fibers
Wing case:	Tip of iridescent green peacock body feather
Eyes:	Black mono eyes

LeRoy Cook recommends filling the gap in the Draper H3ST flat-bodied hook with a piece of burlap twine. In forming the body he twists the tail feather fibers to form a rope after securing their tips at the top of the hook bend to form the tail. He then wraps the rope over the hook shank to form the body. Counterwrapped wire ribbing secures the body and adds to its durability. Dragonfly nymph patterns should be in the fly box of anyone fishing stillwaters in the Greater Yellowstone Area.

DRAGONFLY NYMPH

Hook:	#4 Dai-Riki 700
Thread:	Black 6/0 UNI-Thread
Underbody:	Medium peacock chenille wrapped back and forth on shank to form body
Overbody:	Dyed olive pheasant philoplume
Collar:	Pheasant "church window" feather wrapped soft-hackle style
Eyes:	Black bead chain
Head:	Medium peacock chenille

Tim Blount ties and secures eyes onto the front of the hook first. To form the body of this almost realistic pattern, Tim leaves the tying thread forward of the chenille wraps completed for this purpose. He then spirals the tying thread though the chenille to the rear of the body, wraps dyed philoplumes around the thread, then dubs this combination through the body. He adds the collar and head to finish the fly. The result is a deadly early season pattern for stillwaters.

DUBBED DRAGON

Hook:	#6 Partridge H3ST
Thread:	Olive 3/0 Danville Monocord
Eyes:	Small olive monofilament

Body:	Olive seal or Angora goat dubbing
Legs:	Golden pheasant tail fibers
Wing case:	Iridescent peacock back feather
Thorax:	Olive seal or Angora goat dubbing

Dragonfly nymphs live in the quiet, vegetated edges of stillwaters and streams. They crawl and climb through the vegetation and other structures vigorously searching for prey. Their prey are almost any life-form, from nymphs to tadpoles and small fish. They propel themselves through the water by gulping water and expelling it through contractions, resulting in a darting motion gaining several inches at a time. This motion can be simulated by a twitching retrieve through the shorelines dragonfly nymphs inhabit. John Newbury offers this pattern as an alternative to his Peacock Dragon.

ELK MANE DAMSEL

Hook:	#8 Dai-Riki 710
Thread:	Light olive 6/0 Danville Flymaster
Tail:	Small tuft of light olive marabou
Rib:	Fine copper wire
Underbody:	Butt ends of elk mane used for shellback
Body:	Medium olive/orange variegated chenille
Shellback:	Dark elk mane
Wing:	Tips of elk mane used for shellback
Legs:	Elk mane hairs pulled out on each side and trimmed

According to Chuck Collins, the wing over the fly should extend to the bend. After testing it in many of the southeast Idaho irrigation reservoirs, he recommends that it not be weighted but fished with an intermediate line. To be most effective, present it using a slow troll through the water.

FG'S DAMSEL NYMPH

Hook:	#10-14 Daiichi 1170
Thread:	Olive 70-denier UTC Ultra Thread
Tail:	Olive marabou fibers
Eyes (optional):	Olive small dumbbell
Body:	Olive marabou plume fibers
Wing:	Olive marabou fibers
Head:	Butts of marabou fibers used to form wing

After observing damselfly nymphs, Joni Tomich wanted an easily tied pattern that would mimic their body movements. Originally, she tied this using an ostrich herl body with great results, but its color would fade. She tried marabou for the body and loved how easy it was to work with, found it did not fade, and is in more reliable supply. This pattern can imitate several aquatic insects. Make the tail shorter, and it is a great scud or a shrimp. While fishing Henry's Lake with fish keying on leeches, Joni noted that their movement was similar to that of this fly. She tied it in black, brown, and gray versions on larger hooks to imitate leeches there with successful results. Now it is producing in several Montana stillwaters.

MOHAIR DRAGON

Hook:	#6-8 Dai-Riki 285
Thread:	Olive 6/0 Danville Flymaster
Eyes:	Black plastic dumbbell
Body:	Olive blood mohair
Rib:	Gold Ice Dub

Mohair has been available for decades and most fly tiers use it to create leech patterns. Recognizing its "buggy" properties, Tom Banyas uses it in a different manner. He forms the mohair body of this pattern first, then ribs it with a broad band of Ice Dub. After adding eyes to complete the fly, he carefully picks out the mohair body with either a ceramic rake, a bodkin, or the looped side of Velcro. The result of this process is mohair fibers coming out radially and trailing the fly, giving lifelike motion during a retrieve.

POND #4

Hook:	#10-14 TMC 5263
Thread:	Orange 3/0
Bead:	Gold, 3/32-inch
Tail:	Grouse neck hackle fibers
Rib:	Fine gold wire

Body:	Amber Whitlock SLR dubbing
Thorax:	Gray Whitlock SLR dubbing
Hackle:	Folded grouse neck tied in by tip

Fred Petersen's inspiration for this fly came from two sources: Dave Whitlock's squirrel tail nymph pattern and large eager rainbows in Fremont County, Idaho's Sand Creek Ponds. Fred tied a leaner body and used grouse hackle fibers to form a softer tail. He added a bead to get the fly a bit deeper around vegetation in these off-the-beaten-path ponds. The result is an effective damselfly nymph pattern that should be effective anywhere damselflies are present.

P. W. NYMPH

Hook:	#6-12 Mustad 3906
Thread:	Black
Tail:	Mallard flank feather fibers
Rib:	Peacock herl
Body:	Yellow floss
Thorax:	Peacock herl
Wing case:	Mallard flank feather segment
Hackle:	Mallard flank feather fibers

Pat Barnes originally intended this enduring pattern to be a dragonfly nymph, and it worked superbly well as such in the many stillwaters around West Yellowstone. Eventually fly fishers used it for other purposes by scaling down its size. Over the years it has been used on still and moving waters for many purposes, from mayfly and damselfly nymphs and to caddisfly pupae and stonefly nymphs. It remains as a great choice from the bins of all West Yellowstone fly shops. The author tied the pattern pictured above.

ROAD WARRIOR DAMSEL

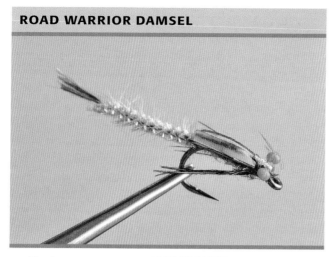

Hook:	#12 TMC 2488H
Thread:	Olive 140-denier UTC Ultra Thread
Extended body:	Pearl Core Braid
Tail:	Three dyed olive ostrich herls
Wing case:	Dyed olive turkey biot
Thorax:	Olive Antron damsel dubbing
Eyes:	Olive monofilament dumbbell eyes
Legs:	Dyed olive ring-necked pheasant rump fibers

Doug McKnight forms the extended body using Pearl Core Braid from which core fabric is removed, and singes the butt end to prevent unraveling. Using a bobbin threader, he pushes three ostrich herls through the empty Core Braid. He trims the ends of the herls to form tails about a quarter-inch long. After mounting this at the top of the hook bend, he ties in butts of the turkey biots, dubs the thorax, and ties in eyes near the hook eye. He forms the wing case by bringing biots over the thorax and tying off behind the eyes. Advancing the thread in front of the eyes, he brings the biots to it, returns the thread behind the eyes, and folds the biot back to be tied off there, forming a head. He ties in legs at this point and whip-finishes a superbly creative adult damselfly imitation.

SIMPLE DAMSEL (KNIGHT)

Hook:	#12 Daiichi 1710
Bead:	Gold, 1/8-inch
Weight:	Ten turns at midshank of 0.020-inch-diameter lead-free wire
Thread:	Olive UNI-Thread
Tail:	Tips of marabou plume used to form body
Body:	Dyed olive blood marabou or color to match natural
Hackle:	Dyed olive hen or color to match natural

This is Buddy Knight's favorite damselfly nymph pattern. He uses a single plume to form the tail and body. To do this, he ties in the tips of the plume to form the tail. Then he forms a tight noodle around the tying thread with the remainder of the plume until the stem becomes too thick to wrap efficiently. He spirals the noodle tightly around the shank to just behind the bead and trims the excess. He makes a single soft-hackle-style wrap of the hackle to finish this fly. He prefers fishing this fly with short strips on either a floating or intermediate line.

SIMPLE DAMSEL (MCKNIGHT)

Hook:	#10 Dai-Riki 075
Thread:	Brown-olive 70-denier UTC Ultra Thread
Rib:	Chartreuse fine wire
Tail:	Olive sparse marabou
Body/thorax:	Olive SLF squirrel dubbing
Wing case:	Ring-necked pheasant tail feather segment

Doug McKnight dubs a tapered body and builds the thorax to be a bit thicker. He prefers fishing this easily tied pattern two at a time, on a 9- to 12-foot leader and uses a slow hand-twist retrieve. He also suspends this pattern under an indicator and allows any wave action to give it motion. He uses either method in shallow still or slowly moving waters over submerged vegetation. Doug also has a chocolate brown version of this pattern.

SWAN LAKE DAMSELFLY NYMPH

Hook:	#12 Mustad 3665
Thread:	Black 8/0 UNI-Thread
Rib:	Fine copper wire or tying thread
Tail:	Ring-necked pheasant rooster tail fibers
Body:	Olive Superfine Dubbing
Overbody:	Butt ends of rooster tail fibers

Wing case:	Turkey tail section, 3/16-inch wide
Eyes:	Small black bead chain
Thorax:	Peacock herl
Legs:	Pheasant tail or partridge feather fibers

Jim Johnson prefers to tie this pattern on a Limerick bend hook because of the resulting profile. He first covers the shank with tying thread, then attaches rib material on top it. He adds rooster tail fibers, making the tail length the same as the hook gap. He anchors these in place with a turn of ribbing material. A tapered dubbed body covers the rear two-thirds of the shank. It is followed by tying in the butt end of the wing case formed from a section of turkey tail feathers after cutting away the top inch of that section. After tying in the eyes, forming the thorax, and finishing the wing case, he ties legs in front to complete this pattern.

TWISTED BODY DAMSEL NYMPH

Hook:	#10 Daiichi 1480
Thread:	Black 8/0 UNI-Thread
Body:	Olive yarn
Eyes:	Black Float Foam

Bob Trowbridge ties in doubled body material to the top of the shank, leaving free ends of length equal to shank extending to front, and doubled end six to eight inches extending to rear. He ties in a short section of Float Foam with figure-eight wraps at head position on shank, wraps thread to rear of shank, and tightly twists body material twelve to fifteen times. He pulls twisted body material to rear and secures at top of bend with thread wraps forming extended body portion. He wraps remaining body material to just behind eye and secures with thread. He pulls thread and body material between eyes and secures at hook eye. He returns thread and body material behind eyes and secures body material. He returns thread to front to whip-finish. He trims trailing body material even with bend, forming wing case. He trims eyes even with body.

VAN'S DRAGON

Hook:	#10 Daiichi 1710
Bead:	Gold, 1/8-inch
Weight:	Ten turns of 0.020-inch-diameter lead-free wire
Thread:	Red 6/0 UNI-Thread
Tail:	Two dyed black goose biots
Rib:	Small red UTC wire
Body:	Four dyed black ostrich herl and two natural peacock herls
Legs:	Dyed black goose biots
Collar:	Tying thread

Weight gets this fly to the bottom where dragonfly nymphs reside. After wrapping the lead-free wire, push it into the bead to distribute weight properly in this fly. Tie in the biots for the tails in a forked position and form the body. Tie in biots for legs. Then form the collar over their butts. Buddy Knight fishes this pattern using an intermediate line. He allows it to sink to the bottom and retrieves it slowly. Takes happen most when the fly rises from the bottom.

WIGGLE DAMSEL

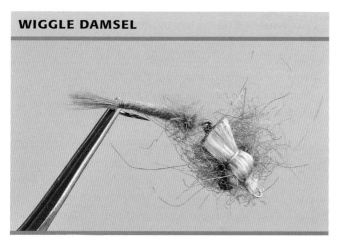

Hook:	#14 Mustad 9672
Thread:	Olive 3/0 Danville Monocord
Tail:	Golden olive marabou fibers
Abdomen:	Dubbed golden olive marabou fibers
Hinge:	Stainless-steel wire staple

Wing case:	Golden olive Swiss Straw strip
Eyes:	Small olive mono eyes
Thorax:	Olive seal or Angora goat dubbing

Looking for a damselfly nymph pattern with motion? This is it. John Newbury dubs the abdomen on the 9672 hook and dubs a bit of thorax behind its eye. He sets this aside and folds staple legs closed, forming an "eye" on each end. He clamps one "eye" of this staple in his vise with remainder exposed for finishing the fly. He slides the open staple leg through the eye of the 9672 hook, rests it on top of his vise, closes that leg, and bends it perpendicular, connecting it with the hook. He ties on eyes, Swiss Straw butt, and dubs the thorax and around the eyes. He crimps the Swiss Straw strip to extend rear enough to hide the hook-staple joint, then pulls it ahead and secures it behind the eyes. He extends the Swiss Straw over the eyes and ties off and trims it, finishing the fly.

WILL TAN NYMPH

Hook:	#10-12 Mustad 9671
Thread:	Olive 6/0 Danville Flymaster
Tail:	Golden brown immature hackle fibers
Rib:	Fine brass wire
Body:	Yellow floss
Thorax:	Light olive chenille
Hackle:	Light ginger saddle one size over standard for hook

From his years guiding for Bud Lilly in West Yellowstone and owning the first full-service fly shop in Last Chance, Idaho, to the present, Will Godfrey has treasured Centennial Valley waters. One of his favorite times to fish these flies is during the damselfly emergence from Valley waters. Whether from larger waters such as Elk and Hidden Lakes to smaller waters such as MacDonald Pond and Culver Spring, this simple pattern produces for him during that event. At other times in the Valley, he also finds this pattern to be effective, but what fish are taking it for is a mystery. But then, damselfly nymphs are always in the waters.

X-MAS TREE

Hook:	#6-12 TMC 5263
Thread:	Olive 3/0
Tail:	Olive marabou
Body:	Olive/red Crystal Chenille
Hackle:	Brown saddle

Several patterns have been named "X-mas Tree." Arrick Swanson, owner of Arrick's Flies in West Yellowstone, Montana, touts his X-mas Tree as a Hebgen Lake favorite for imitating migrating damselfly nymphs. This pattern could have been placed in our attractor section, but it has a reputation for producing on other area stillwaters when damselflies emerge. This includes the famed Henry's Lake emergence and relatively obscure, but important emergences on Elk Lake and Hidden Lake.

ADULT PATTERNS

ANDRE'S DAMSEL SPECIAL

Hook:	#10-12 TMC 5263
Thread:	Black 6/0 UNI-Thread
Tail:	Tips of three peacock swords
Rear hackle:	Grizzly saddle
Rib:	Single peacock herl
Body:	Blue poly yarn
Wings:	Badger hackle tips
Front hackle:	Grizzly saddle

Considering the array of synthetic materials available today for tying dry damsel patterns, this one is quite unusual. Except for its body, it is tied totally from traditional natural materials. Easily tied from readily available materials, it is popular with tiers fishing in remote locations. Some of the remote stillwater locations on which this pattern originated by Eugene Andre and tied by Phil Turck is effective include Elk Lake in Montana's Centennial Valley and Sand Creek Ponds in eastern Idaho's Fremont County.

ARF HI-VIS DAMSEL

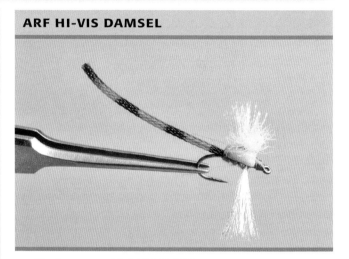

Hook:	#12-16 TMC 2488
Thread:	Black 8/0 UNI-Thread
Abdomen:	Braided monofilament leader dyed blue/black
Wing:	Clear white organza
Post:	Chartreuse Para Post yarn, Hi-Viz
Wing case:	Blue 2-mm-thick closed-cell foam
Thorax:	Blue Superfine Dubbing

Al Ritt adds a drop of superglue to the butt end of the braided leader to prevent unraveling of the abdomen. He ties in the organza spent wing on the bottom of the hook shank. The foam strip for the wing case is split before being tied in, and upon being tied in, is pulled forward on each side of the post and tied down. The result is a delicate, yet effective and highly visible pattern for simulating adult damselflies.

BALSA DAMSELFLY

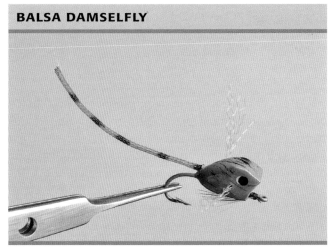

Hook:	#10 Dai-Riki 1750
Thread:	Black 8/0 UNI-Thread
Abdomen:	Dyed blue/black braided leader
Thorax:	Balsa wood carved and sanded to shape, primed, airbrushed or marking penned blue with irregular black stripes, and lacquered to finish
Wings:	Pearlescent FisHair strands
Eyes:	Painted black and yellow
Legs:	Beard-style coachman brown hackle fibers

Gerry "Randy" Randolph's pattern begins with cutting, shaping, and sanding high-quality balsa wood into a thorax form. Next comes painting and lacquering the form. After drying, he paints the eyes. After they dry, he drills holes for wings and abdomen, cements them in place, and attaches the beard-style legs. Looking for an adult damselfly pattern that is sure to float? This is it.

BOSTIC DAMSEL

Hook:	#10-12 Daiichi 1280
Thread:	Blue 14/0 Giorgio Benecchi
Tail:	Black moose body hairs
Body:	Dyed fluorescent blue peccary bristle

Thorax:	Fluorescent blue Superfine Dubbing
Post:	White Para Post
Hackle:	Grizzly saddle

Here is another product demonstrating Shawn Bostic's ability to dye almost any material any color. Dying peccary bristles is one of his specialties, and the body of this adult damselfly pattern illustrates the elegant fluorescent blue color he has achieved. Because of the bristle buoyancy, this pattern floats high enough to support a small submerged nymph in a two-fly rig. Shawn generously gifts other tiers with dyed peccary bristles (see Purple Peccary by Gary Barnes and Olive Drake by Bruce Staples) and encourages them to create uses from them.

DAMSEL ADULT

Hook:	#10-12 Dai-Riki 320
Thread:	Blue 6/0 UNI-Thread
Extended body:	Clear HMH tubing and blue Krystal Flash
Wing:	Blond elk rump hair
Thorax:	Blue Superfine Dubbing
Hackle:	Grizzly saddle
Head:	Blue Superfine Dubbing
Eyes:	Black small foam cylinder

Dean Reiner's unique part of this pattern is the extended body. He inserts a blue Krystal Flash strand within it and ties the extended body onto the hook shank. He secures the extended body butt with a drop of cement to secure the Krystal Flash within. He wraps black thread up and down the body to give a segmented effect. The result gives a subtle sparkle not commonly observed in other adult damselfly patterns.

DEAD DAMSEL

Hook:	#10-12 Daiichi 1150
Thread:	Black 8/0 UNI-Thread
Body:	Blue rubber legs
Thorax:	Blue Antron
Wing/indicator:	White poly yarn
Legs:	Sparse black hackle
Eyes:	Monofilament tippet, melted

Blue rubber leg material is well known to bass fly tiers. Gerry "Randy" Randolph tied these flies while on the Bass Pro circuit years ago. Now a stillwater trout angler by preference, he realized that most damselfly adult patterns are rigid and therefore needed improvement to be more lifelike. Thus he adapted the blue rubber leg material to form a thinner and more flexible body. He added black stripes to the body material with a marking pen. Because a dead damselfly adult lies very low on the surface, he added the poly yarn indicator for visibility. The resulting pattern works extremely well on his favorite stillwaters when damselflies mate, drop eggs, then die on the surface.

FLUTTERING DAMSEL

Hook:	#12 TMC 9300
Thread:	6/0 UNI-Thread, color to match body
Body:	Red, blue, or tan braided monofilament tubing about $1\frac{1}{4}$ to $1\frac{1}{12}$-inch long

Wing case:	Closed-cell foam, $\frac{1}{16}$-inch wide, color to match body
Wing:	Brown bear hair
Hackle:	Grizzly saddle

Attach thread at hook shank midpoint, and attach braided monofilament piece. Burn the butt end of this piece to prevent unraveling. Tie in matching color closed-cell foam, then at least 25 to 30 bear hairs on either side, tips facing rear, and shorter than the body. Split bear hair evenly to form wings on either side of body. Tie in the hackle and make four to five turns of it toward the hook eye, leaving enough room to secure foam behind the hook eye. Bring foam over top of the hackle, tie it down behind the eye, and trim to form a head. Not much need to discuss where and when this highly visible, durable pattern by Tim Tollett is effective. All one needs to see is fish taking adult damsels, and the fun begins.

KG'S KILLER DAMSEL

Hook:	#14 Dai-Riki 125
Thread:	Olive 8/0 UNI-Thread
Extended body:	Olive marabou strands, wrapped with tying thread
Shellback:	Olive Thin Skin
Thorax:	Palmered-dyed olive marabou
Eyes:	Melted red monofilament

A flexible and delicate appendage results from Kelly Glissmeyer's method for forming an extended body for this pattern. He spirals tying thread up the olive marabou strands, then back down. The result simulates the elongated damselfly body quite nicely. No cement is needed and if used would result in a stiffer, less natural body. Medium-sized monofilament is best for melting to result in eyes in proportion to the hook size. Kelly has proven this fly on several of the region's numerous stillwaters.

LOVIN' DAMSELS

Hook:	#12-16 Daiichi 1260
Thread:	Light cahill 8/0 UNI-Thread
Male body:	Braided monofilament dyed blue/black
Female body:	Braided monofilament dyed olive/black or gray/black
Male shellback:	Blue closed-cell foam
Female shellback:	Gray or tan closed-cell foam
Male thorax:	Blue Superfine Dubbing
Female thorax:	Gray or tan Superfine Dubbing
Wings:	Calf tail mixed with pearlescent UV Flash Fibers
Legs:	Moose mane fibers
Eyes:	Black closed-cell foam cylinder

Here is a mouthful for stillwater trout during damselfly mating season. During his stillwater angling experience, Shawn Bostic observed damselflies making love. This fly is the result, with the rear of the male pattern attached to the top of the thorax of the female (frequently olive or gray in color) pattern. The effectiveness of this pattern is obvious. Shawn also notes that a mating pair of damselflies attracts a crowd of males, usually blue in color, resulting in a cluster much akin to those of midges. Certainly a pattern simulating this swarm would be effective, but how does one tie such a swarm on one hook?

SPENT DAMSEL

Hook:	#14 Daiichi 1167
Thread:	Blue 70-denier UTC Ultra Thread
Body:	Braided monofilament dyed blue/black
Wing post:	Light blue dun poly yarn
Thorax:	Blue steel Ice Dub
Hackle:	Grizzly saddle

There is not a stillwater or a stream in the Greater Yellowstone Area that does not host damselflies. On waters such as Henry's Lake, Elk Lake, and Chesterfield Reservoir, nymph fishing during emergence is a happening in the regional stillwater fly-fishing world. But more experienced fly fishers, Gary Barnes included, look with just as much anticipation to fishing adult patterns on the surface of favorite stillwaters. One of those locations for Gary is near the spring creek inlets on the south end of Ennis Lake. Here subsurface vegetation abounds, hosting countless numbers of damselflies. When spent males and egg-laying females collapse to the surface, large trout come in to feed at these locations. Wind-free mornings and evenings can provide some unforgettable fishing then.

CHAPTER 4

LEECH AND AQUATIC WORM PATTERNS

Leeches and aquatic worms populate most waters of the region, and they do so in huge numbers. Until fairly recently, aquatic worms had not been given much attention by fly tiers. Now with widespread knowledge that they are a staple food item for trout both in moving water and along stillwater shorelines, patterns for them are being introduced in large numbers. Annelids, the technical name for aquatic worms, populate streambeds where there is generous rubble acting as overhead cover and hosts on which to burrow and cling. Well-oxygenated water is also required for their existence.

During times of scouring flow, aquatic worms, along with earthworms washed into the stream, are the major food item for resident salmonids. Thus during the runoff season, as well as before it when aquatic insects are less active, patterns for these should be well represented within the fly boxes of anglers. Another excellent time to use these patterns is soon after thundershowers occur. Thunderstorms, which are common in the Greater Yellowstone Area throughout the season, impact streams by increasing water flow that erodes banks and streambeds, releasing aquatic worms. Clearing and ebbing flows afterward are the signal for when to present worm patterns. In a similar manner, wave action along still-water shorelines releases annelids to become available to foraging salmonids.

Leeches are more familiar to fly fishers and fly tiers than aquatic worms because they are free swimmers in stillwaters and many streams, whereas aquatic worms tend to remain under cover unless a scouring flow sends them adrift. Or is it that in the human mind leeches are repulsive? In any case, they are annelids like earthworms and aquatic worms. And they are not all bloodsuckers: some eat larvae, nymphs, and other aquatic insect forms. They are flat bodied, and their presence in a water body is evidence of a generous food chain. It is difficult to find a beaver pond in the region that does not host them. That fact alone should tell the angler that paying attention to beaver ponds can be profitable when seeking good salmonid populations.

Without the chitin used to form the exoskeletons that many aquatic and terrestrial insects have, earthworms, aquatic worms, and leeches are "easy protein" for salmonids. Foraging salmonids rarely refuse them because they are totally and easily digested. Any leech pattern can be suspended under a strike indicator and/or dead-drifted to simulate an earthworm eroded from a bank and drifting in the current or awash in the wave action of a stillwater body.

BLACK COPPER

Hook: #4-10 Mustad 9672
Thread: Black 6/0 Flymaster
Tail: Black marabou fibers
Hackle: Black saddle
Body: Rusty brown Krystal Flash

Fly patterns do not have to be complicated to be successful. Bill Schiess, the dean of Henry's Lake fly fishers, proves this year after year through creating easily tied patterns. This pattern, one of his most recent, results from experimentation with color combinations. Bill tries various combinations throughout the season, and this one has proven effective at many locations on Henry's Lake. Try it at the creek mouths around the lake. Bill's success in creating fly patterns is not limited to Henry's Lake. Many, such as this one, are effective on waters such as Cliff Lake, Hebgen Lake, and Elk Lake, all not far into Montana from Henry's Lake.

BRUSKI

Hook: #8-10 Daiichi 1720
Bead: Gold, 1/8-inch
Thread: Black 8/0
Tail: Purple marabou with two or three pearl Krystal Flash fibers

Body: Purple Flashabou overwrapped with ginger Thin Skin
Thorax: Two turns of peacock herl followed by collar of purple Angora rabbit
Head: Black Angora rabbit dubbing

Being a proponent of stillwater fly fishing, it is not surprising that Gerry "Randy" Randolph has created a leech pattern. In the early season, this is another go-to pattern for Randy. It takes a backseat when gulpers look for Speckled Dun emergers and adults. But being true to his creations, Randy returns it to use during the late season when Speckled Duns are no more. It is named for the author of this work who introduced Randy to many of the region's fabulous waters.

CRAZY WORMS

Hook: #4 Eagle Claw Classic 374F Treble
Thread: Brown 210-denier Danville
Body: 10 to 12 brown or burnt orange 2-inch Ultra Chenille sections
Beads: Three 8/0 brown glass seed beads per chenille section

Anchor beads together and to each chenille piece with superglue. Tie each in at the same hook shank point. Seal and taper ends of chenille pieces with a butane lighter. Fly fishers can observe annelid clumps drifting in Greater Yellowstone Area streams during spring runoff. Harley Reno has witnessed similar clumps drifting in swollen streams in various parts of this country. On scanning scientific literature for information on "clumping behavior in aquatic annelids," he found no references. He and other fly fishers postulate that clumping behavior is likely a colonial sexual orgy, wherein mated pairs of worms bind into a mucous cocoon, then these pairs confederate, secreting a mucous envelope around the party. As waters rise, worm clumps dislodge and drift to become tempting morsels to large trout. That behavior might explain why bait fishermen habitually wad night crawlers on a hook instead threading them over the hook. Crazy Worms is the fly fishers answer to this practice!

E. M.

Hook:	#6-12 Dai-Riki 135
Bead:	Oversized gold tungsten ($^3/_{16}$-inch for #8 hook)
Weight:	0.020-inch-diameter lead-free wire
Thread:	Olive 6/0 UNI-Thread
Tail:	Sparse olive-brown marabou fibers
Rib:	Fine copper wire
Spot:	Light olive Krystal Flash clump
Body:	Olive Krystal Chenille
Hackle:	Olive Whiting Farms dry-fly saddle

After placing the bead, wrap the wire weight and slide its front under the bead. Tie in about 20 strands of Kyrstal Flash on top of bend, then cut off even with bend. This forms a target spot and minimizes the tail from fouling on the hook. Tie in the marabou tail two and a half times longer than the hook shank. Tie in rib and Krystal Chenille. Wrap the body to the bead and tie off. Tie in the hackle at the bead. Make a few turns there, then wrap back to bend in five turns to rear. Catch the hackle with the wire rib, trim it, then counterwrap the wire forward through the hackle to be tied off behind the bead. The pusher motion of the body of this pattern by Mike Andreasen causes the tail to fluctuate on the retrieve and the fly dives on the pause.

KG'S LEECH

Hook:	#6-8 Dai-Riki 710
Thread:	Black 8/0 UNI-Thread
Tail:	Sparse dyed olive marabou with a few strands of red Flashabou
Rib:	Small red UNI-Wire
Body:	Tightly wrapped fine olive chenille through which sparse, spiky hare's ear dyed olive is dubbed

Eastern Idaho offers the widest variety of irrigation reservoirs in the Greater Yellowstone Area. Many of these have existed for several decades and have reputations for producing very large salmonids. Richly endowed with food forms, these reservoirs remain mostly the domain of resident anglers, and they serves as "proving grounds" for locally originated fly patterns. Kelly Glissmeyer's leech pattern is one of these patterns tried on many local reservoirs and proven to be effective.

KG'S SAND CREEK LEECH

Hook:	#6-8 Mustad 9671
Thread:	Olive 8/0 UNI-Thread
Tail:	Olive Simi Seal dubbing, sparse and shank length
Body:	Picked out sparse Olive Simi Seal dubbing over red Crystal Chenille base

Tucked away in eastern Idaho at the interface of Island Park Caldera and Snake River Plain is a stillwater angling treasure like few others in the Greater Yellowstone Area. Four ponds—designated Sand Creek Ponds—were formed from nearby springs to supply water for irrigating alfalfa and hay raised to feed wintering elk herds. Rainbow trout growing to double-figure poundage and brook trout inhabit these ponds. An important item in the food base in these ponds is an olive-colored leech that Kelly Glissmeyer has simulated with this pattern. After forming the red Crystal Chenille body base along the hook shank, spiral the tying thread back to the top of the bend and add the sparse dubbing. With its subtle red flecks and easy motion on being retrieved, this pattern is effective in still and moving waters.

KNIGHT KRAWLER

Hook:	#12 Dai-Riki 135
Bead:	Spirit River copper, 1/8-inch
Thread:	Red 6/0 UNI-Thread
Rib:	Ultra Wire (brassie)
Body:	San Juan red Spirit River Squirmy Wormie

Steven Rendle specifies this bead because of its wide, hollowed-out orifice. He mounts it hollow end facing forward on the hook and positions it at the hook bend. He then pushes one end of a Squirmy Wormie piece through the wide orifice to the rear, with the other end extending past the eye at least one-half inch. Next he pulls the bead forward on the shank to the eye over the Squirmy Wormie, the front end of which hangs out through the bead. He ties in the rib and end of a second Squirmy Wormie piece at the bend and secures both forward along the shank with thread wraps and front end of the piece forward. He snugly (not tightly!) spirals the front end of this piece back to the bend, leaving at least half an inch extending backward, and ribs it going forward with the copper wire, tying off at the bead. He trims front and back pieces to about half an inch in length.

PIG PEN LEECH

Hook:	#4-8 Dai-Riki 720
Bead:	Black tungsten
Thread:	Olive 6/0 UNI-Thread
Tail:	Burnt orange marabou over olive marabou with a few strands of pearl Flashabou on sides
Body:	Dyed olive variant chinchilla

Doug McKnight's Pig Pen Leech is full of action. He recommends this pattern be presented on an intermediate line for fishing in shallow, weedy lakes. He has proven it on nearby Dailey Lake, Martinsdale Reservoir, and Bair Reservoir, where it seems deadly for big rainbows. It has also produced in the Madison River above and below Hebgen Lake.

SHOSHONE LAKE LEECH

Hook:	#10 Mustad 32833-BLN
Bead:	Tungsten, 1/8-inch
Thread:	Black 70-denier UTC Ultra Thread
Tail:	Dyed black pine squirrel strip
Body:	Dyed black pine squirrel strip

Yellowstone Park is a lead-free fishing area, so tungsten-weighted flies can be legally fished. With a density about 90 percent of lead's, tungsten is essentially as effective in getting to depth as lead. Aware of this, Shawn Bostic places a painted black tungsten bead at the head of a straight pin painted black, and secures its shaft to the shank of a jig hook with tying thread and fine steel wire wraps. He then ties in the butt end of a dyed black pine squirrel strip over these wraps. The result is this fly that gets to depth and has the jigging action of a swimming leech. It was first proven effective around the productive weed beds in Shoshone Lake in Yellowstone Park, thus its name.

SPEY LEECH

![Spey Leech fly pattern]

Hook:	#4 Daiichi 1720
Weight:	0.03-inch-diameter wraps of lead or lead-free wire, covering middle third of shank
Thread:	Red 6/0 UTC Ultra Thread
Tail:	Whiting Farms chickabou, color to match rear color of Bird Fur used for body; two Flashabou or Krystal Flash strands on either side
Body:	Three layers of two or three Whiting Farms Bird Fur feathers for each color
Facing:	Whiting Farms soft grizzly dyed brown (dyed magenta for black and magenta version)

Richard Munoz designed this robust fly to be a leech pattern, but it is also a superb streamer. Tie in Bird Fur at top of shank in front of lead wraps and distribute fibers around it with thumb and fingers. Whiting Farms Bird Fur imparts excellent motion when this fly is stripped, and Bird Fur durability is much better than that of marabou. Richard ties this pattern in three different color schemes (rear color first and front color second): olive and brown, brown and olive, black and magenta.

STRETCH FLEX WORM

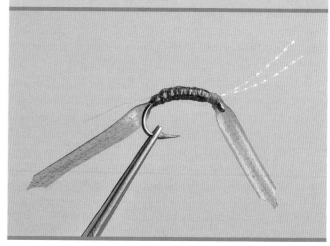

Hook:	#12 TMC 2457
Weight:	0.015-inch-diameter lead-free wire
Thread:	Fire orange 8/0 UNI-Thread
Rib:	Pearl UV Krystal Flash strands
Body, body extension, and tail:	Red ⅛-inch-wide, 4-inch-long Stretch Flex strip

Fold Stretch Flex strip in two and tie while pinching, quarter-inch-long looped end forward, with thread wraps between hook eye and front lead wrap. Leave two Stretch Flex strip ends extending to rear. Tie in two 2-inch-long Krystal Flash strands and Stretch Flex strip over wire wraps with thread spirals to rear. Spiral thread forward to hook eye. Using tension, spiral one strip forward over wire wraps, and rib it with one Krystal Flash strand. Ramp Stretch Flex loop and two Krystal Flash strand ends upward with thread wraps, which form a "hot spot." Cut one end of loop at base and trim a tapered end. Cut a taper in the tailing end of strip. According to Nick Jones, Stretch Flex stretches more readily than Scud Back, and when fully stretched, such as in this pattern, imparts a translucence to it. Several colors are available. Fish this fly as you would any annelid pattern.

SUEDE JUAN WORM

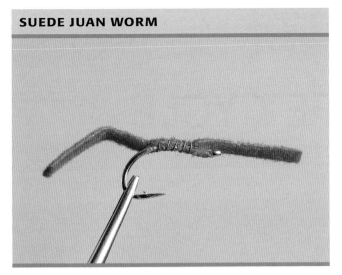

Hook:	#14 1155 Daiichi
Thread:	Hot red 8/0 UNI-Thread
Rib:	Fine gold UNI-Wire
Body:	Hot pink or color to match natural strip of 3-mm suede

In past years Spirit River marketed a spooled suede product labeled "Suede Body." Initially Greg Messel used this product in the lace worm red color to tie this pattern, but this product is no longer available. So, as with many tiers, Greg frequented craft shops and found an alternative to "Suede Body." This pattern is as easily tied as traditional the San Juan Worm, except that Greg ribs the body attached to the hook shank with fine gold tinsel. Experience tells him that this pattern is at least as durable as the traditional San Juan Worm. The suede that Greg uses is available in ten or fifty yard spools online at http://www.tropicari.com/suedeleather-cord.html

TRIPLE S LEACH

Hook:	#6 Targus 7979
Thread:	Red 70- or 140-denier UTC Ultra Thread
Body:	Olive Simi Seal picked out
Overwing:	Strip of olive-dyed pine squirrel skin, $^1/_8$ inch wide, tied in at head, and at top of bend

New to the area, Shawn Bostic is designing effective flies for the region. According to Shawn, this leech pattern is intended for stillwaters, but it also has potential as an excellent streamer pattern. When fished in stillwaters early in the season, this pattern could also prove to be a good one for dragonfly nymphs.

CHAPTER 5

MAYFLY LIFE CYCLE

Mayflies are surely the most romantic aquatic insect in the minds of fly fishers. Patterns for them go back centuries in European fly-fishing literature, with the British being the biggest advocates for mayflies as a salmonid food. This interest came across the Atlantic to be engrained in the minds of fly fishers residing in the Eastern states, and then onto the salmonid waters of the Western states. Certainly attention to mayflies is appropriate in the Greater Yellowstone Area because of the number of species present. There are around two hundred species here, with burrowers, clingers, crawlers, and swimmers well represented.

We mention mayflies in this manner because most of their lives are spent as "nymphs" living underwater, behaving in one of these four characteristics. The remainder of their lives as emergers, duns, and spinners are short in duration, measured in no more than a few days. In this work, nymph patterns will be well represented, and the behavior and lifetime facts given above are the key to their importance and how they should be designed. So many fly fishers enjoy dry-fly fishing more than fishing below the surface. Thus it would be amiss not to have in this work a good representation of the mayfly life-cycle stages that are fished in this manner.

The springtime emergence of mayflies in the Greater Yellowstone Area typically begins in April and peaks in June, depending on elevation. Emergence can occur at any time of day, but water temperature as well as time are the dominant factors in determining when it takes place. In general, mayfly emergences (number of species and total individuals) wane noticeably after midsummer, but return with a lesser autumn emergence peak, then taper off until only *Baetis* (BWO) remain emerging through the winter season. Mayflies populate all water types here. *Callibaetis* (Speckled Dun) dominate in stillwaters with some BWOs, Pale Morning Duns (PMD), and Brown

Drakes also hosted there. The BWO and PMD are the most enduring in moving waters, but there are numerous other important species hosted in these waters. The most widespread species may be BWOs and PMDs, but the most glamorous are the Drakes: Brown, Gray, and Green. Arguably that of the Green Drake is the most sought after of the mayfly emergences in the region. At the top of locations where this takes place is that from the Harriman State Park reach of the Henry's Fork.

Not long after René Harrop and Mike Lawson had suggested how to be successful during the Green Drake hustle on the Harriman reach years ago, I noticed something else happening. While Green Drake populations were growing, a few large stoneflies were around. Wind had blown some of their dwindling numbers in from Box Canyon above and Cardiac Canyon below. All I needed was to see was a large trout take one fluttering on the water, and I began carrying imitations with me. Sure, I received scorn, and I did not land as many fish as those fly fishers not looking at the "big picture." But when those folks observed the size of the trout I fooled, they scorned me no more! For decades I have carried adult large stonefly patterns where the Green Drake and large stonefly emergences overlap. But the Green Drake on the Harriman reach of the Henry's Fork is a bit of an exception, much to the surprise of many fly fishers. Let's look at why this exception has a significant impact on fly-fishing strategies.

This exception comes about because the Harriman reach is a tailwater fishery, Island Park Reservoir being just a few miles upstream. This relatively shallow reservoir acts to store heat in its impounded water. Water warms easily here, cools at a rate much slower than moving water, and is therefore released at temperatures close to that needed for the Green Drake emergence to begin. Thus the Harriman Green Drake emergence is usually a morning event. About 30 miles to the east in Fall River Basin, the Green Drake emergence on Bechler and Fall Rivers is a midafternoon event. Without heat stored in an upstream water body here, more time is required each day to raise water temperatures to the point where the emergence begins. The same is the case for renowned Green Drake emergences happening on Yellowstone Park's Lewis River and Yellowstone River and Slough Creek, the Madison River, and the South Fork reach of the Snake River. Yes, there are upstream lakes on some of these streams, but they are deep and therefore colder than the shallow reservoir on the Henry's Fork.

It is worth mentioning that the PMD colors on emergence vary, because this widespread and numerous mayfly is an important food form for regional salmonids and therefore impacts fly-fishing strategy. On the Henry's Fork, duns tend to a rusty olive color. On Fall River Basin streams, they tend to chartreuse, and on the South Fork reach of the Snake River, they have a pinkish cast. Other variations are present. We will address them in the discussions below.

NYMPH PATTERNS

ARF TUNG-SYN PT

Hook:	#12-18 TMC 3769
Bead:	Tungsten copper
Thread:	Black 8/0 UNI-Thread
Tail:	Root beer over pearl Krystal Flash
Abdomen:	Root beer Glitter D-Rib
Wing case:	Mirage Tinsel
Thorax:	Hare's ear Ice Dub, peacock herl

Al Ritt is fond of using natural materials and tying traditional style flies. But he also enjoys tying and experimenting with the vast array of new synthetics. He appreciates their effectiveness, durability, and convenience and has used them in many of his patterns. His Tung-Syn PT is a synthetic version of an old classic, the Pheasant Tail Nymph. It's a productive fly fished in the same situations and manner as the Pheasant Tail Nymph, especially when a little extra flash and reflectivity is desired to attract extra attention.

BANGIN' BAETIS

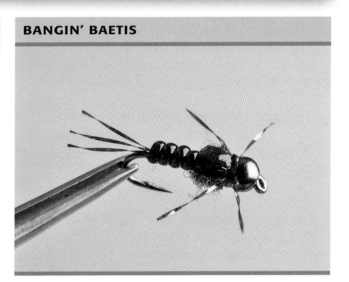

Hook:	#16-22 TMC 3761
Bead:	Black copper
Thread:	Olive 8/0 UNI-Thread
Tail:	Three black Krystal Flash fibers
Abdomen:	Small brownish olive D-Rib
Wing case:	Brownish olive Medallion Sheeting strip
Thorax:	Brown/olive Superfine Dubbing
Legs:	Black Krystal Flash

The lower Henry's Fork and the Madison River below Hebgen and Quake Lakes are famed for hosting both spring and autumn BWO emergences. Both rivers at these locations are very accessible, so many dry-fly enthusiasts look forward to each of these seasonal emergences. As with most waters, the best fishing occurs when the weather is not the best. Paul Stimpson offers his Bangin' Baetis nymph, which has produced on rivers during both of the BWO seasons.

BWO REDEMPTION NYMPH

Hook:	#16-20 Dai-Riki 125
Bead:	Silver
Thread:	Tan 8/0 Danville
Tail:	Tan pheasant tail fibers
Rib:	Fine chartreuse wire
Abdomen:	Nature's Spirit dyed BWO stripped bleached peacock herl
Thorax:	Nature's Spirit dyed BWO unstripped bleached peacock herl
Wing case:	Mirage Tinsel strip
Legs:	Hungarian partridge flank feather fibers

The South Fork reach of the Snake River and the lower Henry's Fork host superb late season BWO emergences. Beginning in late September and into October, these activities become destination events on overcast or stormy days. Easily tied, Tim Woodard's pattern has proven effective for fishing these events and for late winter BWO emergences on the lower Henry's Fork and the middle Madison River.

HICKEY'S AUTOMATIC EMERGER

Hook:	#16 TMC 2457
Bead:	Black tungsten, 5/64-inch
Thread:	Olive 6/0 UNI-Thread

Rib:	Small copper UNI-Wire
Tail:	Ring-necked pheasant tail fibers
Body:	Three strands of brown Krystal Flash
Thorax:	Sculpin olive SLF dubbing
Wing pad:	Medium pearl Mylar Tinsel
Wing:	Dark dun CDC oiler puffs

Wrap a thread base behind the bead to the start of the hook curve. Tie in six or seven pheasant tail fibers with tips about three-quarters of shank length. Tie in the wire rib. Tie in Krystal Flash strands and return thread to just behind the bead. Wrap the Krystal Flash strands and tie off behind the bead. Wrap five turns of wire and secure. Coat body evenly with Hard As Nails. Allow to dry. At the same point tie in a CDC oiler puff, then a Mylar Tinsel strand. Apply dubbing wax to three inches of thread followed by a small amount of dubbing. Build a bulbous thorax to the bead. Pull the Mylar over the thorax and tie in at the bead. Trim the CDC wing to just shorter than the body. This is the BWO version of Jim Hickey's Automatic Emerger series for emerging nymphs.

HOLLOW BODY MAYFLY NYMPH

Hook:	#10-14 Daiichi 1260
Thread:	Light cahill 8/0 UNI-Thread
Rib:	Tying thread
Body:	Thin polyethylene grocery store produce bag, double-faced transparent craft tape, and Superfine microdubbing
Tail:	Ostrich miniplumes
Wing pad:	Swiss Straw
Thorax:	Fine and Dry Dubbing
Legs (optional):	Small barred rubber legs

To create this fly by Kenshiro Shimazaki and tied by Kuni Masuda, follow directions for forming Shimazaki Hollow Body Mayfly (page 120) but use the straight body form tool. Peel backing paper from two pieces of double-sided tape and sandwich these over body. Carefully trim excess tape. Attach three ostrich plume feathers for tails to top of body. Wrap segmented ribs along the body. Dab body with Superfine microdubbing. Remove extra dubbing with a brush dusted with Dry-Shake powder. Gently remove finished hollow body from the tool. Saddle the formed body over hook in vise about one-quarter of shank length behind the eye. Trim excess body material. Secure body to shank with thread and apply head cement to these wraps. Secure a piece of Swiss Straw (excess pointing to rear). Dub thorax and apply legs. Wrap Swiss Straw over the thorax and tie off behind head. Bend a tab of straw backward and trim to form pronotum.

HOT HEADED HARE'S EAR

Hook:	#14-16 Dai-Riki 285
Bead:	Small fire orange glass Killer Caddis
Thread:	Brown 70-denier UTC Ultra Thread
Tail:	Brown Hungarian partridge rump feather fibers
Rib:	Brown Krystal Flash strand
Body:	Hare's ear Krystal Dub
Wing case:	Peacock herl
Thorax:	Dark hare's ear Krystal Dub

Doug Kinney ribs only the body of this pattern and pulls the peacock herl wing case over the top of thorax. After completing this pattern Doug teases out the thorax to achieve a buggy look. He intends this pattern to be a mayfly nymph and varies its size to simulate any species. For example, he carries it in two sizes while fishing the South Fork reach of the Snake River in September when Mahogany Dun and BWO emergences overlap.

KORN'S TNT GREEN DRAKE NYMPH

Hook:	#12 Mustad 9671
Bead:	Toho green 6/0 glass
Thread:	Olive 6/0 UNI-Thread
Tail and shellback:	Ten wild turkey tail feather fibers
Rib:	Large copper wire
Body:	Parks' Fly Shop DK#7 Green EMT dubbing
Legs:	Pheasant aftershaft feather

When Green Drakes are emerging from streams in the northeast corner of Yellowstone National Park, Doug Korn's pattern is just the ticket. He ties it in the same manner as his Korn's TNT Golden Stone Nymph (see page 140). He also ties these TNT Drakes for brown and gray drakes, all in size 12. To fish any of these in deeper waters, use copper, gold, or black metal beads. Other TNT variations include smaller sizes for Yellow Sallies and small mayfly nymphs.

OLIVE NYMPH

Hook:	#16 Mustad 94840
Thread:	Olive 70-denier
Tail:	Barred lemon wood duck flank fibers
Body:	Olive Krystal Flash fiber
Wing:	Tips of olive marabou
Wing case:	Dyed black turkey biot
Thorax:	Coarse olive dubbing

The wing on Ron English's pattern goes near the hook bend. Being made from marabou gives it lifelike action. He doubles the biot wing case over to minimize pullout. He ties another version on a Dai-Riki 300 hook that has a slightly shorter shank than the Mustad 94840. This is Ron's preferred BWO nymph pattern for southwestern Montana streams, particularly the Beaverhead, Madison, and Ruby Rivers.

PMD FLOATING NYMPH

Hook:	#16-20 TMC 100
Thread:	Camel 8/0 UNI-Thread
Tail:	Wood duck flank fibers
Body:	Z-Lon PMD emerger dubbing

Shellback:	Black closed-cell foam
Abdomen:	Same as body

After this fly is completed and removed from the tying vise, rough up the bottom of the abdomen with a dubbing brush, which pulls out fibers to simulate legs. This simple pattern by Blue Ribbon Flies and tied by Bucky McCormick imitates an important stage in any BWO emergence. Floating nymphs attract feeding salmonids any time a hatch is in progress, thus anglers fishing one should have these patterns available.

PMD REDEMPTION NYMPH

Hook:	#14-18 Dai-Riki 125
Bead:	Gold
Thread:	Tan 8/0 Danville
Tail:	Tan pheasant tail fibers
Rib:	Fine gold wire
Abdomen:	Nature's Spirit dyed PMD stripped bleached peacock herl
Thorax:	Nature's Spirit dyed PMD unstripped bleached peacock herl
Wing case:	Mirage Tinsel strip
Legs:	Hungarian partridge flank feather fibers

Tim Woodard observed that many PMD Nymph patterns seem too bulky in imitating the natural. He thus searched for a better material to result in a more representative tie. He settled on stripped bleached peacock herl to form the abdomen and unstripped peacock herl to form the thorax of this fly. The result is a thinner, sparser pattern that more closely resembles a living PMD nymph. Tim suggests that his pattern, when tied without a bead, can be presented as an effective emerger.

SOS NYMPH

Hook:	#16-20 TMC 2487
Bead:	Silver tungsten, $^3/_{32}$-inch
Thread:	Black 10/0
Tail:	Black pheasant tail fibers
Rib:	Small silver Ultra Wire
Body:	Tying thread
Wing case:	Two strands of red floss
Legs:	Black Krystal Flash
Thorax:	Black hare's ear dubbing

Spencer Higa's SOS Nymph is a versatile pattern used throughout the Greater Yellowstone Area and beyond. It has proven effective before, during, and after BWO, PMD, and other mayfly hatches. It is a superb searching pattern and produces when the hatch is uncertain. It is effective when fished as a dropper off a dry fly or deep drifted under an indicator. Whether on big rivers or small streams, this fly is a "must-have" in the fly box. When a picky fish is encountered, try an SOS.

STEWIE FLY

Hook:	#10-16 TMC 3761
Bead:	Gold
Thread:	Olive dun 8/0 UNI-Thread

Tail:	Six Hungarian partridge barbs
Body:	Light hare's ear dubbing brush (or substitute light hare's ear dubbing)
Hackle:	Hungarian partridge neck feather
Collar:	Peacock herl

R. L. "Stew" Stewart is a frequent visitor from northern California to stillwaters around western Montana and eastern Idaho. His favorites include Hebgen Lake, Quake Lake, and Springfield Reservoir, particularly when gulpers are beginning to work on emerging Speckled Duns (*Callibaetis*). He uses this effective pattern, rarely seen and just recently used in the region, to begin the day nymphing before fish take to the surface for Speckled Dun emergers and duns.

STONE CLINGER

Hook:	#14-18 TMC 100
Bead:	Gold
Tails:	Partridge feather fibers
Thread:	Olive dun 8/0 UNI-Thread
Rib:	Chartreuse Ultra Wire (small)
Abdomen:	Olive brown Hare's Ear Plus Dubbin
Thorax:	Peacock Ice Dub

Clinger mayflies, such as *Epeorus albertae* are common in Greater Yellowstone Area streams. Michael Snody created this pattern to be a successful representative of this type of nymph. The Stone Clinger seems especially effective during the morning drift. To best fish that drift, Michael recommends a two-nymph rig using a Euro-style presentation. On finishing tying this pattern, pick out the thorax to produce sparkles that simulate tiny bubbles.

TODDLER

Hook:	#10-18 Dai-Riki 135
Bead:	Copper
Thread:	Olive 8/0 UNI-Thread
Tail:	Two mallard biot tips
Body:	Olive 8/0 UNI-Thread
Wing case:	Strand of silver holographic tinsel
Thorax:	Olive dun dubbing

This is Todd Allen's pattern in small sizes for BWO nymphs, or in larger sizes for Flav (Western Green Drake) nymphs. *Baetis*, or BWO emergences, are numerous and well known throughout the area, and surprisingly, so are those of Flavs. Flav emergences occur at different times of the year on streams, depending on their warming profile. On tailwater fisheries, such as the Henry's Fork in Harriman State Park, they occur in early July. On colder streams such as Big Elk and Palisades Creeks, both Snake River tributaries, they occur in August.

WEISE'S SHIMMER NYMPH

Hook:	#14-18 Montana Fly Company 7077
Bead:	Gold
Thread:	Rusty brown 8/0 UNI-Thread
Tail:	Lemon wood duck flank fibers
Abdomen:	Rust Midge Diamond Braid twisted into a rope
Wing case:	Pheasant tail fibers
Legs:	Divided extensions of pheasant tail fibers used to form wing case
Thorax:	Rusty brown Ice Dub

Walter Weise suggests this pattern for PMD nymphs active on the Firehole, Lamar, and Madison Rivers. He also offers a brown version for autumn BWO nymphs. Wrapping the abdomen of this pattern from tightly twisted Midge Diamond Braid suggests segmentation. He also offers versions of this pattern with a black or a chartreuse abdomen.

WEISE'S SKINNY NYMPH

Hook:	#14-20 Dai-Riki 125
Thread:	Rusty brown 8/0 UNI-Thread
Tail:	Natural brown partridge
Rib:	Gold wire
Abdomen:	Rusty brown 8/0 UNI-Thread
Wing case:	Lagartun pearl flat braid
Thorax:	Pheasant tail Ice Dub brushed out to form legs

Walter Weise's brown version of this fly for PMD nymphs is discussed and pictured above. He also offers an olive (using olive tying thread) version for simulating *Baetis* nymphs. Closely spaced wire ribbing in either version suggests segmentation. He suggests that this fly, either brown or olive, is a great choice for use on spring creeks or during late summer and autumn when waters, such as on the Lamar River, are low and fish are spooky. On completing this pattern, coat the wing case with superglue to increase durability and sparkle.

EMERGER AND CRIPPLE PATTERNS

BAETIS SOFT HACKLE EMERGER

Hook:	#18-22 TMC 900BL
Thread:	Olive or red 8/0 UNI-Thread
Tail:	Wood duck flank feather fibers
Body:	Olive-gray Superfine Dubbing
Hackle:	Mallard shoulder feather

To create this fly by Nick Nicklaus and tied by Bucky McCormick, tie in tail, and dub body to just behind hook eye. Tie in a mallard flank feather by the tip. Take one to one-and-a-half turns of this feather just in front of the body. Here is a great example of an easily tied fly that is superbly effective anywhere when the most widespread mayflies in the area, *Baetis* (also known as BWOs), are emerging.

BOE GREEN DRAKE EMERGER

Hook:	#10-12 TMC 206BL or equivalent
Thread:	Olive dun 8/0 UNI-Thread
Tail:	Z-Lon loop around grouse neck hackle tip fibers

Underbody:	Yellow thread underwrap
Overbody:	Olive and yellow CDC dubbing in front of Flexi Floss
Thorax:	Clear glass bead
Hackle:	Golden olive-dyed grizzly
Wing:	Dyed black snowshoe rabbit hairs

Howard Cole gives the body of this pattern a segmented effect by covering the hook shank with a yellow thread wrap. In wrapping the overbody, he leaves enough space between turns to reveal the yellow thread in narrow bands, thus obtaining the segmented effect. The Z-Lon loop that encloses the grouse hackle fibers is tied in vertically when forming the tail.

BOOM EMERGER

Hook:	#12-16 Daiichi 1180
Thread:	Tan 70-denier UTC Ultra Thread
Tail:	Six to eight wood duck flank fibers
Body:	Dyed Callibaetis stripped peacock eye quill
Thorax:	Dyed Callibaetis UV Ice Dub
Wing case:	Bull elk hairs tied in tip first
Hackle:	One and a half turns of partridge

Shawn Bostic's Boom Emerger for the speckled dun is proving effective around the region. For presentation Shawn dresses only the butt ends of the elk hair with floatant. This allows the rest of the fly to submerge and the hackle fibers to float on the surface, simulating legs. Shawn fishes this fly in a slow troll, or still with an occasional twitch to submerge it. The slow rise to the surface after a twitch frequently brings strikes.

BOOTY'S HECUBA EMERGER

Hook:	#10-12 Dai-Riki 135
Thread:	Clear mono
Shuck:	Brown Z-Lon
Abdomen:	Dark brown fine thread or Danville Monocord coated with Zap-A-Gap, superglue, or fast-drying epoxy
Wing:	Sand EP Fibers
Wing post:	Brown 2-mm closed-cell foam, cut into a V at one end to fit around the wing
Legs:	Brown Z-Lon
Hackle:	Brown rooster saddle
Thorax:	Ginger bleached squirrel dubbing

In Booty's Hecuba Emerger, inspired by Ken Burk-holder's Hangdy-Downdy Emerger, Boots Allen uses the notched piece of closed-cell foam to support the wing in a 45-degree forward position. After it and the wing are tied in, he dubs the thorax above their base. Hecuba live in moderately fast streams and emerge during late summer throughout the region. Salmonids can be selective with respect to taking duns or emergers, so it is important to have patterns for both these life stages ready when Hecuba are emerging.

BOOTY'S MAHOGANY EMERGER

Hook:	#10-16 Daiichi 1170
Thread:	Black 6/0 or 8/0 UNI-Thread,
Shuck:	Dyed brown ostrich herl
Abdomen:	Brown camel dubbing
Rib:	Fine 5-grain gold or copper wire
Thorax:	Brown 1-mm or 0.5-mm closed-cell Razor Foam
Hackle:	Brown rooster saddle
Wing:	Dark gray EP Fibers

Use this fly by Boots Allen during the much antici-pated Mahogany Dun emergence in the Greater Yellow-stone Area. September is the month to expect the major part of the autumn mayfly emergence peak. Look for the emergers to be in slower waters of regional streams, with midmorning to late afternoon holding peak activity when feeding can be selective. Consider that Mahoganies will also inhabit and emerge from stillwater shorelines that have strong wave action.

BOWEN PMD CRIPPLE

Hook:	#14-18 TMC 101
Thread:	Yellow 8/0
Tail:	Pheasant tail fibers and a single strand of UV pearl Krystal Flash
Rib:	Single strand of UV pearl Krystal Flash

Body:	Pheasant tail fibers
Thorax:	Cream dubbing
Hackle:	Grizzly dry-fly saddle
Wing:	CDC post (tilted forward)

Inspired by the Quigley Cripple, Paul Bowen adapted new materials and some of his own ideas to come up with this pattern. Paul lives on the lower South Fork reach of the Snake River, and he occasionally guides on the Henry's Fork and South Fork. The PMD activity on both rivers is a major event, and for Paul, an award-winning fly tier, this pattern is becoming a standard go-to pattern during their long season. Try the larger size for Flavs and the smaller size for PMDs.

BURKUS BAETIS EMERGER

Hook:	#16 Daiichi 1130
Thread:	Gray 6/0 Danville
Shuck:	Amber Z-Lon fibers
Legs:	Front end of Z-Lon fibers used for shuck
Abdomen:	Great blue heron biot
Thorax:	Slate Nature's Spirit wool dubbing
Wing:	Four white-tipped Canada goose CDC feathers

The hook used gives a natural curve to this pattern, Ken Burkholder's favorite for a BWO emerger or cripple. The heron biot gives this pattern correct color. Ken first wraps a short thread base behind the eye. Over the bottom of this base, he ties in the Z-Lon fibers, the front of which will form legs. Turning the rest of the fibers to the top of the hook and catching them beneath the thread base advanced to the rear forms the shuck. He wraps the biot abdomen, then reinforces it with back-and-forth thread wraps. He dubs a thorax and ties legs into position in front of it, leaving room to tie in the CDC wing feathers, tips forward. He ramps these feathers upward with thread wraps and trims the butt ends over the thorax. He trims legs to the hook point and shuck to abdomen length completing the fly.

BURKUS MAHOGANY EMERGER

Hook:	#16 Daiichi 1130
Thread:	Black Pearsall's Gossamer silk
Trailing shuck:	Brown Antron fibers
Rib:	White tying thread
Body:	Claret Pearsall's Gossamer silk
Thorax:	Mahogany Nature's Spirit wool dubbing
Legs:	Amber Antron fibers
Post:	Fine polar bear underfur
Hackle:	Light dun Whiting saddle

This particular pattern by Ken Burkholder is highly effective on the South Fork reach of the Snake River during the fall season. It also works well on the Wyoming portion of the Snake River. It is seeing a greater use among anglers in the Jackson Hole One Fly who are comfortable presenting small flies. In the 2011 One Fly Contest, the winning amateur used this fly the second day from Moose to Wilson and scored over 500 points.

BWO STUDENT

Hook:	#16-22 Dai-Riki 075
Thread:	Olive dun 8/0 UNI-Thread
Tail:	Natural dun TroutHunter CDC fibers
Body:	Tying thread
Wing:	Natural dun TroutHunter CDC feather

Frank Johnson suggests using a wet fly/nymph hook for added strength when tying this pattern. He ties in the tail, five or six fibers together, and then begins the body at a point on the shank directly above the hook point. Tail length is twice the distance of the hook gape. He carefully wraps the tying thread forward to a point one hook-eye length behind the eye to form the body. At front end of body, he ties in butt end of wing feather with tip pointing over hook eye. He pulls butt end of feather to rear to adjust wing height. He trims butts and cover ends with tying thread to produce a slightly tapered body. He ramps wing upright with thread turns in front of its base and whip-finish. Frank uses only a micro amount of CDC oil to dress CDC wings on his flies. He dries them with chamois or amadou. Using a full-dress dry fly in front of this pattern provides an "indicator."

CALLIBAETIS EMERGER

Hook:	#12-14 Dai-Riki 060
Thread:	Brown-olive 70-denier UTC Ultra Thread
Rib:	Fine silver UNI-Wire
Tail:	Lady Amherst pheasant tippet fibers
Body:	Natural gray SLF squirrel dubbing
Wing case:	Ring-necked pheasant tail segment
Thorax:	Same as body

This is Doug McKnight's favorite Speckled Dun emerger pattern for fishing lakes in Paradise Valley. Around midsummer the peak activity of Speckled Dun (*Callibaetis*) mayflies begins, and fish key on them. Doug presents this pattern behind a floating adult Speckled Dun pattern and uses a very slow strip, which is more effective than fishing this pattern under an indicator.

CDC FLAV CRIPPLE

Hook:	#14 TMC 900BL
Thread:	Iron gray 8/0 UNI-Thread
Tail:	Three dyed black mallard flank fibers
Rib:	Yellow 8/0 UNI-Thread
Body:	Dyed olive twisted CDC
Thorax:	Peacock Ice Dub
Hackle:	Grizzly saddle dyed golden olive with turmeric solution
Wing:	Blue dun CDC feathers
Head:	Black Orvis dubbing

The Flav emergence on the Harriman State Park reach of the Henry's Fork during early July evenings is legendary. Sumi Sakamaki's emerger pattern for meeting this hatch has proven effective regardless of weather conditions. Thus it is worth trying during Flav emergences anywhere. Sumi's use of a warm turmeric solution to dye grizzly hackle golden olive is unique and easy to perform. Add half a cup turmeric powder to a cup of hot water. Allow hackle to soak for two days, then rinse and dry.

CIRCLE K

Hook:	#12-18 Mustad 94840
Thread:	8/0 UNI-Thread, color to match natural
Tail:	Z-Lon loop

Body: HOH PMD Superfine Dubbing or HOH
                    dubbing color to match natural

Wing: Clump of CDC feathers

This is Kieran Frye's go-to mayfly pattern for use during his visits to Greater Yellowstone waters. It is easily tied and uses the House of Harrop (HOH) materials that he favors. Before a visit to fish regional waters, Kieran determines which mayfly species will be emerging, then selects the HOH dubbing and CDC colors that best match the duns and emergers of the species. The Circle K thusly tied in the proper size has resulted in many successes. Shown and described above is the PMD emerger version.

CW'S FOAM GREEN DRAKE EMERGER

Hook: #10-12 TMC 2488
Thread: Olive 70-denier UTC Ultra Thread
Shuck: March brown Antron dubbing fibers
Underbody: Olive dubbing
Body: Goose or turkey biot dyed BWO
Wing case: Gray Razor Foam
Wing post: Goose CDC
Thorax: BWO Superfine Dubbing
Hackle: Whiting Farms speckled badger saddle

To create Chris Williams's fly, wrap tying thread halfway up shank. Pinch wrap in a clump of March brown dubbing fibers at bend. Tie in biot with notch facing hook eye to achieve a furled body. Before wrapping biot, dub underbody to middle of shank. Wrap biot over dubbing. Tie in split piece of gray Razor Foam for wing case. Secure it facing rear with thread wraps. Use a bodkin to make a hole through both pieces of foam at midpoint. Slide tips of opposing CDC feathers into a dubbing threader. Gently pull them through holes, adjust to shank length, and secure butts. Tie in hackle. Dub thorax around base of butts. Tie in two hackle wraps. Pull foam over thorax, forming wing case, position wing at 45-degree angle to rear, then tie down and trim foam. Whip-finish and clip "V" in hackle bottom.

CW'S PMD EMERGER

Hook: #16-18 TMC 2488
Thread: Yellow 70-denier UTC Ultra Thread
Shuck: Dyed March brown Antron dubbing
                        fibers
Body: PMD dyed turkey or goose biot over
                        olive dubbing underbody to midshank
Wing case: Transparent dun Razor Foam forming
                        shellback
Thorax: PMD Superfine Dubbing
Hackle: Whiting Farms speckled badger saddle
Wing: Goose CDC, concave sides facing

To create this pattern by Chris Williams, after tying in shuck, tie in biot with notch facing hook eye. Dub underbody to shank midpoint. Wrap biot forward, making a furled body, and trim excess. Tie in a piece of translucent gray Razor Foam at midpoint. Pull both foam ends to rear and secure with two thread wraps to hold them back. Use a bodkin to make a hole through both pieces of foam at wing case midpoint. Slide CDC tips into a dubbing threader and gently pull them through the holes. Adjust the wings to correct length (about shank length) and secure butts on shank with two thread wraps. Tie in two wraps of hackle, pull foam over thorax, and position wing at a 45-degree angle pointing rear. Whip-finish and clip "V" in hackle underneath fly.

CW SOFT HACKLE EMERGER SERIES

Chris Williams fishes throughout the season on Greater Yellowstone waters. He observes the season-long progression of emerging mayfly species and notes that on or near the water surface, emerger patterns are most effective in catching trout. His favorite waters to fish are spring creeks and rivers producing large trout. Chris therefore designed this easily tied series of patterns to appear as duns just crawling out of the nymphal shuck on these waters. He presents these with as light of tackle as possible, uses a powder desiccant on the wing and soft-hackle, and fishes each fly dry with the tail and abdomen in the surface film.

To tie the patterns below, first place a thread base on the hook shank. Tie in the ribbing and goose biot pair tails. Rib the thread body to give a segmented appearance. Tie in the post-style wing and cover its butt end with the dubbed thorax. Wrap two turns of hackle in front of the wing.

CW's Soft Hackle BWO Emerger

Hook:	#18-22 TMC 2487
Thread:	Olive 70-denier UTC Ultra Thread
Tails:	Two BWO dyed goose biots
Rib:	Two or three strands olive Iceabou, one strand black Flashabou, and extra fine gold wire twisted together and wrapped over thread base
Body:	Tying thread base
Wing:	Dun Iceabou mixed 1:1 with dun poly yarn
Thorax:	Peacock Ice Dub
Hackle:	Two wraps of dun hen

CW's Soft Hackle Callibaetis Emerger

Hook:	#14-16 TMC 2487
Thread:	Dun 70-denier UTC Ultra Thread
Tails:	Two natural dun goose biots
Rib:	Two or three strands gray Iceabou, one strand black Flashabou, and extra fine silver wire twisted together and wrapped over thread base
Body:	Tying thread base
Wing:	Dun Iceabou mixed 1:1 with dun poly yarn
Thorax:	Dun Ice Dub
Hackle:	Two wraps of Whiting Farms Coq de Leon silver speckled hen

CW's Soft Hackle Green Drake Emerger

Hook:	#10-12 TMC 2487
Thread:	Olive 70-denier UTC Ultra Thread
Tails:	Two olive-brown dyed goose biots
Rib:	Two or three strands olive Iceabou, two or three strands brown Iceabou, one strand black Flashabou, and fine copper wire twisted together and wrapped over thread base
Abdomen:	Two brown and two BWO bleached and dyed stripped peacock herls twisted together and wrapped with ribbing

Wing:	Dun Iceabou mixed 1:1 with dun poly yarn
Thorax:	Olive seal substitute dubbing
Hackle:	Two wraps of Whiting Farms dun hen

CW's Soft Hackle Mahogany Emerger

Hook:	#14-18 TMC 2487
Thread:	Rust brown 70-denier UTC Ultra Thread
Tails:	Two dyed rusty spinner goose biots
Rib:	Two or three strands brown Iceabou, one strand claret Iceabou, one strand black Flashabou, and extra fine copper wire twisted together and wrapped over thread base
Body:	Tying thread base
Wing:	Brown Iceabou mixed 1:1 with dun poly yarn
Thorax:	Dark brown Ice Dub
Hackle:	Two wraps Whiting Farms dark barred ginger hen

CW's Soft Hackle PMD Emerger

Hook:	#16-18 TMC 2487
Thread:	Rust brown 70-denier UTC Ultra Thread for abdomen, yellow 70-denier UTC Ultra Thread for thorax

Tails:	Two rusty spinner dyed goose biots
Rib:	Two or three strands brown Iceabou, one strand claret Iceabou, one strand black Flashabou, and extra fine copper wire twisted together and wrapped over thread base
Body:	Tying thread base
Wing:	Yellow Iceabou mixed 1:1 with tan poly yarn
Thorax:	Yellow Ice Dub
Hackle:	Two wraps Whiting Farms honey dun hen

CW's Soft Hackle Trico Emerger

Hook:	#20-24 TMC 2487
Thread:	Brown 70-denier UTC Ultra Thread for abdomen, olive 70-denier UTC Ultra Thread for thorax
Tails:	Two dark BWO dyed goose biots
Rib:	Two or three strands dark olive Iceabou, one strand black Flashabou, and extra fine gold wire twisted together and wrapped over thread base
Body:	Dark brown tying thread base
Wing:	Clear Iceabou mixed 1:1 with light dun poly yarn
Thorax:	Caddis green Iceabou twisted on olive tying thread
Hackle:	Two wraps Whiting Farms pale dun hen

DK SOFT HACKLE DRY

Hook:	#14-16 TMC 200R
Thread:	70-denier UTC Ultra Thread, color to match natural
Tail:	Natural mallard flank fibers
Rib:	Single pearl Krystal Flash strand
Body:	Superfine Dubbing, color to match natural
Thorax:	Natural ostrich herl
Wing:	Natural dun CDC feathers
Hackle:	Speckled partridge flank feather

Doug Kinney ties and uses this pattern for any mayfly emerger by changing hook size and thread and body color. Perhaps his favorite version is for the South Fork reach of the Snake River PMDs for which he uses pink callibaetis Superfine Dubbing and pink thread. He has a wet version of this pattern in which a shuck of amber Montana Fly Company Z-Yarn fibers replaces the mallard flank fiber tail and UV callibaetis dubbing fibers replace the CDC wing.

EZY EMERGER

Hook:	#10-22 Daiichi 1130
Thread:	Tan 8/0
Tag (optional):	Tying thread

Shuck:	Ginger hackle
Body:	Ginger dubbing
Rib:	Fine copper wire
Wings:	Ginger hackle
Indicator:	Yellow closed-cell foam
Head:	Darker dubbing than used for body

This fly by Al Beatty represents an emerging insect that has almost completed its entry into the world of sky and air. The waste ends of the wings represent the shuck as the insect struggles to escape its clutches; this part of the fly can easily be trimmed should the angler need to change his presentation profile while on the water. Colors can be changed to match a natural insect.

EZY OCCASION

Hook:	#10-22 Daiichi 1130
Thread:	Tan or color to match natural 6/0 or 8/0 depending on hook size
Tag (optional):	Tying thread
Body:	Ginger dubbing or color to match natural
Rib:	Thread or optional wire or tinsel
Wings:	Ginger or color to match natural
Hackle:	Brown or color to match natural

Gretchen Beatty's pattern combines the looped wonder wing and Hans van Klinken's Klinkhammer Special concepts. The Beattys form a looped wonder wing by not tying the stem to the hook shank, only the fibers. The result is more flexible, which minimizes leader twist compared to the traditional wonder wing. For best presentation, put floatant on wings and hackle and Fly Sink on the body. This positions the fly in the film with the hook bend and body below the surface. Wings and hackle float above the surface, giving a highly visible late-stage emerger pattern. Through changing material colors and hook size, any mayfly emerger is simulated by this pattern.

FLAV CRIPPLE

Hook:	#12 TMC 100
Thread:	Olive 8/0 UNI-Thread
Tail:	Dyed dark olive EP Fibers
Rib:	Fine gold wire
Body:	Dyed dark olive pheasant tail fiber
Overbody:	Olive Z-Lon fibers
Thorax:	Dark olive Superfine Dubbing
Wing:	Blue dun EP Fibers
Hackle:	Sparse chartreuse dyed grizzly saddle

During low light afternoon conditions Flavs emerge in numbers that attract feeding salmonids. According to Mike Lawson, salmonids key more readily on cripples during these times because partially submerged emerger bodies come into their sphere of sight on the surface before duns do. Thus his pattern is designed to ride with the tail and body breaking the surface and the remainder above it. The slender, wire-ribbed body aids in this setting. He suggests adding a strand of olive marabou to the Z-Lon overbody to create subtle motion and a buggy appearance natural to a molting insect.

FORNEY'S WOVEN EMERGER

Hook:	#12-20 TMC 2487
Thread:	6/0 Danville flat-waxed nylon, color to match natural
Shuck:	Rainbow Blending Thread (Glissen-Gloss fibers), color to match natural
Abdomen:	Nylon thread tied in overhand weave, colors to match natural
Wing:	Saddle hackle, tied paraloop style over the thorax
Thorax:	Dry-fly dubbing, color to match natural

Russ Forney's Woven Emerger is ideal when emerging mayflies begin to ride the surface. Select color and size matching naturals, or use a generic, subdued color scheme. To keep the semisubmerged fly in the surface film and visible, rub a touch of floatant into its hackle. Russ fishes this emerger in a drag-free drift, edging it along current seams and in bank-side slower waters. A wet retrieve often brings a strike. This pattern takes time to tie because of the weave and paraloop. Olive, tan, and gray (with an Adams hackle) are standard color schemes; variations in cream, brown, red, and black, sizes 18-20, take trout when midge and other minutiae are on the water.

GALLOUP'S CRIPPLE

Hook:	#16-20 Daiichi 1170, bent to shape
Thread:	Olive 50-denier GSP
Tail:	Grizzly dyed olive hackle fibers
Body:	Dyed olive turkey biot (tied in with notch facing hook eye) or olive dun Superfine Dubbing
Wing:	Blue dun Z-Lon
Hackle:	Grizzly dyed olive

This is Kelly Galloup's pattern for simulating a "knockdown dun." Since mayflies struggle to emerge, nearly half of them drift with one wing on the water surface. They are also clumsy fliers, again many of them landing with a wing on the surface. All this makes it wise to have knockdown patterns available during any mayfly emergence. Kelly gently bends the hook shank horizontally in his vise before tying this fly on it. He ties the Z-Lon wing on one side of the shank. Through changing size and color, the Galloup Cripple can be used to imitate any mayfly dun. A BWO knockdown cripple is described here.

GENERIC PT DRY

Hook:	#12-18 Daiichi 1120
Thread:	Black 8/0 UNI-Thread
Tail:	Pheasant tail fiber tips
Rib:	Extra small gold wire
Abdomen:	Pheasant tail fibers
Thorax:	Peacock herl
Post:	White Antron
Hackle:	Parachute grizzly

To create this fly by Nick English, tie in pheasant tail fiber tips the length of the shank. Ensure they are angled down off the hook bend. Tie in gold wire and wrap the pheasant fibers forward about two-thirds up the shank. Tie off and rib with gold wire. Tie in peacock herl. Then tie in the post, leaving extra length untrimmed. Tie it in facing up and out the back so the fly will ride in the surface film with tail and part of body underwater. Tie in hackle to match size of hook. Form the peacock herl thorax and tie off at hook eye. Wrap hackle parachute style around the post four to five times. Tie off at eye and whip-finish. Trim post to be about three-quarters the body length. Fish this fly with floatant on the post only. It should ride in the surface film for best results.

GET-R-DUN

Hook:	#14-20 Daiichi 1640
Thread:	Olive, light cahill, or gray 8/0 UNI-Thread
Tail:	Olive or brown Antron yarn
Body:	Tying thread
Overbody:	Gray/olive, McCheese, light yellow, black, and other colors to match natural McFly Foam strip
Wing:	Light elk hair
Hackle:	Blue dun, grizzly, brown, or ginger

After tying in the tail of this fly by Tim Tollett, wrap thread two-thirds up the shank, tie in McFly Foam, color of choice, on top of shank, securing it with thread wraps back to bend, then forward to tie-in point, thus forming body. Pull McFly Foam back over body, forming humpback, and secure. Tie in elk hair, tips facing forward. Tie in hackle, color of choice, and advance thread to behind eye. Make three or four wraps of hackle, then tie off. Trim elk-hair butts to form small extension over body. Through changing colors and size, the Get-R-Dun cripple pattern can be used during any mayfly emergence.

KG'S BWO HALFBACK FOAM EMERGER

Hook:	#16-20 Dai-Riki 125
Thread:	Olive 70-denier UTC Ultra Thread
Shuck:	Amber olive Arizona Simi Seal dubbing
Abdomen:	BWO dyed goose biot tied rough (notch up) to two-thirds point of shank
Thorax:	Brown olive Nature's Spirit Fine and Dry Dubbing
Wing pad:	Packing foam strip, $1/32$-inch thick
Legs:	Medium dun CDC puff

HARE'S EAR EMERGER

Hook:	#12-20 Daiichi 1120
Bead:	Copper or black metal
Thread:	Black or brown 6/0 Danville flat-waxed nylon
Trailing shuck:	A sparse loop of cream Antron fibers extending about one-quarter the length of the body
Body and thorax:	Hare's ear dubbing
Legs:	Hackle fibers tied to each side of the body
Wing:	Ostrich herl tied paraloop-style

This is the BWO version of Kelly Glissmeyer's Halfback Foam Emerger. To form legs, he ties in the base of CDC puff stem with loose wraps behind hook eye. He pulls it through forward and distributes fibers on either side to form legs in proportion to hook size. He developed this pattern on the flats below the Heise Bridge over the South Fork reach of the Snake River. Here prolific September to November BWO emergences attract all salmonids present.

Russ Forney's pattern is a simple variation of the venerable Hare's Ear Nymph. The curved hook shank, midthorax bead, and ostrich paraloop help convey the appearance and behavior of an emerger, an individual caught in the transition from nymph and adult. The off-axis weighted bead placement enhances movement on the drift. Russ suggests replacing a brass bead with one of tungsten for a faster drop or when fishing in a heavy current.

KG'S PARASOL JUMPER

Hook:	#14-18 Dai-Riki 125
Thread:	Cahill yellow 8/0 UNI-Thread
Tail:	Rust colored Arizona Scud Dub tied as a shuck
Abdomen:	Rust-dyed goose biot tied rough
Thorax:	PMD Superfine Dubbing
Wing:	Medium to dark dun CDC puff

This is the PMD version of Kelly Glissmeyer's Parasol Jumper. It is an omnibus pattern that can be used to simulate any mayfly emerger simply by changing size and colors. It is tied with and without a parasol. When tied with a parasol, the base is tied in at the thorax position. Kelly prefers the CDC puffs for forming immature wings because of their natural bulk. Of course PMD emergers, as well as duns, inhabiting different drainages may have different color tinges, thus Kelly varies the colors accordingly. The *Callibaetis* version is tied on a size 14 Dai-Riki 125 hook and has proven very effective during afternoon Speckled Dun emergences.

KG'S PMD HALFBACK FOAM EMERGER

Hook:	#14-16 Dai-Riki 125
Thread:	Light cahill 8/0 UNI-Thread
Shuck:	Yukon orange Arizona Simi Seal dubbing

Abdomen:	Rust-dyed goose biot tied rough (notch up) to two-thirds point of shank
Thorax:	PMD Nature's Spirit Fine and Dry Dubbing
Wing pad:	Packing foam strip, 1/32-inch thick
Legs:	Pale yellow CDC puff

This is the PMD version of Kelly Glissmeyer's Halfback Foam Emerger. He forms the legs in the manner described in his KG's BWO Halfback Foam Emerger (see page 93). In both patterns Kelly places a drop of cement at the base of the biot and along the shank for durability. This is his go-to PMD emerger on all waters he fishes.

KG'S SMOKE JUMPER VARIATION

Hook:	#14 Dai-Riki 125
Thread:	Olive dun 8/0 UNI-Thread
Tail:	Chartreuse Z-Lon fibers
Rib:	Fine gold wire
Body:	Tying thread
Thorax:	Brown-olive Nature's Spirit dubbing
Shellback:	Olive-gray CDC puff
Wing:	Tips of CDC puff

Kelly Glissmeyer has a world of experience fly fishing from the waters around West Yellowstone, where he lived during the 1990s, and eastern Idaho, where he has lived for the last several years. He numbers spring creeks and stillwaters as his favorites to fish. This pattern is his Speckled Dun emerger, and it has a growing reputation for producing on regional stillwaters. Kelly dead-drifts it on the surface to gulpers during the first stages of their activity. He does the same on spring creeks when Speckled Duns emerge.

MAYFLY LIFE CYCLE **95**

LITTLE JIMMY

Hook:	#14 TMC 200RBL
Thread:	Light brown 6/0
Tail:	Eight to ten wood duck or dyed wood duck flank, extending hook gap length
Rib:	Fine gold wire
Abdomen:	Clear $1/8$-inch wide Thin Skin over dubbed gray wood duck fiber to cover rear two-thirds of shank
Thorax:	Apply Hard As Nails polish over front third of shank, then wrap 4 or 5 peacock herls to cover
Legs:	Gray wood duck flank or lemon-dyed mallard fibers extending to hook point

Callibaetis mayflies are the major food form during the gulper phenomenon on so many Greater Yellowstone Area stillwaters. Gulpers attract fly fishers from all points. Tom Cundith is one of these, and gulpers have inspired him to create flies to simulate their life cycle. This is his pattern for emergers. Not only is it easily tied, but it has proved to be very effective.

LOOP WING PURPLE PHAZE EMERGER

Hook:	#14-18 TMC 100
Thread:	Purple 8/0 UNI-Thread
Shuck:	Golden brown Widow's Web or brown Z-Lon

Body:	Purple Wonder Wrap
Wing bud:	Light gray Razor Foam loop, $1/16$-inch wide
Indicator:	Orange Para Post wing
Hackle:	Dun badger or medium dun trimmed underneath

Walter Weise suggests this pattern for the heavy autumn gray *Baetis* emergences that peak in September. He uses a dun hackle on this pattern rather than the Purple Haze Cripple and Adams-style mixed brown and grizzly to better approximate the overall color of the fall *Baetis*. The foam loop that forms the wing bud helps this pattern float for long periods of time. The orange Para Post indicator ensures visibility on a broken surface.

MADISON GUIDE CRIPPLE

Hook:	#14-16 TMC 2488
Thread:	Light cahill 8/0 UNI-Thread
Shuck:	Epeorus dyed Z-Lon fibers
Body:	Tying thread
Thorax:	Two dyed purple peacock herls
Wing:	White poly yarn
Hackle:	Tannish-brown grizzly saddle

Tie in the poly yarn wing on top of the front of thorax and leave a small portion of the wing's butt on top of the thorax. Wrap two turns of hackle in back of and in front of the wing. After the fly is completed, cut a "V" in the bottom of the hackle in order for the fly to ride lower in the surface film. This pattern by Craig Mathews has proven to be a great searching pattern on area streams.

MCLELLAN'S EP EMERGER

Hook:	#16 Dai-Riki 125
Thread:	Cahill 70-denier UTC Ultra Thread
Shuck:	Rust Z-Lon
Body:	Tying thread
Thorax:	Superfine PMD dubbing
Wing:	Light dun-dyed CDC
Overwing:	Light dun EP Fibers

Marty McLellan is another proponent of EP Fibers for winging mayfly emerger patterns. They create less bulk than other available synthetics, are easy to apply, and result in visible patterns. His CDC "hunchback" wing case simulates that of a struggling emerger. After tying in the shuck, tie in the body, then the CDC feather by the tip at the front of the body. Dub the thorax. Pull the CDC feather over the top to tie in at the front of the thorax near the hook eye. Tie in an inch-long piece of EP Fibers at the same point. Once tied in, pull the EP Fibers over the CDC and trim them, forming the overwing. Marty's PMD version is featured here, but through changing color and size, any mayfly emerger can be simulated.

MR. SCRUFFY

Hook:	#8-12 Dai-Riki 125
Thread:	Gray 6/0 UNI-Thread
Monofilament:	Six-inch piece of 10-pound test
Parachute wing:	Soft deer hair
Tail:	Natural deer hairs
Abdomen:	Olive dubbing or Kreinik gold braid

LeRoy Cook intends this pattern to be scruffy, and as such it is a great large mayfly emerger. Working from front to back, dub over a small portion of the shank behind the eye. Behind the dubbing, tie in midpoint of monofilament piece, having an open overhand knot in section extending forward. Over location where monofilament is tied onto shank, tie in a clump of stacked deer hair, tips forward, with length about that of hook. Trim butts. Pass tips through knot (a post material to create an indicator may be placed into the knot before pulling it into the deer hair) and using monofilament section extending to rear, pull knot down to hair tie-in point. Tighten knot, which spreads deer hair radially over shank in a manner similar to parachute hackling. Trim monofilament extending to rear, tie down front monofilament piece extending from knot and trim. Tie in tail and dub abdomen.

PMD SOFT HACKLE EMERGER

Hook:	#18-22 TMC 900BL
Thread:	Pale yellow 8/0 UNI-Thread
Tail:	Three or four wood duck flank feather fibers
Body:	Pale yellow Superfine Dubbing
Hackle:	Mallard shoulder feather

After tying in tail, dub a tapered body to just behind the hook eye. Tie in a mallard flank feather by the tip. Take one to one and a half turns of this feather just in front of the body. Here is a superb example of an easily tied fly created by Nick Nicklaus and tied by Bucky McCormick that is extremely effective anywhere PMDs are emerging in the area.

PMD STUDENT

Hook:	#14-18 Dai-Riki 075
Thread:	Orange 3/0 Danville Monocord
Shuck:	Yellow gold Antron yarn fibers
Body:	Tying thread
Thorax:	Amber or sulfur orange Superfine Dubbing
Wing:	Light tan or cream TroutHunter CDC feather

Frank Johnson prefers a wet fly/nymph hook for added strength when tying this pattern. He also prefers unwaxed thread, as it stays clean and retains color better. The dubbed thorax adds floatability and visibility to Frank's larger Student patterns. The Antron yarn shuck adds sparkle and perhaps a little floatability. Tie in the shuck. Begin the body at a point on the shank directly above the hook point. Carefully wrap the tying thread forward to a point half the distance to the hook eye to form the body. At one hook eye distance behind the eye, tie in the butt end of wing feather with tip pointing over hook eye. Pull butt end of feather to rear to adjust wing height. Trim butts and cover ends with dubbing to form the thorax. Ramp wing upright with thread turns in front of its base and whip-finish.

PMD UNUSUAL EMERGER

Hook:	#14-18 TMC 100
Thread:	Rust brown 8/0 UNI-Thread
Tail:	Wood duck flank fibers over amber Z-Lon fibers
Body:	Furled dyed rust brown turkey biot
Thorax:	Cream fur dubbing
Wing:	Light tan snowshoe rabbit hair
Hackle:	Sandy dun saddle

The Z-Lon fibers in the tail should be about half as long as the wood duck flank fibers. Howard Cole recommends a thread wrap underneath the base of these tail components to hold them in position. After tying in the tail, body, thorax, and wing, lift the wing and place the first wrap of hackle behind it. Next, hackle wraps should be in front of the wing. This pattern is highly visible even when dead-drifted in the surface film. Howard suggests changing its colors to match those of the PMD emergers in the waters you fish.

PURPLE PECCARY

Hook:	#12-18 Daiichi 1480
Thread:	Black 70-denier UTC Ultra Thread
Tail:	Wood duck flank feather fibers
Body:	Dyed purple peccary body hair
Thorax:	Olive-brown UV Ice Dub
Wing:	Two pearl Krystal Flash fibers behind partridge speckled flank fiber wrapped soft-hackle style

Gary Barnes presents this easily tied pattern as a mayfly emerger in the surface film about eight inches behind a dry attractor. He experiences great success with this rig on the upper Ruby River during mid and late summer. Resident brown trout, rainbow trout, and grayling seem to take it in larger sizes during the summer Mahogany Dun emergence. In early summer he has used it effectively in smaller sizes on the river and on the Beaverhead River during the PMD emergence.

RANDOLPH T-C CALLIBAETIS EMERGER

Hook:	#14 Dai-Riki 300
Thread:	Dark gray 8/0
Tail:	Two pieces of white thread
Rib:	Dark gray 8/0 thread

Body:	White tying thread and gray Thin Skin
Thorax:	Light tan dubbing
Legs:	One turn of dun hen hackle with top fibers cut away
Wing:	Sparse Hungarian partridge fibers tied in on top of hook shank
Head:	Dark gray tying thread

This pattern is Gerry "Randy" Randolph's go-to fly when *Callibaetis* emergences are in full swing. He relies on it during his visits to favorite stillwaters throughout the gulper season. He fishes it slowly in shallow water with an intermediate line and four feet of 5X tippet as soon as he observes cruising fish.

SCUDDLE MUDDLE

Hook:	#10-22 Daiichi 1130
Thread:	Tan 8/0
Tag (optional):	Tying thread
Extension/shuck:	Ginger untrimmed waste from wings
Body:	Tan dubbing
Rib:	Fine copper wire
Wings:	Ginger
Front hackle:	Elk or deer
Head:	Clipped elk or deer hair

This fly by Al Beatty represents a stuck-in-the-surface-film emerger and is particularly effective in slow-moving waters like Slough Creek or Bechler River in Yellowstone Park. In faster water, present it on a dead drift quartering upstream and when the fly starts to drag, pull it under and fish it like a wet fly as it swings across the current on its trip downriver.

SOUTH FORK PMD EMERGER

STICH GREEN DRAKE CRIPPLE

Hook:	#12-16 TMC 100
Thread:	Pink 8/0 UNI-Thread
Tail:	White spade hackle fibers
Rib:	Silver UNI-Wire (extra small)
Abdomen:	Mixture of nonspiky pink dubbing and small amount of nonspiky yellow dubbing
Underthorax:	Gray Antron dubbing
Overthorax:	Gray Sparkle Yarn
Hackle:	White or cream saddle

Michael Snody designed this fly for fishing riffles in eastern Idaho's South Fork reach of the Snake River. PMDs emerging from this part of the Snake River have a distinct pinkish tinge, and the most successful emerger, cripple, stillborn, and duns fished there will have this color. Michael forms the thorax in a manner similar to Gary LaFontaine's method used in the emergent caddis pupa, in which sparkle yarn envelops the "underthorax," except that he ties in strands of gray sparkle yarn on either side in front of the abdomen to form the "overthorax." Next he dubs the underthorax, leaving room to finish the overthorax and wrapping hackle. He finishes the overthorax by pulling the strands of sparkle yarn forward, distributing them evenly around the hook shank, then tying them down. He trims their excess, then wraps the hackle over their butts.

Hook:	#10-12 Daiichi 1170
Thread:	Olive 6/0 UNI-Thread
Shuck:	Tip of body CDC feather
Body:	Dyed light olive CDC
Wing:	Elk body hair
Hackle:	Grizzly saddle

When Green Drakes emerge, an effective and quickly tied pattern is desired. No one wants to tie complicated patterns when a simple one means less time at the vise and more time to get ready for the great action Green Drakes can bring. This pattern fills the bill. It is composed of only four easily obtained components along with hook and thread. Aaron Stich trims some of the CDC fibers from the body, but leaves enough for the buggy look of an emerger. He also trims hackle fibers from the bottom of the fly, allowing it to sit lower in the water as an emerger would.

TLF DEER HAIR EMERGER

Hook:	#16-20 Partridge 15BN Klinkhamer
Thread:	Rusty dun 8/0 UNI-Thread
Shuck:	Tan or light gold Antron fibers
Body:	Brown Danville Stretch Floss
Rib:	Fine silver wire
Thorax:	Pink Ice Dub
Wing:	Fine natural deer hair, tied in up-wing with butts trimmed to shape over thorax
Hackle:	Saddle color to match natural

Jerry Criss offers this pattern for the *Callibaetis* emergence on any stillwater you may fish. It has accounted for numerous fish in the Greater Yellowstone Area as well as in his central Oregon stillwaters. He applies floatant to the wing and hackle, allowing only the shuck and body to hang Klinkhammer style deep in the surface film.

TLF QUILL WING EMERGER

Hook:	#16-20 Partridge 15BNX Klinkhamer
Thread:	Dun 8/0 UNI-Thread to 14/0 Benecchi
Shuck:	Pair of lemon wood duck fibers
Body:	Light brown tying thread doubled up

Rib:	Fine silver wire
Thorax:	Pink Ice Dub
Wing:	Duck quill tied upright and divided
Hackle:	Saddle color to match natural

Jerry Criss created this pattern to supplement his Deer Hair Emerger. Like the Extreme Klinkhamer, the quill wing and hackle, when dressed with floatant, sit very well on the surface, and the body and shuck, both not treated with floatant, go deep into the surface film. Expect subtle takes on this pattern, requiring attention to any movement below the fly.

WEISE'S HAZE CRIPPLE

Hook:	#12-20 TMC 100
Thread:	Purple 8/0 UNI-Thread
Shuck:	Golden brown Widow's Web or brown Z-Lon
Body:	Purple Wonder Wrap (Spandex)
Wing:	White Widow's Web
Hackle:	Brown and grizzly saddles trimmed underneath

Walter Weise offers this DOA- or Quigley-style pattern as a very effective fly during autumn BWO emergences. It works well when these hatches are sparse as well as an attractor whenever mayfly hatches are expected. Besides the purple version described and pictured above, Walter also offers this fly in a PMD color as well as in spring BWO (olive) and autumn BWO (gray).

DUN AND SPINNER PATTERNS

ALIEN BWO

Hook:	#10-14 TMC 2302
Thread:	Olive dun 8/0 UNI-Thread
Tail:	Deer hair
Rib:	Copper Krystal Flash strand
Abdomen:	Bluish olive Superfine Dubbing for rear half, olive Superfine Dubbing for front half
Wing:	Deer hair mixed with rainbow Krystal Flash
Legs:	Black Larva Lace Super Floss
Hackle:	Barred blue dun saddle
Thorax:	Black peacock Ice Dub

This is an unorthodox pattern for a BWO dun, but it works better than you may think! Mike Snody suggests trying it on broken water when BWO duns are active. It is highly visible here, and there are plenty of the faster waters in Yellowstone country where BWOs are present.

ANDRES HATCHMATCHER SERIES

Decades ago the Darbee family in New York State's Catskill Mountains originated the "Hatchmasters" to simulate mayfly duns. (They were originally named "Hatchmasters" by the Darbees, but Doug names his variations "Hatchmatchers.") Eventually Dick Alf of Ketchum, Idaho, brought them west for use on Silver Creek. They languished in relative obscurity until creative tiers such as Doug Andres applied alterations to them using currently available tying products. Easily tied, highly visible, and effective, a new generation of hatchmatchers is emerging in this area.

To tie these patterns, first place a thread base on the hook shank. Select a symmetrical duck flank feather and

pull back all fibers, except some at the tip, in the same manner as preparing a reverse wrapped wing. Position the reversed wrapped feather on top of the hook shank so that a body portion proportional to the hook size extends beyond the bend, and secure it to the shank. Wrap the thread back toward the bend of the hook, then forward so that a thread body is created on the rear two-thirds of the hook shank. Cut away the tip of the feather extending from the rear, leaving a fiber or two on either side, depending on the hook size, to form a split tail. At this point, part of the stem and hackle fibers from the reversed portion of the flank feather is secured under the thread body. The remainder of the stem and tips of the fibers extend forward and parallel to the top of the shank. Lift the stem and tips of the fibers straight up to begin forming a wing. Ramp these to a vertical position with thread wraps, cut away the stem, and use a few figure-eight wraps to divide the fibers. Trim the fibers to a wing length proportional to hook size. For added durability, apply head cement to the split tails, extended body, and thread body. Allow to dry. Hackle the fly with one turn behind and two in front of the wing. Whip-finish a head.

Adams Hatchmatcher

Hook:	#14-22 Daiichi 1110
Thread:	Gray 8/0 UNI-Thread
Body:	Tying thread
Tail:	Dun-dyed mallard flank feather
Hackle:	Cree or brown/grizzly saddle mix

Brown Drake Hatchmatcher

Hook:	#10-12 Daiichi 1110
Thread:	Dark brown 8/0 UNI-Thread
Body:	Tying thread
Tail:	Dark brown dyed mallard flank feather
Hackle:	Cree or brown/grizzly saddle mix

Olive Hatchmatcher

Hook:	#16-22 Daiichi 1110
Thread:	Olive or light olive 8/0 UNI-Thread
Body:	Tying thread
Tail:	Olive-dyed mallard flank feather
Hackle:	Medium or dark dun saddle

Callibaetis Hatchmatcher

Hook:	#12 Daiichi 1110
Thread:	Dark brown 8/0 UNI-Thread
Body:	Tying thread
Tail:	Natural mallard flank feather
Hackle:	Brown saddle

Pale Morning Dun Hatchmatcher

Hook:	#14-18 Daiichi 1110
Thread:	Light cahill or yellow 8/0 UNI-Thread
Body:	Tying thread
Tail:	Natural mallard flank feather
Hackle:	Medium dun, light ginger, or grizzly saddle

Trico Hatchmatcher

Hook:	#20-24 Daiichi 1110
Thread:	Olive or black 8/0 UNI-Thread
Body:	Tying thread
Tail:	Drake gadwall breast feather or similar small white feather
Hackle:	Grizzly or cream saddle

ARF HAREY PMD THORAX

Hook:	#14-18 TMC 101
Thread:	Cahill yellow 8/0 UNI-Thread
Tail:	Medium dun Mayfly Tails tied long and split
Abdomen:	Saddle hackle quill dyed Pale Morning Dun
Wing:	Snowshoe hare, medium dun hair from back feet
Thorax:	Pale Morning Dun Superfine Dubbing
Hackle:	Dun saddle tied Marinaro thorax style

Al Ritt admires the sparse elegance of Catskill-style dry flies. The modified thorax style hackling commonly used today is effective, but there are times when a more sparsely dressed fly seems best for attracting fish. Thus, Al prefers the sparse Marinaro style (original) thorax hackling that floats well and is stable when combined with split tails. (Search www.flyanglersonline.com for instructions on this technique.) He utilizes a favorite wing material: snowshoe hare. It is not hollow, so it does not waterlog. It is softer than calf tail, and therefore easier to tie in. It is also less bulky, with a similar crinkly texture that maximizes the outline of the wing while requiring less material. Al dead-drifts this pattern during a PMD emergence. This fly can be twitched subtly if the tippet remains on the surface.

ARF LIFE & DEATH CALLIBAETIS

Hook:	#14-18 TMC 101
Thread:	Tan 6/0 UNI-Thread
Tail:	Grizzly hackle fibers split into two tails with thread wraps
Abdomen:	Stripped gray quill
Wing:	White organza
Post:	Chartreuse Hi-Viz Para Post
Thorax:	Adams gray Superfine Dubbing
Hackle:	Dry-fly quality grizzly saddle

Among other attributes, Al Ritt's pattern is highly visible, a blessing when fishing on sun-drenched stillwaters. Both the Hi-Viz post and the organza wing reflect light superbly. Most gulper fishing ends when wind roughs the water surface, reducing visibility of drifting spinner patterns. This one, however, would likely be the last to fade from view.

BEAR HAIR HECUBA

Hook:	#12 Daiichi 1190
Thread:	Gray 8/0 UNI-Thread
Body:	Rainy's Tube Bodiz TB-201204, Adams gray mayfly body
Dubbing:	Fly-Rite #37, gray drake/gray fox extra fine poly dubbing
Wing:	Light brown brown bear hair
Hackle:	Brown and grizzly

To create this fly by Ken Burkholder, wrap a thread base from hook eye to shank halfway point. Insert a round toothpick into the body tube for a mandrel. Use a claret marking pen to make segments on the tube. Impale the mayfly body tube over the hook point and slide over the shank. Superglue thread base, slide tube over thread, and immediately bind with thread to fix in place. Tie on the bear-hair wing. Tie hackles on behind wing and dub thorax. Wind hackles forward through thorax and clip bottoms flat. Color tying thread with claret marker and form a generous head. Superglue head to finish.

BROWN DRAKE HACKLE SPINNER

Hook:	#10-12 Daiichi 1280
Thread:	Tan 6/0 Flymaster, waxed
Tail:	Moose body hairs

Body:	Tan Superfine dubbing
Rib:	Brown 2/0 thread
Wings:	One brown and one grizzly neck hackle, with fibers shank length
Thorax/head:	Tan Superfine Dubbing

To create this pattern by Nelson Ishiyama, tie in small dubbing ball above barb. Tie in six or eight moose body hairs in front of ball, allowing half to split to each side. Tie in ribbing thread in front of ball. Dub slender tapered body to point two-thirds of way from bend to eye. Counterwrap thread rib. Tie in hackles and wind in narrow band at front of body. Using both hands, gather fibers into equal clumps on sides of the hook. Use figure-eight thread wraps to further gather clumps. Post each with thread wraps. Use thinly dubbed thread for further figure-eight wraps around wing, building up a thorax and keeping wings horizontal and 90 degrees from hook. Whip-finish. Soak wing fibers with Flexament one-eighth inch from thorax. Allow to dry until no longer sticky. Using flat-nosed pliers, squeeze wing bases flat, causing fibers to fan horizontally. Start squeezing next to thorax and work outward.

BUFF STUFF

Hook:	#14-16 TMC 900BL
Thread:	Gray brown 70-denier UTC Ultra Thread
Tail:	Wood duck flank feather fibers and a few bison undercoat fibers
Abdomen:	Dyed gray-olive goose biot
Thorax:	Bison undercoat or bison down
Wing:	Bison down
Hackle:	Grizzly dry-fly

According to Bob Starck, bison down is easily worked and durable. Once cleaned, the bison down fibers are aligned and tied in Quigley style for the wing. He saw few references where bison down had been used on dry flies, so this pattern is his answer. Among Bob's favorite fly-fishing events is the Hebgen Lake gulper activity. Thus he applied this fly to the very selective gulpers with great success. He trims hackle on the bottom of the fly flush with the hook point to get a lower ride on the surface. Bison down absorbs water quickly, so be sure to thoroughly dress an example before presentation.

BWO PARAWULFF

Hook:	#12-16 Dai-Riki 300
Thread:	Olive 8/0 UNI-Thread
Wing:	White calf tail, upright and divided
Rib:	Pearl Krystal Flash strand
Body:	Olive Antron dubbing
Hackle:	One grizzly and one brown saddle

Tie in the wing first on this pattern by Jack Dennis. Next, tie in the tails and rib. Dub the body to just forward of the wing and rib it. Tie in the hackle butts at the wing base, and wrap hackles there. This is a newer member of the Parawulff series. Others are the PMD Parawulff and the Gray (Hecuba) Parawulff. Any mayfly can be simulated with the Parawulff technique (search www.fly-anglersonline.com for instructions on this technique.). These are highly visible flies for fast-moving rivers in the region.

CDC COMPARADUN

Hook:	#12-22 Dai-Riki 075
Thread:	8/0 UNI-Thread, color to match natural
Tail:	Antron fibers, color to match natural
Body:	Superfine Dubbing, color to match natural
Wing:	CDC tied Compara-dun style, color to match natural

The Compara-dun concept has been around for decades. This pattern represents a major variation where Antron fibers are used for the tail, and, most significantly, the wing is formed of CDC Fibers. Any mayfly dun can be simulated with concept variation. Pictured above is Frank Johnson's popular CDC Baetis Compara-dun in which amber Antron fibers make the tail, olive-gray Superfine Dubbing form the body, and CDC dyed blue form the wing.

CDC DRAKE

Hook:	#10-12 Dai-Riki 280
Thread:	Gray 70-denier UTC Ultra Thread
Tail:	Dark moose mane hairs
Body:	Stripped Coq de Leon hackle stem
Wing:	Natural dun CDC feather pairs
Thorax/head:	Gray Superfine Dubbing

Soak the stem to minimize splitting during wrapping, tie it in by the tip, natural curve down, and dull side facing. The result is an elegantly tapered body. Coat it with superglue to add durability. Dandy and Dean Reiner use a pair of CDC feathers for each wing. Each pair is mounted convex side out. The stems of each pair are folded to the rear to act as stabilizers on each side of the body. CDC feathers extending from the wings also help stabilize this pattern, which can be used to imitate the spinner stage of any drake mayfly.

CHAPMAN MAYFLY DUN

Hook:	#14-18 Mustad 3399
Thread:	Black 6/0
Wing:	Light blue dun hackle tips, upright and divided
Tail:	Blue dun hackle fibers
Body:	Dubbed beaver fur
Hackle:	Blue dun

Scotty Chapman was for decades (1920s–1980s) the premier resident fly tyer in Yellowstone National Park. A full-time ranger based mainly in Mammoth and Gardiner, he fished all Park waters and guided contemporary celebrities to the best fishing the Park offered. His fly patterns are based on experiences on Park waters that have no equal. Thus it is appropriate to have one of his patterns here. Craig Mathews and Bob Jacklin attest to the value of Scotty's contributions to the fly-tying world. The original of this BWO pattern is in the box of flies tied by Scotty that son Bill and Loretta Chapman own. It is also in the collection framed by Fred LaTour for Jim O'Toole. The author tied the fly pictured above using materials available during Scotty's era.

CRONK'S TEABAG DUN

Hook:	#18 Dai-Riki 060
Thread:	Black 6/0 Danville Flymaster
Tail:	Split dun Microfibetts
Body:	Dark sorrel horse tail
Wing:	Reuseable white teabag material
Hackle:	Medium blue dun saddle

Chuck Collins prefers to coat the horse hair for the body with head cement to add a gloss on finishing. He uses a burner to form the wings from the fine-mesh teabag material, but offers that a wing cutter can also be used or the wings can be cut by hand. This material is easily colored with a marking pen to match a natural. Likewise, Chuck uses a white horse hair and colors it with a marking pen to match a natural color. On completing this fly, trim a "V" in the bottom of the hackle. The Trico version of this pattern is featured above.

CW'S CALLIBAETIS DUN

Hook:	#14-18 TMC 100
Thread:	White 8/0 UNI-Thread
Tail:	Divided light pardo Whiting Farms Coq de Leon fibers
Body:	Natural goose biot
Wing:	Deer body hair post

Thorax: Light dun Superfine Dubbing
Hackle: Cree or speckled badger saddle

Apply a thread base to shank and tie in and divide tail fibers. Tie in goose biot with notch toward tail to obtain a smooth body and wrap to halfway point of shank. Tie in the deer-hair wing post and wrap the hackle. This high floating, yet delicate Callibaetis Dun pattern by Chris Williams is a great choice during gulper activity anywhere.

CW'S GREEN DRAKE DUN

Hook: #12-14 TMC 100
Thread: Olive 70-denier UTC Ultra Thread
Tail: Whiting Farms dark Coq de Leon
feather fibers
Body: Dyed olive goose biot tied in with
notch toward tail for a smooth body
Wing: Goose CDC feathers
Hackle: Dyed olive grizzly
Thorax: Olive Superfine Dubbing

CW'S CALLIBAETIS SPINNER

Hook: #14-18 TMC 100
Thread: White 8/0 UNI-Thread
Tail: Light pardo Whiting Farms Coq de
Leon fibers
Body: Light dun turkey or goose biot tied in
with notch toward tail for a smooth
body
Wing post: Translucent dun Razor Foam
Hackle: Cree or speckled badger saddle
Thorax: Light dun Superfine Dubbing

After tying in and dividing tail, tie in biot and wrap it to just forward of shank midpoint. Fold in two, then tie in Razor Foam just forward of biot and wrap thread up both sections to form a post. Tie in hackle on post, dub thorax, and wrap hackle parachute style. Divide hackle fibers to either side, pull top of post forward, and tie off at head. This pattern by Chris Williams is excellent for spring creeks and during the widespread gulper event season in the Greater Yellowstone Area.

Wrap a thread base along the shank, tie in 10 to 12 Coq de Leon feather fibers and divide into a right and left tail with thread wraps. At the top of the bend, tie in the turkey biot with notch toward tail for a smooth body. Wrap the biot to just past the halfway point on the shank. Tie in the butt end of the hackle. Select two goose CDC feathers of the same size, tie them in, convex sides facing, at the thorax midpoint on the shank. Stand these feathers vertically with thread wraps. Dub a thorax behind and in front of the tied-in wing. Wrap two turns of hackle in back and in front of the wing. Trim a "V" out of the hackle underneath the thorax. In size 14, this pattern by Chris Williams imitates the Western Green Drake (Flav).

CW'S GUINEA WING CALLIBAETIS

Hook:	#14-18 TMC 100
Thread:	White 8/0 UNI-Thread
Tail:	Light Whiting Farms Coq de Leon feather fibers
Body:	Natural goose biot
Wing post:	Tips of two speckled Guinea hen body feathers
Thorax:	Light dun Superfine Dubbing
Hackle:	Cree or speckled badger saddle

Wrap a thread base along the shank, tie in ten to twelve Coq de Leon feather fibers and divide into right and left tails with thread wraps. At top of the bend, tie in the turkey biot with notch toward tail for a smooth body. Wrap the biot to just past halfway point on the shank. Tie in and post tips of two guinea hen body feathers just in front of the body. Tie in butt of hackle, and dub a thorax behind and in front of post and tied-in hackle. Wrap hackle parachute style around post and tie off. Certain speckled duns emerging during gulper action have darker wings. Chris Williams uses this pattern tied with guinea feather wings when he observes these Speckled Duns being taken by feeding trout.

CW'S RUSTY SPINNER

Hook:	#18-24 TMC 100
Thread:	Rusty brown 8/0 UNI-Thread or 70-denier UTC Ultra Thread
Tail:	Divided Whiting Farms Dark Coq de Leon fibers
Body:	Rusty brown turkey or goose biot tied in with notch toward tail for a smooth body
Wing:	Dun-colored Whiting Farms Coq de Leon feather over dun-colored floating poly yarn
Thorax:	Rusty brown Superfine Dubbing

After tying in the tail and forming the body, tie in about 10 poly yarn fibers just in front of the body. Pull back on the yarn fibers to angle them in a horizontal "V" shape and anchor their tie-in point with thread wraps. Clip evenly just past the bend. Tie in a Coq de Leon feather just in front of poly wing and divide fibers into left and right bunches with figure-eight wraps. These should extend to the rear on each side at 45 degrees. Dub a thorax over the wing tie point. This pattern by Chris Williams can be used for PMD and BWO spinners and has accounted for many large trout.

DARK WING FLAV

Hook:	#14 TMC 100
Thread:	Brown 8/0 UNI-Thread
Tail:	Mayfly brown Z-Lon
Rib:	Dark brown 3/0 thread
Body:	HOH BWO dubbing
Hackle:	Dark dun saddle
Wing:	Black EP Fibers

Don Martinez originally championed that contrasting a dark-colored fly component with a light-colored one enhances a pattern's visibility. John Hudgens applies this concept to his dark-wing mayfly dun patterns where black- or dark-winged flies hatch best in low-light conditions. His use of black EP Fibers creates that effect in his Dark Wing Flav. Change only the dubbing to HOH dark brown and the hackle to grizzly saddle and you have John's Dark Wing March Brown. Clip hackle from the bottom of the fly for a lower silhouette.

DOWNSTREAM DUN

Hook:	#16-20 1270 Daiichi
Thread:	Olive 6/0 Danville Flymaster
Wing:	Bleached calf elk

Body:	Fly-Rite dubbing, color to match natural
Trailing shuck:	Gray Antron

Noting that mayflies drift headfirst downstream, Ron Hicks created this pattern. He fishes variations of this concept pattern during any mayfly emergence and changes colors and size to match those of the adult life-cycle stage. He varies it further by using a CDC wing, but finds when he does this, he must tie in a few turns of hackle at the hook bend to keep this material in an upright position. He has also tied this pattern with a tail of hackle fibers split into a "V" shape.

GALLOUP'S BROWN DRAKE

Hook:	#10 TMC 534
Thread:	Wine 6/0 Danville
Tail:	Moose body hair tips
Body:	Natural brown moose body hair
Wing post:	White deer hair
Hackle:	Dyed brown grizzly

Through changing material colors and hook size, any drake can be imitated by this concept drake pattern. Moose body hair is Kelly Galloup's favorite material for making bodies in patterns such as this. He secures it to the hook shank with figure-eight tying thread wraps and leaves a short extension. He leaves a few uncut hairs to form tails off the extension. The result is a durable, buoyant, and lifelike fly.

GALLOUP'S COMPARA SPINNER

Hook:	#12-24 TMC 100 or 101
Thread:	6/0 or 8/0 Danville, UNI-Thread on smaller sizes, color to match body
Tail:	Four to six strands of Micro-fibetts
Body:	Superfine Dubbing, or tying thread on sizes 18 or smaller, color to match natural
Front wing:	White or light dun Hi-Viz tied Compara-dun style
Second wing:	White or light dun Hi-Viz tied spent style behind front wing
Thorax:	Superfine Dubbing, color to match natural

This concept pattern can be altered by size and component colors to simulate the spinner stage of any mayfly. It is unique in that Kelly Galloup applies two wing styles, resulting in visibility and stability while riding on the water surface.

GB'S MIGHTY MAY

Hook:	#12-28 Daiichi 1480
Thread:	Tan 70-denier UTC Ultra Thread
Tail:	White Darlon fibers

Body:	Callibaetis waxed stripped peacock herl
Shellback:	Wood duck CDC
Thorax:	Callibaetis UV Ice Dub
Wing:	White, light dun, and black poly yarn
Indicator:	Extension of CDC used to form shellback

Gary Barnes designed this as a concept pattern that, by changing component colors, size, and proportions, can be used to simulate three life-cycle stages of any mayfly. As shown and described above, it is a *Callibaetis* dun pattern effective for gulpers. Through cutting back the wing material to a shorter length, it can be an effective emerger pattern. Lengthen the wing, and it can be a spinner. From the South Fork of the Madison River to the South Fork reach of the Snake River and Yellowstone National Park streams, Gary has had great success with this pattern by changing components to match the hatch.

GIB'S GREEN DRAKE

Hook:	#8-10 Dai-Riki 300
Thread:	Yellow 3/0 Danville Monocord
Tail:	Deer hair tips
Rib:	Tying thread
Body:	Dyed olive mule deer hair
Hackle:	Dyed olive grizzly

Several extended body Green Drake patterns have come out of the Greater Yellowstone Area. This one from Doug Gibson is the easiest to tie and has fewer components. Mule deer hair is available in abundance in the area, and techniques for dying it while retaining durability have been developed here.

Through many years of guiding, Doug has experienced Green Drake emergences throughout the area. This go-to pattern is the recent result from modifications coming from his experience during this famed emergence.

GRAY DRAKE SPINNER (HARROP)

Hook:	#12 TMC 5212
Thread:	Tan 8/0 UNI-Thread
Tail:	Black moose body hairs
Body:	Dark tan dyed turkey biot
Wings:	Speckled Hungarian partridge neck feather tips
Thorax:	Dark tan TroutHunter dubbing
Hackle:	Grizzly saddle wrapped over thorax

A renowned Gray Drake spinner fall occurs later in June on the Chester Dam backwater reach of the Henry's Fork and below. This evening spinner fall attracts trout of all sizes to feed with gusto, and it occurs practically on René Harrop's doorstep. Thus it is fitting that he offers an elegant pattern in the House of Harrop tradition for meeting this event. Significant Gray Drake emergences occur from several Greater Yellowstone Area waters. Some of these that bring notable attention from trout are from Yellowstone Park's Duck Creek, Shoshone Lake tributaries, flooded meadow reaches of Fall River Basin streams, Teton River in Teton Basin, and from Star Valley's Swift Creek.

GRAY DRAKE SPINNER (HUDGENS)

Hook:	#10-12 TMC 200R
Thread:	8/0 UNI-Thread, color to match natural
Tail:	Coq de Leon flank feather fibers
Rib:	Dark brown tying thread
Body:	Dark tan René Harrop Professional Dubbing
Hackle:	Grizzly saddle
Wing:	Pearlescent EP (Enrico Pugliese) Fibers tied spent
Head:	Dark tan René Harrop Professional Dubbing

To add durability but remain as delicate and buoyant as CDC, John Hudgens searched for the right winging material for completing his Gray Drake Spinner pattern. He found these properties in EP Fibers, with their ability to hold together under repeated use. Now his Gray Drake Spinner pattern enjoys superb popularity in the Greater Yellowstone Area. Through changing tying thread and body material color, John's pattern can be used to simulate any larger drake spinners so common in season on Greater Yellowstone waters. John suggests brownish-green dubbing for tying Green Drake Spinner patterns and yellowish-brown for Brown Drake Spinner patterns. Because Brown Drake spinners are mostly encountered under low-light conditions, he uses black EP Fibers for winging these to achieve visibility from color contrast.

HECUBA PARACHUTE DUN

Hook:	#8-10 Dai-Riki 300
Thread:	Tan 3/0
Tail:	Grizzly hackle fibers
Rib:	Brown embroidery floss strand or brown tying thread
Body:	Light hare's mask dub
Wing post:	White Hi-Viz
Hackle:	One brown and one grizzly saddle

A resident of well-oxygenated rivers, Hecuba is distributed throughout the Greater Yellowstone Area. It evolved in aqueous environments having silt from glacial or volcanic sources. Its late summer to early autumn emergences can take place from late mornings to late afternoon, depending on stream temperatures. Green Drake dun imitations will work for it during these times; however, more specific imitations, such as Jay Buchner's, are favored by most fly fishers. Notable populations of Hecuba occur in such area streams as the Snake River and its drainage, Lamar River, Soda Butte, and Slough Creeks, and the drainage of the Yellowstone River through Paradise Valley.

HECUBA SPINNER

Hook:	#12-18 Dai-Riki 320
Thread:	Gray 8/0 UNI-Thread
Tail:	Coq de Leon feather fibers

Body:	Grizzly hackle stem
Shellback:	Gray Float Foam
Hackle:	Oversized grizzly saddle

After soaking the stem to minimize splitting during wrapping, tie it in by the tip, natural curve down, and dull side facing. Wrap the stem in close spirals to form the body. Tie it off halfway up the shank, then coat it with superglue. Tie in the Float Foam butt in front of the body, Tie in and wrap the hackle. Bring the Float Foam over the top of the hackle and tie it down at the hook eye. Trim it, leaving enough to form a head, and tie off. Trim hackle fibers away from the bottom. Dean Reiner meant this pattern to be a Hecuba spinner, but it can be used for the spinner stage of any drake mayfly.

H&L VARIANT THORAX

Hook:	#13-19 TMC 103BL
Thread:	Black 8/0 UNI-Thread
Tail:	Split dun Microfibetts
Body:	Stripped peacock herl
Thorax:	Peacock herl
Hackle:	Brown saddle tied thorax style
Wing:	White turkey flats

Tom Harman recommends fishing this pattern any time mayfly drakes are on the water and attracting fish. Change its size accordingly. He has particular success with it on riffle and run reaches such as the Ruby, Big Hole, and Beaverhead Rivers. This is also his favorite searching pattern for any stream in the Greater Yellowstone Area. Split the Microfibetts tails with a dubbing ball, which can double as an egg sac.

HI-VIS EPEORUS SPINNER

Hook:	#16 TMC 900BL
Thread:	Tan 8/0 UNI-Thread
Tail:	Four Coq de Leon fibers
Body:	Epeorus spinner Superfine Dubbing
Wing:	White Z-Lon
Overwing:	Black EP Fibers

First Bucky McCormick ties in the tails and lifts them upright with a thread wrap between the shank and their tie-in point. He dubs a tapered body on the rear three-quarters of the shank, then ties in divided Z-Lon wings. He dubs in a bit of Superfine to keep the wings divided, then ties in the black EP Fibers between them for lifting support. This method produces a relatively bulky spinner pattern that is a proven pattern for the Madison River. Using rusty colored dubbing to form the body, this pattern can be a great spinner pattern for general use.

HUDGENS BROWN DRAKE SPINNER

Hook:	#10 TMC 5212
Thread:	Brown 8/0 UNI-Thread
Tail:	Coq de Leon hackle fibers
Rib:	Dark brown 3/0 thread
Body:	HOH tannish-yellow dubbing

| Hackle: | Oversized grizzly saddle |
| Wing: | Black EP Fibers |

John Hudgens applies his dark wing technique to a Brown Drake spinner because the natural is usually on the water during low-light conditions, typically during early July evenings in the Greater Yellowstone Area. Brown Drake spinner falls can be very concentrated and may offer some superb fishing. Through guiding on the Henry's Fork, John has had ample opportunity to show that this is an effective pattern. Clip hackle from the bottom of the fly to achieve the lower spinner silhouette.

IDAHO HEX

Hook:	#10 Dai-Riki 320
Thread:	Yellow 70-denier UTC Ultra Thread, GSP for head
Tail:	Moose body hair
Extended body:	Dyed yellow elk underneath mottled oak turkey fibers secured by brown thread rib
Wing:	White McFlylon
Thorax:	Spun deer hair clipped to shape
Head and legs:	Spun natural deer hair with tips forming collar

Some *Hexagenia* populations can be found in the Greater Yellowstone Area. Perhaps the best population lives in the silted bottom sections of the Snake River below the Henry's Fork confluence and in the extreme lower Henry's Fork. These mayflies emerge around dusk, and their duns can be found on adjacent buildings. In tying his pattern, Shawn Bostic secures the wing between the spun deer-hair thorax and the spun head to hold the wing upright. He cuts away deer hair in the collar to simulate legs flaring out at the sides.

JACKLIN'S BROWN DRAKE

Hook:	#10-12 Dai-Riki 285
Thread:	Brown 70- or 140-denier Flymaster
Tail:	Five or six fine tan bull elk mane hairs
Rib:	Dark brown silk buttonhole twist, size E
Body:	Light tan dubbing
Wing:	Compara-dun style natural dark gray deer body hair tied full and high
Hackle:	Oversized dyed brown grizzly tied thorax style
Head:	Light tan body dubbing

Bob Jacklin recommends a small dubbing ball tied in at the top of the bend to prop the tails in a slight uplift. Flat nylon tying thread of same size can also be used instead of Flymaster. Bob uses light tan dubbing to match the underside color of the newly emerged Brown Drake dun. Fine elk hair dyed dark dun gray can be used instead of deer hair for the wing. He suggests trimming hackle flat on the underside to give the proper silhouette.

JACKLIN'S BROWN DRAKE PARA-SPIN SPINNER

Hook:	#10-12 Dai-Riki 285
Thread:	Brown 70- or 140-denier Flymaster
Egg sac:	Dark brown or black dubbing
Tail:	Five or six fine tan bull elk mane hairs
Rib:	Golden yellow flat nylon tying thread
Body:	Tan to dark brown or rusty dubbing
Wing:	White Antron Para-Spin style parachute wing
Hackle:	One or two oversize grizzly or grizzly dyed light brown neck

Bob recommends a small dubbing ball tied in at the top of the bend to simulate an egg sac and to prop the tails in a slight uplift. He uses oversize hackle to represent the spinner wing. See discussion of Bob's Rusty Paraspinner (page 119) for details on tying his Para-Spin wing. He recommends tying the body very thin to represent that of the spent insect. This fly floats in the surface film like the natural insect, particularly when the hackle is trimmed away from the bottom of the fly.

JACKLIN'S SLATE WING OLIVE

Hook:	#12 Dai-Riki #280
Thread:	Olive 70- or 140-denier Flymaster
Tail:	Short, stiff natural dun hackle fibers

Rib:	Dark brown silk buttonhole twist, size E
Body:	Light to dark olive brown dubbing.
Wing:	Compara-dun style natural dark gray deer body hair tied full and high
Hackle:	Two very stiff natural or dyed dun gray, tied Compara-dun style
Head:	Same dubbing as used for body

As with Bob Jacklin's Brown Drake patterns, use a small dubbing ball tied in at the top of the bend to prop the tails in a slight uplift. He notes that the natural body color of this mayfly varies from river to river and the area fished with a very light olive body on naturals in some rivers to a tan body on naturals in others. This is an important early autumn insect closely resembling the Green Drake hatching on the same waters in late June and early July. Bob suggests trimming the hackle flat on the underside to give the proper silhouette.

KG'S GRAY DRAKE SPINNER

Hook:	#12 Dai-Riki 125
Thread:	Black 8/0 UNI-Thread
Tail:	Tips of elk hock used for body extension
Body:	Natural rusty red elk hock hair
Thorax:	Rusty brown Nature's Spirit Fine and Dry Dubbing
Hackle:	Oversized two times (#8 for #12 hook) coachman brown saddle

Gray Drake spinners on the Henry's Fork tend toward a rusty brown color, and elk hock is ideal for simulating this color. Kelly Glissmeyer uses size 6/0 tying thread because it is sturdy enough to withstand pressure needed to form the extended body of this pattern. While spiraling the thread up and down the clump of elk hair used to form the body extension, he keeps the body on the sides and on top of the shank. On finishing the extension, he cements the body to keep it in place. After winding the oversized hackle through the thorax, he trims fibers from the bottom for a lower ride in the water. Fibers left on top add to this pattern's visibility.

LAND'S PATTERN

Hook:	#10-12 Dai-Riki 320
Thread:	Brown 8/0 UNI-Thread
Tail:	Pale watery dun hackle fibers
Body:	Stripped brown hackle stem
Thorax:	Brown Superfine Dubbing
Hackle:	Dark brown saddle
Wing:	Pale watery dun hackle tips

After soaking the stem to minimize splitting during wrapping, tie it in by the tip, natural curve down, and dull side facing up. Wrapping the stem results in an elegantly tapered body that appears to be segmented. Coat it with superglue. Tie in the hackle stem butt and dub the thorax. Tie in the hackle tips wings, convex sides facing, and wrap the hackle through the thorax. This elegant mayfly dun pattern by Dean Reiner can be used to simulate mayflies throughout the season beginning with March Browns, moving to Mahogany Duns and on to Hecuba duns.

LOOP WING MARCH BROWN

Hook:	#12-14 TMC 900BL
Thread:	Rusty dun 8/0 UNI-Thread
Tail:	Tan Microfibetts
Underbody:	Rusty dun 8/0 UNI-Thread
Overbody:	Rust Flexi Floss
Loop wing:	Teal flank fibers dyed rust
Hackle:	Cree dyed dark ginger
Head:	Rust brown 8/0 UNI-Thread

Howard Cole gives the body of this pattern a segmented effect by covering the hook shank with a rusty dun thread wrap. In wrapping the Flexi Floss, he leaves enough space between turns to reveal the yellow rusty dun thread in narrow bands, thus obtaining the segmented effect. Throughout the region March Brown is the common name for the *Rhithrogena* species of mayfly. They are the first large mayfly to emerge, usually during the latter half of March. They inhabit well-oxygenated riffles and runs.

MAHOGANY DUN CUT WING PARACHUTE

Hook:	#16 Daiichi 1110
Thread:	Dark brown 8/0 UNI-Thread
Tail:	Four or five dark dun or brown Microfibetts

Body:	Blue Ribbon Flies Tiger Beetle Black dubbing
Wing:	Dark dun turkey flat fibers
Hackle:	Black, dark brown, or brown-dyed grizzly saddle

To create Doug Andres's pattern, wrap thread base on entire shank, place a dubbing ball above hook bend, and wind thread halfway foward on shank. Tie in tailing fibers extending half a shank length to rear. Wind thread back to ball while holding down fibers securely to fan them out. Wrap thread forward to midshank. Pull 10 to 12 fibers off a turkey flat feather. Position them at mid-shank and tie down. Elevate fibers, then apply three or four thread wraps in front of them. Make three or four thread wraps around fibers, and cut to appropriate height. Wrap thread back to hook bend. Wax thread and apply minimum dubbing. Dub a tapered body to just behind the wing. Tie in hackle, concave side up, at wing base. Wrap three turns spiraling downward. Trim while pulling gently against wing. Build head and tie off.

MARCH BROWN

Hook:	#14-16 Dai-Riki 320
Thread:	Black 8/0 UNI-Thread
Tail:	Dark moose body
Body:	Light and dark moose body hairs
Wing:	Deer body hair
Hackle:	Dark brown saddle

To achieve a segmented body effect, Ed Thomas lines up the tip of one moose body hair with the butt of another, then spirals them around the hook shank on which he has wrapped a thread base wetted with a thin layer of cement. On some Montana streams, March Browns emerge at the same time as the Mother's Day Caddis event. Such streams include Rock Creek and the Gallatin River. Ed recommends having this pattern in the fly box when fishing during the Mother's Day event.

OLIVE DRAKE

Hook:	#10-12 Daiichi 1170
Thread:	Light cahill 8/0 UNI-Thread
Tail:	Moose hock hair
Wing:	Whiting Farms Coq de Leon hen hackle tips
Body:	Dyed olive peccary bristle
Hackle:	Whiting Farms gold speckled badger saddle

Whiting Farms Coq de Leon hen capes are one of the most versatile hackling products available today. These contain feathers suitable for forming hackle tip wings, for soft hackles, for featherwing streamers, and for facing on streamer patterns. Tough moose hock hairs are banded brown and an iridescent tan. Tough peccary bristles are easily worked. Speckled badger saddle hackle is spectacular, with occasional black flecks, a nearly black core, and gold tips. These components combine to result in what has proven to be my favorite traditional pattern for Brown Drake and Hecuba duns.

PHIL'S PINK COMPARADUN

Hook:	#14-18 Dai-Riki 300
Thread:	Pink 8/0
Tail:	Sparse rust Antron fibers

Body:	Spirit River "Pink H"
Thorax:	Nature's Spirit ginger cream dubbing
Wing:	Natural CDC fibers

Phil Blomquist was a renowned designer of fly patterns for the South Fork reach of the Snake River. He died in a boating accident on that river in July 2010. This pattern was the last in the series he designed for use during the South Fork's PMD emergence, an event that attracts fly fishers from around the world. Emerging from the South Fork, PMDs have a pinkish tinge in their body colors. This unusual color influences PMD dun and emerger patterns designed for fishing this river.

PMD (CUTTS)

Hook:	#14-18 Daiichi 1130
Thread:	Tan 8/0 UNI-Thread
Tail:	Cream Antron fibers
Rib:	Very fine gold Lagartun wire
Body:	Cream Spirit River stripped peacock herl biot
Wing:	Cream CDC feather
Thorax:	Whitlock red fox squirrel dubbing
Legs:	Grizzly saddle hackle

The counterwrapped wire rib provides reinforcement to minimize the delicate biot from being damaged, thereby increasing the lifetime durability of this pattern. Logan Cutts recommends fishing this effective pattern in riffles or in the nearby surface film during a PMD emergence. He fishes it solo or as the trailing fly in a two-fly rig.

PMD SPINNER

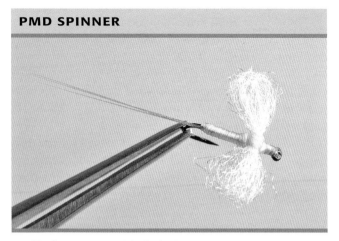

Hook:	#17 TMC 102Y
Thread:	50-denier GSP, color to match natural
Tails:	Microfibetts or Coq de Leon flank feather fibers
Body:	Z-Lon yarn, color to match natural
Wings:	Pearlescent Antron yarn

Pat Gaffney designed this pattern to be quickly tied and durable. After tying in the tails and the Z-Lon, advance the thread forward and tie in the Antron wings. Then coat the hook shank with a small amount of glue before wrapping the body. Wrap the Z-Lon using figure-eight wraps around the wings to add a lifelike taper to the thorax. A supply of this pattern to last for a day of fishing can be easily tied in half an hour. By varying the color of the Z-Lon, any species of mayfly can be quickly and effectively imitated. The bright yellow version pictured above is ideal for early in a PMD hatch, then switch to a rusty-bodied spinner as the hatch progresses.

PURPLE HAMMER STACKER

Hook:	#13-17 TMC 103BL
Thread:	Purple 8/0 UNI-Thread
Tail:	Four or five rooster pheasant tail fibers and 2 or 3 strands of purple Super Hair
Body:	Rooster pheasant tail fiber butts and purple Super Hair twisted to make a rope
Thorax:	Purple Fine and Dry Dubbing ball
Stacker loop:	7X monofilament tippet
Wing:	Stacker-style cree saddle hackle

Tom Harman uses the butts of the rooster pheasant tail fibers tied in for the tail to form the rear body portion. Tie in the stacker loop and wrap hackle on it before dubbing the thorax. Pull the result over the finished thorax and tie down in front of the hook eye. The resulting Bob Quigley stacker-style wing makes this pattern superbly visible. Thus the Purple Hammer Stacker is Tom's go-to dry attractor pattern for such gradient streams as the Big Hole, Madison, and Ruby Rivers. Try it for March Browns, Olive Duns, and BWOs early in the season. Try it for Mahogany Duns and BWOs during the autumn season. Vary the Purple Hammer Stacker size accordingly.

QUICK'N EZY PARA (DM)

Hook:	#10-22 Daiichi 1170
Thread:	Tan or color to match natural 6/0 or 8/0, depending on hook size
Tail:	Ginger hackle fibers or color to match natural
Wings:	Ginger or color to match natural
Body:	Ginger dubbing or color to match natural
Rib:	Thread coated with olive Touch Dubbing
Hackle:	Ginger or color to match natural, parachute style

The Quick'n EZY Para is by Al Beatty, and the DM, stands for LaFontaine's Double Magic dubbing process, which provides highlights as a halo around the regular body color. The DM application often takes any old standard fly and turns it into a new hot pattern. DM has completely changed Beatty's pattern selection; almost all of his personal flies now have some form of DM within their construction.

RUSTY PARASPINNER

Hook:	#12-16 TMC 9300
Thread:	Black 6/0 or 8/0
Tail:	Elk mane
Egg sac:	Closed-cell foam, color to match natural (yellow for Hendrickson spinner)
Rib:	Turkey biot
Body:	Rusty dun dubbing
Thorax:	Same as body
Wing:	Oversized grizzly saddle hackle
Post:	White or brightly colored Antron

Bob Jacklin developed the paraspin concept to combine properties of the parachute wing and the mayfly spinner. He ties the fly in the common manner, including setting the post wing. He wraps the hackle, concave side up, each turn under the last around the post, and ties off at the top of the body. The result is a "cup and saucer" effect for the post and hackle that better supports the fly on the surface. Lastly Bob cements the base of the post and spreads it radially into the hackle, thus binding these together for added durability. The result is illustrated above in a Hendrickson spinner, but this concept can be applied to the spinner stage of any mayfly.

SALT RIVER SPECIAL

Hook:	#10-12 Mustad 94840
Thread:	Black 6/0 UNI-Thread
Tail:	Rooster pheasant tail fibers
Body:	Dubbed muskrat body fur
Hackle:	Dry-fly grizzly and badger saddle

Swift Creek is a major tributary flowing west out of the Salt River Range then skirting the north part of Afton, Wyoming, to the Salt River below. Upstream of Afton, the creek hosts a major Gray Drake emergence near the end of June each year. Public land is plentiful here, thus access to the creek is easy during this emergence. Fly fishers arrive to enjoy trout responding to the numerous spinners. Josh Peavler's fly is the standard Gray Drake spinner pattern for Star Valley fly fishers because of its ability to ride high enough to be seen on broken water. When September rolls around, Josh scales this pattern down to sizes 12 and 14 to be used to simulate Mahogany Duns that emerge from Star Valley streams.

SHIMAZAKI HOLLOW BODY MAYFLY

Hook:	#10-14 TMC 200R
Thread:	Light cahill 8/0 UNI-Thread
Body:	Thin polyethylene grocery store produce bag, double-face transparent craft tape
Tails:	Three moose mane hairs
Thorax:	Micro Superfine Dubbing
Wing:	Wing Sheet
Hackle:	CDC or feather

Using Kenshiro Shimazaki's hollow body tool kit available from Kuni Masuda, sandwich two layers of produce bag pieces over the hollow body form. Cut and fuse the pieces with heated bodkin to form a tapered "sock" over the curved hollow body form. Remove from form and mount butt end in vise. Color to match natural with Prismacolor marker. Peel backing paper from two pieces of double-sided tape and sandwich these over body. Carefully trim excess tape. Attach moose mane hairs for tails to top of body. Wrap segmented ribs along body, also securing tail butts along top. Dab body with micro Superfine Dubbing. Remove extra dubbing with brush dusted with Dry-Shake powder. Ease body off form. Saddle the hollow body over hook in vise, securing it with thread about one-quarter of shank length behind eye. Tie in wings and hackle. The result is an exceptionally buoyant fly with a soft, insectlike texture. The pattern pictured above was tied by Kuni Masuda.

SILVER FOX

Hook:	#14-16 Dai-Riki 300
Thread:	Gray 8/0 UNI-Thread
Tail:	Whiting Farms Coq de Leon fibers dyed dun
Body:	Gray polypro fibers
Wing:	Badger hen cape feathers
Hackle:	Whiting Farms silver badger saddle

In the fly-fishing world, Hebgen Lake seems to be a testing ground for defining *Callibaetis* patterns for attracting gulpers. Such is the case for the Richard Munoz's Silver Fox through Jerry Toft's efforts, but there are many other places around western stillwater fisheries where this pattern is proving its mettle. Jerry Toft is among those "spreading the word" on how effective this pattern is becoming for enjoying the gulper season anywhere. In the Greater Yellowstone Area, the gulper season is anticipated nearly as much as the Green Drake emergence.

SLS SPARKLE DUN

Hook:	#16 TMC 206BL
Thread:	Light cahill 8/0 UNI-Thread
Wing:	Deer hair

Shuck:	Amber Z-Lon
Body:	Tying thread
Thorax:	SLS Z-Lon dubbing

Tie in deer hair for wing at shank midpoint and divide into left and right wing with figure-eight wraps. Tie in Z-Lon piece that will form shuck and midwing. Trim shuck to length and wrap piece under tying thread to form body, with remainder extending between wings. Tie in and trim to same length as wings. Dub thorax, going front to rear and back around base of wings. This fly by Craig Mathews is meant to be an all-purpose pattern for Slough Creek, Lamar River, and Soda Butte Creek during midsummer when many different species of mayflies are emerging.

SNAKE DRAKE

Hook:	#8-12 TMC 100
Thread:	Tan 3/0
Tail:	Dark moose body hair
Rib:	Doubled pale yellow thread
Body:	Natural hare's mask dubbing
Wing:	White calf tail
Hackle:	Two medium dun saddle

Guy Turck recommends his Wulff-style pattern for use in imitating any of the large species of mayfly duns that frequent regional waters at various times during the season, including Green, Brown, and Gray drakes as well as the late summer *Timpanoga hecuba*, commonly named Blue-Wing Red Quill. Dub a robust body, and make two turns with both hackles behind the wing, then three or four turns in front. Fully hackled flies float best, and the calf tail wings add visibility to patterns meant for use on waters of gradient such as that encountered around Jackson Hole.

TRICO CDC WINGED PARACHUTE

Hook:	#20-24 Daiichi 1110 big-eye "ring-eye"
Thread:	Black 8/0 UNI-Thread
Tail:	White Microfibetts or fine monofilament
Body:	Trico René Harrop Professional Dubbing
Wing:	Reversed white CDC feather, top and butt ends clipped
Hackle:	White saddle

The Trico emergence from Greater Yellowstone Area still and moving waters is consistent and dense. It provides reliable morning fishing from August to October. Males, black to dark brown in color, emerge en masse as spinners at night to await equally numerous olive-colored females emerging in the early morning. The female emergence can be fished, but it is the spinner fall after mating that provides the best fishing. See discussion for tying Doug Andres's Mahogany Dun Cut Wing Parachute (page 116) for tips on tying this pattern.

TRICO CUT WING PARACHUTE (FEMALE)

Hook:	#20-22 Daiichi 1110
Thread:	Olive 8/0 UNI-Thread
Tail:	Three or four white Microfibetts
Dubbing:	Light olive René Harrop Professional Dubbing
Wing:	White turkey flat fibers
Hackle:	Grizzly saddle

Using materials given above, apply technique Doug Andres describes for tying his Mahogany Dun Cut Wing Parachute (page 116). After mating, female Tricos immediately drop to the water surface to lay eggs. This usually happens in the midmorning hours, but can be later in the day as October advances. The experience of many fly fishers is that trout feeding on Trico spinners seem to key more on egg-laying females than on males.

TRICO CUT WING PARACHUTE (MALE)

Hook:	#20-22 Daiichi 1110
Thread:	Dark brown 8/0 UNI-Thread
Tail:	Three or four white Microfibetts
Dubbing:	Trico René Harrop Professional Dubbing

Wing:	White turkey flat fibers
Hackle:	Grizzly saddle

Using materials given above, apply technique Doug Andres describes for tying his Mahogany Dun Cut Wing Parachute (page 116). This parachute pattern seems superior because it lays low in the water. It is best fished early in the day to midmorning when male spinners are most available. Fishing it can be successful but frequently its effectiveness is confounded by the number of female spinners laying eggs on the surface.

TRICO SPINNER

Hook:	#18-20 Daiichi 1310
Thread:	White for female, black for male 8/0 UNI-Thread
Tails:	Stiff hackle fibers
Abdomen:	Superfine Dubbing, grayish white for female, black for male
Wings:	Clear organza
Thorax:	Black Superfine Dubbing

To create this pattern by Nelson Ishiyama, tie in tiny dubbing ball above barb point. Tie in four to six tailing fibers, one and a half shank-length, splitting them on sides of dubbing ball. With figure-eight wraps, tie in wing fibers, right angles to shank, at point two-thirds from bend to eye. Post wings, then wrap thread around shank, gathering fibers securely at right angles to shank. Wings should be twice shank length. Dub a robust tapered abdomen (white for female, black for male) to just behind wings. Use thin black dubbing to figure-eight around wings, building a robust thorax ending at eye. Whip-finish. Coat wing fibers with Flexament for about one-sixteenth inch out from thorax. Allow to dry until no longer sticky. Use flat-nosed pliers to squeeze wing fibers, working outward from thorax, into a flat horizontal fan. Trim wings to about one and a quarter body length, rounding rear corners. Sometimes picky fish take the female in preference to the all-black male.

TUPS INDISPENSIBLE STACKER

Hook:	#13-19 TMC 103BL
Thread:	Orange 8/0 UNI-Thread
Tail:	Split dun Microfibetts
Body:	Yellow floss
Thorax:	Spirit River Golden Stonefly Mottled Nymph dubbing
Stacker loop:	7X monofilament tippet
Wing:	Stacker-style blue dun saddle hackle

Tom Harman's favorite version of this pattern is for a PMD as described and pictured above. He changes color and size to conform to other emerging mayfly species. His emerger version is tied in the same manner except for a shuck of tan Antron instead of the hackle fiber tail and on a TMC 206BL hook. Split the Microfibetts tails with a dubbing ball. Note the length of the tails. Note also that Tom uses orange thread in tying this pattern. He does this because he has observed that PMD duns in the southwestern Montana rivers he fishes have orange eyes. Thus, he offers that this color may offer a "hot spot" for fish to key on.

USD PARADUN VARIANT (CALLIBAETIS)

Hook:	#12-14 Mustad 94842
Thread:	Camel 8/0 UNI-Thread
Tail:	A few dyed dark dun grizzly hackle fibers
Rib:	Stripped quill from dyed dark dun grizzly saddle
Hackle loop:	4X monofilament
Hackle:	Grizzly saddle dyed dark dun
Wings:	Trimmed Hungarian partridge pair, concave sides out
Abdomen:	Nature's Spirit Callibaetis dubbing
Thorax:	Nature's Spirit dark honey dubbing

Mike Snody forms a perpendicular hackle loop below the wing tie-in point by securing monofilament loop legs along the bottom of the shank. One monofilament tip extends past the bend. The other tip will be covered by the body. After forming the tail, tie in the hackle stem tip forward along bottom of the shank. A ribbed body and abdomen are formed, and wings mounted. Turn the fly upside down in the vise, and attached a parachute tool to the hackle loop. Wind four turns of hackle around the base of the loop. Pass the hackle tip through the loop and pull its exposed tag to rear to secure the hackle turns at the bottom of the shank. Trim excess hackle and loop tag end.

Z-DUN

Hook:	#11-17 Tiemco 102Y
Thread:	Tan 12/0 Benecchi
Tail:	Cree hackle barbs
Rib:	Tying thread
Wing/shuck:	Light tan Z-lon
Abdomen:	Tan rabbit, natural gray rabbit, and olive synthetic dubbing in equal parts
Hackle:	Cree saddle
Thorax:	Tan rabbit, natural gray rabbit, and olive synthetic dubbing in equal parts

Hans Weilenmann uses a single segment of light tan Z-Lon to fashion the shuck, shellback, and wing for this pattern. He also suggests that the material for dubbing the body and thorax can be varied to match the natural color of the mayfly dun being simulated. He trims the hackle flush underneath body to obtain a lower ride on the water surface.

CHAPTER 6

SCUD, SHRIMP, AND WATER BUG PATTERNS

This looks like a catchall chapter, and in some sense it is. But there is reason for it—the life forms here have attracted nowhere near the attention garnered by those in other chapters of this work. Think of the attention given to caddisflies, mayflies, midges, and stoneflies: all are the subject of numerous books and media articles. Many of the insects addressed in this chapter have gained attention only within the last decade or two. One thing all in this chapter have in common is that they are overwhelmingly denizens of still or slow-moving waters with weedy shallows and vegetated shorelines. But they are all food forms, and they therefore deserve attention from fly tiers.

Freshwater shrimp, commonly called scuds, are actually crustaceans. They are the most numerous of the "insect forms" discussed in this chapter. Not predators, they live on decaying plant and animal matter. They are available as a food form year-round, and their presence is evidence of waters rich in the bicarbonates needed to build exoskeletons. Explore the weeds of scud-rich stillwaters and it will be common to find the outside surface of your waders coated with them. They are so numerous in weedy shallows that they can be the equivalent of an above-water midge or caddis swarm. Poor swimmers, they cling to vegetation, and trout can be seen burrowing and tailing in weeds to release them for easy feeding. In some stillwaters and spring creeks, they make up half of the diet of resident salmonids. Thus they are now targeted by fly tiers.

Scuds' body color depends on their surroundings, so it is prudent to determine the color of the scuds in the waters you will be fishing before creating patterns. As with other crustaceans, scuds molt regularly as they outgrow their exoskeleton. Newly molted scuds tend toward delicate bluish colors, thus some patterns for them should be in this color, regardless of fishing location.

Mysis shrimp are the exception to the above discussion on scuds. Introduced decades ago around the region as forage for salmonid in impoundments, they have escaped to populate immediate tailwaters in huge numbers. Salmonids living in such waters as those below Jackson Lake Dam and Palisades Dam on the Snake River grow to huge sizes feeding on these crustaceans.

Water boatmen and backswimmers occur most commonly in ponds and along the edges of lakes, both being well vegetated. Some are predaceous and feed on mosquito larvae and other small aquatic insects, helping to control aquatic pests. Both surface to take air that forms a bubble underneath their wings and along their abdomens. This bubble allows submergence for many minutes and should be targeted by fly tiers. Although not as numerous as scuds, both are important prey for salmonids.

Like other insects discussed here, aquatic beetles inhabit weedy waters, including weedy moving waters such as the Madison River along Yellowstone National Park's West Entrance Road. Like some water boatmen, backswimmers, and aquatic wasps, aquatic beetles are predators, feeding on submerged insects. They are air breathing and surface to form a bubble, which extends their submergence time and prevents them from going too deep.

Aquatic wasps have terrestrial relatives in ants, bees, and wasps. They are parasitic, feeding on a variety of aquatic insects and living in the same water types as the insects discussed above. Emergence is in the spring, making them available through summer and early autumn. Of all the insects discussed here, they are the least known, but are numerous enough to be a food form for salmonids.

Since little is know about aquatic wasps compared to other aquatic insects, they are relatively new to fly fishers. René Harrop, in his superb *Learning from the Water*, is the first in angling media to address their importance in any detail. But René admits that their significance and behavior remains a riddle. What René offers throughout his book is detail that adds depth to our knowledge in matters concerning fly-fishing success.

BEETLE LARVA (BLOUNT)

Hook:	#6-12 Daiichi 1710
Thread:	Black 6/0 UNI-Thread
Tail:	Pair of extra small olive/brown Centipede Legs
Trailing bubbles:	One strand pearl micro Krystal Flash
Body:	Olive Hareline Dubbin Woolly Chenille
Collar:	Dyed olive ring-necked cock pheasant philoplume

Tim Blount ties in the strand of pearl micro Krystal Flash along the hook shank and ties in the tails. He wraps the body, clips a forward taper on it, then tightly, but gently wraps the philoplume collar, pressing fibers to the rear. Tim's pattern simulates the larva of the numerous predaceous beetles that inhabit weed beds. These larva take a year to develop into adults, thus they are present throughout the season. Tim recommends fishing this pattern around weed beds and through weed channels.

BILL'S CRAYFISH

Hook:	#1/0 Gamakatsu 90 HW
Weight:	0.030-inch-diameter lead-free wire
Cone:	Large black nickel
Thread:	Mono thread and white 140-denier UTC Ultra Thread
Rib:	Medium silver wire
Claws:	Pine squirrel strips
Antennae:	Black/olive Sili Legs
Body and abdomen:	White (with pinch of olive) UV dubbing mixture
Legs:	Black barred silver Sili Legs
Belly:	Barred olive rabbit strip

To create this fly by Bill Fenstermaker, push wrapped wire into cone. Dub body forward to above hook point. Tie in pine squirrel strip claws on sides of shank here with UTC thread. Pull each out to spread and cut to make inch-long claws. Attach wire rib, tie in inch-and-a-half long antennae, and change to mono thread. Dub abdomen to cone. Back-wrap mono thread to shank midpoint and tie in three pair of three-inch long legs. Spread these and reverse hook in vise. Pull rabbit strip skin end at center point over hook point and pull to body. Turn hook over and poke hole in front of strip. Pull it through hook eye. Rib with wire to secure strip to body. Whip-finish behind cone and superglue rabbit strip butt to form tail extending past hook eye and under cone.

BOSTIC FLASHBACK SCUD

Hook:	#12 Daiichi 1150
Thread:	Light olive 70-denier UTC Ultra Thread
Underbody:	0.020-inch-diameter lead or lead-free wire, 10–12 wraps on shank
Tail:	Arizona scud blend in equal proportions: olive, tan, orange, or yellow-olive
Rib:	Fine monofilament
Back:	Yellow flashback
Shell:	Light olive Scud Back
Body:	Dubbed with same blend as used in tail

When tying scud patterns, it is important to maintain the same color throughout the pattern being tied. Shawn Bostic wraps wire, forms the tail, then secures the back and shell along the shank. He dubs the body, forms back and shell, then ribs all these with at least six turns of monofilament. After finishing the head, he picks out legs to extend downward no further than the hook point.

BOSTIC SNAIL VERSION 2 (BSV2)

Hook:	#10-14 Daiichi 1150
Thread:	70-denier gray UTC Ultra Thread
Shell:	Moose body hair coated with Devcon 5 Minute Epoxy

Eyes:	Natural small rubber leg segments with tips painted black
Body:	Peacock herl

An important part of all salmonid diets, snails are present in almost all stillwater weed beds. They can also be found adhering to rocks and logs as well as in weed beds in nutrient-rich streams. Relatively overlooked by fly fishers, snail patterns like the BSV2 by Shawn Bostic are beginning to appear. When fish are seen "tailing" or working weed beds, a good strategy is to dead-drift a snail pattern under an indicator near working fish and allow it to slowly sink through the water column with a tight line.

CHUCK'S BACKSWIMMER

Hook:	#15 TMC 102Y
Thread:	Tan 3/0 Danville Monocord
Weight:	0.020-inch-diameter lead or lead-free wire
Body:	Light hare's ear dubbing
Shellback:	Black moose body hair
Shell:	Clear Scud Back
Paddles:	Natural dun hackle
Legs:	Black moose body hair
Head:	Light tan Superfine Dubbing

To create this pattern by Chuck Echer, lay a thread foundation on the middle third of the hook shank. Wrap weighting wire over these wraps. Taper wire ends with thread and superglue. Tie in the Scud Back at hook bend. Cut away tips from stacked moose hair and tie in the remaining ends over the Scud Back. Reverse hook in vise and using figure-eight wraps, tie in and superglue prepared paddles at midshank. Return hook in vise and dub body to front of lead wraps. Form a shellback over body, pull the Scud Back over it and tie in at same location. Select two moose hairs on each side from shellback butts. Tie these down to form four front legs. Dub a head. Trim all excess and bend legs to form joints and to be positioned under body. Use a marker to make eyes on the dubbed head.

CRAY FRESH

Hook:	#8-10 Dai-Riki 075
Weight:	0.020-inch-diameter lead-free wire
Thread:	Orange 70-denier UTC Ultra Thread
Antennae:	Blond elk body hair
Claws:	Two sets of Spanflex barred brown with red tips
Rib:	Fine orange UNI-Wire
Legs:	Hungarian partridge
Body:	Tan Antron dubbing picked out
Back:	Ring-necked pheasant tail segment
Tail:	Butt end of pheasant tail fibers used to form back

After weighting the hook shank with wire wraps, tie in the antennae and rib at the top of the bend. Tie in the butt end of the pheasant tail segment at the bottom of the bend, and dub a small portion of the body. Tie in the legs and claws at each side, and finish dubbing the body to the hook eye. Bring the pheasant tail segment forward under the body, and tie off with butts forming the tail at the hook eye. Spiral the wire rib forward, securing the pheasant tail segment to the dubbed body. Trim the wire and tie off. Fish any crawfish pattern like this one by Doug McKnight around bottom structures such as submerged logs and rock crevices.

DEPTH CHARGE SNAIL

Hook:	#12-16 TMC 2488H
Weight:	0.015-inch-diameter lead-free wire
Thread:	Cream 70-denier UTC Ultra Thread
Body:	Painted brass cone
Hackle:	Brown saddle

Doug McKnight's Depth Charge Snail is aptly named. It is sure to get to depth! He paints the cone in a theme to imitate a snail, usually a model paint mixed with copper and black glitter. He spirals wire on the front portion of the shank and builds up thread on the rear wraps. He pushes the reversed cone onto the rear of the wire-thread wraps and superglues these together. He adds a few turns of hackle in front of the reversed cone. Want this pattern to go deeper faster? Use a tungsten cone instead of a brass cone.

DISCO SCUD

Hook:	#14-18 Mustad C 495
Thread:	Black 6/0 UNI-Thread
Tail:	One gray goose biot tip
Shellback:	Pearlescent Thin Skin
Rib:	Black tying thread
Body:	Sparkle dubbing brush

Scuds do best in shallow waters, and they are rarely found in rivers. They are most active at night, hiding in aquatic plants and under bottom features during daytime. Scuds are scavengers, feeding on dead plant and animal matter and walk on or swim close to the bottom in search of these foods. They are also a favorite food for fish, including trout.

Thus their presence is desirable for fish as well as for cleaning water. Fish scud imitations such as this one by Kieran Frye close to the bottom or in and around aquatic plants.

KG'S MOLTING SCUD

Hook:	#14-16 Dai-Riki 125 or equivalent
Thread:	Clear 0.004-inch-diameter monofilament
Tail:	White dubbing
Rib:	Pearl Krystal Flash fiber, regular size
Shellback:	Plastic bag (Ziploc) strip, $^1/_8$ to $^1/_{16}$ inches wide depending on hook size
Body:	White Arizona dubbing picked out and trimmed to simulate legs

When scuds molt, they temporarily have a bluish-white color. Eventually they turn to their normal color as their carapace hardens. During this temporary stage, however, their color is a signal to predators of their less chitinous character, which means they are more easily digested. Thus it is wise for any fly fisher presenting scud patterns to have a few of the molting color like this one by Kelly Glissmeyer in the fly box.

KG'S MYSIS SHRIMP

Hook:	#14-16 Dai-Riki 125 or equivalent
Thread:	Clear 0.004-inch-diameter monofilament
Tail:	Pearl Ice Dub
Back:	Large opal Mirage Tinsel
Body:	Pearl Ice Dub
Eyes:	Small black Wapsi mono eyes

After tying in the tail of this fly by Kelly Glissmeyer, tie in eyes at the top of the bend. Sparsely touch pearl Ice Dub onto the thread coated with dubbing wax, and dub immediate front and back of eyes using figure-eight wraps around the eyes. Tie in tinsel in front of eyes using thread with dubbing, then using thread with dubbing, secure in back of eyes. Build up body around eyes, and use less dubbing to form taper toward hook eye. Bring tinsel over top of body and tie off behind hook eye. Pick out dubbing to form a few legs underneath eyes. Dress the entire fly with one coat of Sally Hansen Hard As Nails.

KG'S SPRING CREEK SCUD

Hook:	#12-14 Dai-Riki 125 or equivalent
Thread:	Woodchuck 8/0 UNI-Thread
Tail:	Amber dubbing
Rib:	Pearl Krystal Flash fiber, regular size
Shellback:	Plastic bag (Ziploc) strip, $1/8$ to $1/16$ inches wide depending on hook size
Body:	Amber colored Arizona dubbing picked out and trimmed

The Pearl Krystal Flash fiber rib gives the subtle sparkle to this pattern that a wire rib cannot. The plastic bag strip gives a hard carapace look. Dubbing used to form the body should be picked out to a length even with hook point. Kelly Glissmeyer fishes this pattern in all spring creeks he encounters. He also ties an olive version. In each version he maintains color throughout all materials used.

MINCH'S OSTRICH SCUD

Hook:	#12-16 Dai-Riki 060
Thread:	Light olive 6/0 Flymaster
Rib:	Fine gold wire
Tail:	Tip of tannish gray philoplume feather from base of Hungarian partridge flank feather

Body:	Tan and olive ostrich herl
Case:	Tan mottled turkey wing segment over body and under ribbing

Matt Minch's pattern is effective because its ostrich herl body "breathes" while retrieved through the water. It is especially effective in slow currents or when sinking in stillwater. This subtle action gives this pattern a definite edge when picky trout are seeking freshwater shrimp or scuds. This pattern has gained fame for being effective in Trout Lake, which produces the largest cutthroat-rainbow hybrid trout in Yellowstone National Park, but this pattern also produces in any lake, spring creek, or tailwater having a heavy scud population.

MYSIS SHRIMP (TEA)

Hook:	#14 Mustad 3906
Thread:	White 6/0 UNI-Thread
Tail:	Pearl Krystal Flash fibers
Underbody:	Thread, color to match natural
Body:	Pearl Krysal Flash
Hackle:	White saddle

Mysis shrimp patterns are popular among anglers fishing below Jackson Lake Dam and Palisades Dam on the Snake River. Plentiful and nutritious, *Mysis* are targeted throughout the season by trout that can grow to large sizes through foraging on them. Merrill Tea ties his patterns in the predominant colors *Mysis* take: olive, orange, pink, and white. These patterns must be fished deep; thus fly-rod enthusiasts use lead-core lines with split shot, lead wire, or lead-free wire on leaders to get to the bottom, allowing the pattern to twist and roll in the current to attract foraging trout.

NOBLE SCUD

Hook:	#10-16 TMC 2487
Weight:	0.010- or 0.015-inch-diameter lead or lead-free wire
Thread:	Light gray 8/0 UNI-Thread
Front feelers:	Natural duck biots
Tail:	Light gray Sparkle Yarn
Rib:	Medium copper Ultra Wire
Shellback:	Pink Thin Skin
Body:	Mike's Scud Dub
Head:	Tying thread wraps

Mike Snody has fished this scud pattern in spring creeks throughout the Greater Yellowstone Area. He colors the top of the thread wraps with a pink Sharpie permanent marker. On completing the fly, he picks out the lower body to simulate legs. He recommends any dubbing with trilobal components to give a sparkle to the body. With this dubbing, he can vary the color tones from pink, as pictured above, to olive or orange.

OBAMA BEETLE

Hook:	#12-18 TMC 2457
Thread:	Black 8/0
Tail:	Single ¼-inch fiber of peacock Midge Flash

Legs:	Two turns of black hackle around shank with top fibers cut away
Body:	Olive speckled Thin Skin over moose hairs
Head:	Tying thread

Gerry "Randy" Randolph named this fly to celebrate our first African-American president. It appears to be an adult aquatic beetle, and certainly can be presented as such. Randy fishes it wet on a floating line in shallow waters and near banks and weed beds in moving water. In stillwaters he fishes it under an indicator around weedy shallows using a floating line.

RAINBOW SCUD

Hook:	#14 Daiichi 1530
Bead:	Blue tungsten, ⁵/₃₂-inch
Thread:	Blue 6/0 UNI-Thread
Body:	Dark Rainbow Scud dubbing

This is John Taylor's favorite scud pattern for fishing Chesterfield Reservoir east of Pocatello, Idaho, across the Portneuf Range. The abundant shallows of this reservoir are as productive as any in the Greater Yellowstone Area, and when drawdown is minimal for a few years, holdover trout, primarily rainbow, grow to double-figure poundage. Thus Chesterfield Reservoir is as popular a stillwater destination as any in the area. Many fly patterns have been conceived here because of the challenge of catching its large and vigorous rainbows.

SNAIL (EVANS)

Hook:	#4-12 TMC 2457
Bead:	Black glass
Thread:	Black 70-denier UTC Ultra Thread
Tail:	Dark brown marabou fibers
Rib:	Small diameter black wire
Body:	Peacock herl
Shellback:	Black Scud Back strip, ⅛-inch wide

Snails are an indicator of waters holding a rich amount of nutrients needed to build exoskeletons in aquatic life-forms. Irrigation reservoirs in the southeast corner of Idaho are particularly rich in nutrients, and thus hold huge populations of snails. So do Ennis, Hebgen, and Smith Lakes in Montana. Snails are mostly found clinging to submerged vegetation as well as bottom debris. Being another "easy protein" food form, salmonids key on them. Everet Evans presents this pattern under an indicator and near submerged vegetation. Constant observation is required fishing in this manner, but the rewards can be some very large fish.

WATER BOATMAN (ANDREASEN)

Hook:	#8-16 Dai-Riki 075
Thread:	Olive 6/0 UNI-Thread
Trailing bubbles:	Pearl Krystal Flash strand
Underbody:	Pearl Diamond Braid
Shellback:	Mottled Thin Skin
Body:	Light olive dubbing
Legs:	Dyed brown goose biots
Head:	Light olive dubbing

For this pattern Mike Andreasen uses a personal stock of dubbing that combines Antron fibers with rabbit fur. But any light olive dubbing with a sparkle will do. After tying in the trailing bubble strand, attach the butt ends of the Thin Skin and the Diamond Braid at the hook bend, top and bottom respectively. Dub the body to the three-quarter point on the shank and form the Diamond Braid air bubble along the bottom surface and shellback. Tie these off and tie in the biots to form the legs. Dub the head, and you will have a very effective pattern for fishing the shallows of stillwaters and slow-moving streams. Use smaller sizes for water boatmen and larger sizes for backswimmers. Mike has success with this pattern presented on a floating or intermediate line in the shallows of all Greater Yellowstone waters he fishes.

WATER BOATMAN (NEWBURY)

Hook:	#10-12 Mustad 3906B
Thread:	Black 3/0 Danville Monocord
Eyes:	Small black monofilament
Underbody:	Green wool yarn
Body:	Peacock herl
Overbody:	Pearl floral wrap strip; peacock secondary wing quill segment
Legs:	Black rubber hackle
Thorax:	Peacock herl

Melt a piece of black monofilament, such as Maxima tippet material, to form a dumbbell that will become eyes for this pattern by John Newbury. Floral wrap is offered at florist shops, plant nurseries, and department stores with garden and flower departments. John recommends coating the back of this pattern (peacock secondary wing quill segment) with Loon Hard Head to add durability. Water boatmen frequent shorelines of stillwaters and slow-moving streams, especially where vegetation is present. Trout cruising these shallow waters target them. It is prudent to have a Water Boatman pattern available when fishing such waters.

CHAPTER 7

STONEFLY LIFE CYCLE

No aquatic insect's presence indicates water quality more accurately than stoneflies. And perhaps nowhere is there as rich a variety and as dense a population as in the moving waters of the Greater Yellowstone Area. Stoneflies, especially the larger species—Giant and Golden Stoneflies—require high concentrations of dissolved oxygen to live. But this region abounds in cold streams with gradient that allow for abundant riffles and runs. These streams come in all sizes, and even though some may warm to levels where dissolved oxygen is reduced, the flow due to gradient can keep the effective oxygen concentration at hospitable concentrations for stonefly life. A good example is in the Firehole River below Firehole Falls where waters can warm naturally to concentrations low enough to be dangerous for stoneflies, but the gradient keeps the effective oxygen concentration high enough so that a fair population of Giant and Golden Stoneflies survive and have an early season emergence. However, there are streams in the area where, diversion of water for agricultural purposes during summers drastically reduces stonefly populations to the point that some species, mainly the Giant and Golden Stoneflies, have entirely disappeared.

Stonefly emergences can happen almost every month of the year in the region. As early as midwinter, the Skwalas emerge, making for good afternoon fishing on nice days. March and April before runoff seem to be the best months for encountering emerging Skwalas. Reaches of the Madison, Snake, and Yellowstone Rivers remaining open during these times have become destinations for winter-bound fly fishers. In some areas the term "Skwala" has come to mean any small, dark-colored stonefly and is applied to those that emerge throughout the season.

The Yellow Sally is another smaller stonefly that emerges throughout the season and can be rewarding to focus on during emergences. They are present in essentially all regional streams of gradient and are a major prey for foraging salmonids. Some of these emerge on land, and other species emerge in water. The egg-laying female has been called "Mormon Girl" in many places. The combination of yellowish body and reddish egg sac apparently reminded western fly fishers in the past of the colorful dresses worn by young Mormon women during social occasions.

The emergence of few aquatic insects brings such concentrated attention from fly fishers as that of the larger Golden and Giant Stoneflies. In lower elevations of the region, their emergence peaks as early as late May. As springtime advances to early summer, the emergence climbs the elevation ladder in all hosting streams. The Giant and Golden Stonefly emergences overlap nearly everywhere, and likely because they get the attention of even the largest fish, streams hosting this event become major destinations for fly fishers. By early August, Giant and Golden Stoneflies have essentially finished emerging except for the until recently widely overlooked Mutant Golden Stoneflies, those in which the adult does not fly but skitters on the surface to lay eggs. The importance of these creatures, which pupate in water and emerge at night, is relatively new in fly-fishing circles, most likely because of mayfly abundance and the onset of terrestrial insect populations when they emerge.

Shops and guide services in the region literally place observers on streams to monitor when nymphs move and adults fly. On to websites and other media go progress reports of the "Salmonfly hatch." Being able to pass on solid information on the best locations to meet the emergence has huge economic consequences for shops and guides.

The middle Madison River, the middle Yellowstone River, the North Fork of the Shoshone River, the Snake

River in Wyoming, Idaho's South Fork reach of the Snake River, and the Box Canyon, Cardiac Canyon, and Warm River to Ashton reaches of the Henry's Fork all have storied large stonefly emergences. They also have advocates claiming that each has the best possible emergence. Other streams, not so much in the limelight, have the same event. Boating is not allowed on the Fall River Basin streams, the Lewis River, the Lamar River, the Yellowstone River, and the Heart River of Yellowstone Park. But each in time has a large stonefly emergence worthy

of attention of the larger streams outside the Park that allow boating. And if all this is not enough, many small streams of gradient in the region host a large stonefly emergence. Of course, because of the attention paid to the Giant and Golden Stonefly emergence, a huge array of patterns, nymph and adult, have been created in the region. Some of these are several decades old; others are added each year, accompanied with stories championing their prowess.

EMERGER AND NYMPH PATTERNS

BBS STONE

Hook:	#6-12 Daiichi 1530
Bead (optional):	Tungsten gold
Thread:	Camel UNI-Thread, 8/0 for smaller versions, 6/0 for larger versions
Tail:	Goose biot tips
Rib:	Midge UNI-Wire
Body:	Kaufmann's Streamborn dubbing, color to match natural
Wing pads:	Goose biots, dyed color to match natural
Thorax:	Kaufmann's Streamborn dubbing, color to match natural
Legs:	Amber Larva Lace or Flexi Floss pieces tied in at either side of thorax

"BBS" stands for "Biot Back Stone." This is Devin Olsen's omnibus pattern for simulating stonefly nymphs. Devin, a member of Fly Fishing Team USA, recommends fishing this pattern European style or in an indicator rig as the top nymph in a two-fly rig. When fishing shallower riffles, he omits the bead, which is useful for getting this fly down in depth. He varies the material colors

and hook size to simulate the nymph of various stonefly species.

BEAD BROOKS STONE

Hook:	#4-8 Mustad 9672
Bead:	Black copper or tungsten
Thread:	Black 3/0 UNI-Thread
Tail:	Brown marabou fibers
Abdomen:	Peacock Ice Dub
Thorax:	Spirit River dark hare's ear dubbing
Hackle:	Grizzly dyed brown saddle

From the Madison River to the Gallatin River and on to the Yellowstone River and the Henry's Fork, Matt Minch's easily tied pattern has proven its worth in streams hosting Giant Stoneflies. Originally Matt tied this pattern with a tail of dark brown grizzly marabou, but the supply of that material is not as reliable in keeping up with demand as the brown marabou he now uses. Matt named this pattern after his friend and mentor, Charlie Brooks.

BEAD HEAD GOLDEN STONE

Hook:	#8-14 Daiichi 1550
Bead:	Gold
Thread:	Tan 8/0 UNI-Thread
Tail:	Duck biots dyed amber
Body:	Fine gold Sparkle Chenille

Wrapping the Sparkle Chenille tightly is important in making this pattern durable. After wrapping, compress the body by securing the rear of the body between a thumb and forefinger and firmly pushing the Sparkle Chenille to the rear with thumb and forefinger of other hand. If necessary, add more warps behind the bead after compressing. Phil Blomquist used this pattern mainly to simulate Golden Stonefly nymphs, but smaller versions can be use to simulate Yellow Sally nymphs.

BROOKS MONTANA STONE

Hook:	#4-10 Mustad 9672
Weight (optional):	0.015-inch-diameter lead or fuse wire spiraled over shank
Thread:	Black 3/0 UNI-Thread
Tail:	Crow or raven primary fibers
Rib:	Gold wire
Body:	Black fuzzy yarn

Hackle:	Two turns of one natural grizzly saddle and one dyed brown grizzly saddle tied in together, each with fibers stripped from one side
Gills:	Light gray or white ostrich herl wrapped at hackle base

This may be Charlie Brooks's most enduring pattern. Its popularity has not waned in over a half century. All shops in West Yellowstone, Montana, and some in Last Chance, Idaho, offer it. His Yellow Stone Nymph is constructed in a similar manner. Cinnamon turkey primary fiber tails, body of mottled brown yarn, and an antique gold yarn make the difference.

DARK PRINCE

Hook:	#10 TMC 2488
Bead:	White tungsten, $^{1}/_{8}$-inch
Weight:	Five turns of 0.030-inch-diameter lead-free wire
Thread:	Black 6/0 UNI-Thread
Tail:	Pheasant tail fibers
Rib:	Five grain red wire
Abdomen:	Black rabbit dubbing
Wing case:	White goose biots
Hackle:	Soft black hen saddle
Thorax:	Black rabbit dubbing

Practically all streams of gradient with primarily rocky bottoms and good concentrations of oxygen host a variety of stoneflies. This holds true throughout the Greater Yellowstone Area. Scott Urbanski offers this pattern for dark-colored stonefly nymphs for use in any of these waters. The weight gets it to the bottom of streams he fishes. It has proven effective throughout the season.

DELEKTABLE MEGAPRINCE STANDARD FLASHBACK

Hook:	#4-10 Daiichi 1720
Bead:	Copper
Weight:	Tin 0.030-inch-diameter wire
Thread:	Black 6/0 Danville Flymaster
Tail:	Brown marabou under pumpkin/gray Sili Legs
Rib:	Copper wire
Body:	Peacock herl
Legs:	Pumpkin green/orange Sili Legs
Antennae:	White goose biots
Hackle:	Speckled hen back
Flashback:	Pearl Krystal Flash, twenty strands
Head:	Peacock Ice Dub

Dan Delekta first bends a 30-degree angle in the hook at the thorax point to simulate the stonefly nymph shape. After adding the bead, he places Sili Legs in front of it. He places a small dubbing ball behind the hook eye; then ties in Sili Legs, pulls the bead forward, and wraps the thread over the bead to rear. He ties in wire on either side of the shank, or wraps the shank with wire. He sets the legs into this section, then a second set at the hook bend. He winds the thread to rear to tie in the tail, rib, and several peacock herls. He builds the body to hook bend and ties in the flashback. He finishes and ribs the body to bead, and ties in the biots and hackle. He secures the flashback over hackle, biots, and body. He dubs the head with superglue at the dubbing end. He makes one turn around the shank. When the superglued end contacts the dubbing on the shank, the fly is completed. Five-minute epoxy finishes the flashback.

GOLDEN BARNES

Hook:	#6-8 Daiichi 1720
Thread:	Black 70-denier UTC Ultra Thread
Tail:	Brown round rubber legs
Body:	Overhand weave of dark brown Aunt Lydia's Rug Yarn on top, light tan Aunt Lydia's Rug Yarn on bottom
Thorax:	Dubbed Canadian mohair and grizzly hackle
Legs:	Brown round rubber legs
Antennae:	Brown round rubber legs

To form the thorax of his pattern, Gary Barnes lays some mohair in a dubbing loop, then places a hackle, tip facing down, through the loop. He places more mohair in the loop and spins it. On wrapping the spun loop around the shank, hackle fibers extend in all directions, giving an extreme buggy look to the finished pattern. This is Gary's favorite Golden Stonefly nymph pattern and he usually fishes it in front of a small bead-head nymph dropper.

GOLD LARVA LACE STONE

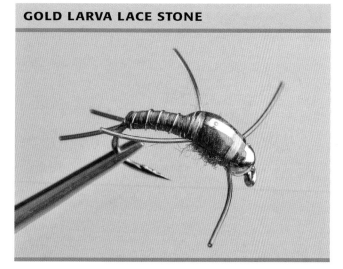

Hook:	#10 Daiichi 1120
Bead:	Gold, 1/8-inch
Weight:	Ten turns of 0.020-inch-diameter lead-free wire
Thread:	Orange 8/0 UNI-Thread
Tails:	Two pieces of pheasant tail color Micro Tubing
Rib:	Small gold UTC wire
Abdomen:	Pheasant tail color Midge Lace
Flashback:	Medium Opal Mirage
Wing case:	Strip of brown Thin Skin, 1/8-inch wide
Thorax:	Ginger dubbing
Legs:	Pheasant tail color Micro Tubing

This pattern by Buddy Knight is unusual because it uses midge lace and Micro Tubing for so many components. In forming the wing case, he ties in the Mirage first, then the Thin Skin. After the dubbing the thorax, he ties in the Thin Skin, then the Mirage over it. To ensure durability, Buddy places a drop of five-minute epoxy on the Thin Skin wing case. He fishes this fly as any nymph, with and without an indicator.

THE GRUNT

Hook:	#4-8 TMC 2302
Bead:	Black tungsten
Weight:	Strip of 0.030-inch-diameter lead or lead-free wire on either side of hook shank
Thread:	Fire orange 6/0 UNI-Thread
Tail ball:	Black Superfine Dubbing
Tails:	Dyed black goose biots
Rib:	Small black Ultra Wire
Abdomen:	Overhand weave of one strand each of black Wapsi Sparkle Yarn and DMC E898 yarn on top, and one strand each DMC 3047 and DMC 3045 and golden russet LaFontaine Sparkle Yarn on bottom
Wing case:	Strip of mottled oak Thin Skin
Legs:	Black Spanflex
Thorax:	Medium black/copper chenille
Collar:	Fire orange 6/0 UNI-Thread
Feelers:	Dyed black goose biots

Here is a rugged Giant Stonefly nymph pattern with subtle flash and a little realism. It's fun to tie and has proven to be quite effective in Yellowstone area streams. Twist all strands to form the top of the abdomen together, and do the same with strands forming the bottom of the abdomen. Then apply the overhand weave to form the abdomen. Mike Snody recommends presenting this fly in a Czech-style drift for best results.

JUDSON STONE

Hook:	#4-14 TMC 200R
Weight:	0.020-inch-diameter lead wire
Thread:	Yellow 8/0 UNI-Thread
Tail:	Turkey biots
Abdomen:	Turkey biots and Kaufmann's dubbing
Rib:	Fine copper wire
Wing pads:	Two turkey biots
Legs:	Whiting barred hen hackle
Thorax:	Kaufmann's dubbing
Head:	Kaufmann's dubbing
Antennae:	Turkey biot tips

To create this pattern by Merne Judson, wrap double layer of lead wire on hook for large flies, single layer for smaller. Flatten wire, wrap with thread, and cement. Dub a small ball to separate biots used for tails. Tie in rib, biots for top and bottom of abdomen, and dub abdomen to shank center. Tie biots in at abdomen top and bottom. Rib them in place. Cut excess from top biot. Tie in two biots, tips facing rear, and hen feather tip (underside facing up) at abdomen front. Dub a third of remaining shank, bring top and bottom biots forward, and tie in place, excess facing rear. Dub remainder of shank. Bring bottom biot and hen feather forward and tie off. Bring top biots forward, cross them to form antennae, dub a head, and tie off. Use colors to match stoneflies in your streams. Merne's golden stone version is pictured and described above.

KORN'S HOLIDAY STONE (GOLDEN)

Hook:	#8-10 Daiichi #1720
Bead:	3.5-mm-diameter gold on #8 versions; 3.0-mm-diameter gold on #10 versions
Thread:	Brown 120-denier Serafil
Tail and legs:	Olive or natural goose biots
Rib:	Clear nylon quilting thread or fine gold wire
Wing case:	Pearl Easter basket Mylar strip
Abdomen:	One-ply mustard yarn
Thorax:	Mustard yarn
Collar:	Loose Parks' Fly Shop DK#21 Golden Nymph dubbing

In the early season, Yellowstone River and other regional streams are frequently discolored through runoff. Doug Korn designed this pattern with abundant flash for visibility when fishing under this condition. He splits the tails with a dubbing ball at top of the bend. He folds the Mylar twice to form two wing cases. Doug also offers the Black Holiday Stone tied on #4-6 Daiichi 1720 with two-ply black yarn, copper wire, or nylon rib, rubber or biot legs and tails, and a 4.0-mm-diameter black bead for #6 versions and 4.5-mm-diameter black bead for #4 versions. Each version can be tied without a bead for trailing behind a dry fly.

KORN'S TNT GOLDEN STONE NYMPH

Hook:	#10 Mustad 9671
Bead:	Toho brown 6/0 glass
Thread:	Tobacco brown 6/0 Danville
Tail:	Wild turkey tail feather fibers
Back:	Wild turkey tail fibers
Rib:	Large copper wire
Body:	Parks' Fly Shop DK#21 Golden Nymph dubbing
Legs:	Pheasant aftershaft feather

Doug Korn uses turkey tail fibers on his extremely effective TNT Golden Stone Nymph (Turkey-N-Tail). The pheasant aftershaft feather gives the fly lifelike movement in the water. During July and August, he almost exclusively fishes this pattern as a trailer behind a dry stonefly pattern on Montana streams hosting large stoneflies. He also ties this pattern as a Black Stone, sizes 6 to 8, with a purple glass bead head. Also try this pattern with copper, gold, or black metal beads in proportion to hook size.

LIL' PRINCE

Hook:	#16 TMC 2488
Bead:	Silver tungsten, 5/64-inch
Thread:	Red 8/0 UNI-Thread
Tail:	Three pheasant tail fibers
Rib:	Red five grain wire

Body:	Black dubbing
Wing:	White goose biots
Hackle:	Brown saddle
Head:	Dark green dubbing

Some species of small stoneflies are most active early in the season. It is not unusual to see them crawling around the tops of snowbanks during nicer days even in February and March and April. One of these, a *Capnia* species, emerges during late winter. Scott Urbanski uses this pattern to simulate the nymphs of these small stoneflies.

MARTY'S GOLDEN STONE NYMPH

Hook:	#2 Daiichi 2340
Thread:	Tan 3/0 Danville
Tail:	Amber goose biots
Rib:	Gold wire
Body and thorax:	Gold, tan, and yellow Angora goat dubbing, blended
Overbody:	Peacock secondary strip
Wing case:	Peacock secondary strip
Legs:	Mottled brown hen hackle
Antennae:	Amber goose biots

Cut an elongated diamond shape from a semihard plastic strip. Secure it to the top of the hook with tying thread and cement. Separate tails with a dubbing ball. Tie in a Flexament-treated peacock feather strip at the bend with wire rib. Twist body dubbing in a loop, then wrap forward to thorax. Pull the peacock feather strip over top and lock into position with open rib turns. Flatten the wire top and bottom with hemostats, creating segmentation. Tie in a second Flexament-treated peacock feather strip for the wing case. Dub a three-section thorax with a set of legs tied in between each. Pull over top and fold the first wing case after completing first thorax section. Tie in the second peacock strip and fold over the remaining thorax section. Tie in antennae split with a dubbing ball. Whip-finish with a small amount of dubbing over second wing case. Marty Howard created this pattern for Madison River pocketwater.

MIKE'S AP NYMPH

Hook:	#14-16 TMC 2487
Weight:	0.010- or 0.015-inch-diameter lead or lead-free wire
Thread:	Camel 8/0 UNI-Thread
Rib:	Small copper wire
Tails:	Turkey biots dyed brown
Abdomen:	Overhand weave of brown (on top) and dark cream (on bottom) DMC yarn
Wing case:	Natural mottled oak Thin Skin
Legs:	Small speckled orange Centipede Legs
Thorax:	Peacock Ice Dub

Mike Snody created this nymph for use in rivers with strong currents, such as the South Fork reach of the Snake River. It seems particularly effective in simulating Golden Stonefly or Mutant Golden Stonefly nymphs. Mike has observed that it is also effective in slower waters for imitating emerging Brown Drake nymphs. After tying this pattern, brush out the thorax to enhance a "buggy" appearance. DMC yarn is available at Michaels Arts and Crafts stores.

MIKE'S YELLOWSTONE GOLD

Hook:	#8 TMC 2302
Bead:	Cyclops gold, $5/32$-inch
Weight:	Strip of 0.020-inch-diameter lead-free wire tied on either side of hook shank
Thread:	Yellow 8/0 UNI-Thread
Tail ball:	Gold Hare's Ear Plus Dubbin
Tail:	Dyed tannish yellow goose biots
Rib:	Chocolate brown DMC sparkle yarn
Abdomen:	Overhand weave with light yellow Antron on top and cream sparkle and dull tan DMC yarns on the bottom
Wing case:	Mottled oak golden stone Thin Skin
Legs:	Orange barred nymph Sili Legs
Thorax:	Light yellow UV Ice Dub
Antennae:	Dyed tannish yellow goose biots

This is Mike Snody's pattern for Golden Stonefly nymphs that inhabit so many Greater Yellowstone streams. He prefers to present it European style and ties it for the durability needed for streams of gradient and rough bottoms that host these stoneflies.

MINCH'S GOLDEN STONE

Hook:	#8-14 Mustad 9672
Bead:	Brass or tungsten
Thread:	Yellow 3/0 UNI-Thread
Tail:	Brown chickabou fibers
Abdomen:	Brown-olive Ice Dub
Thorax:	Spirit River antique squirrel Ice Dub
Hackle:	Grizzly saddle dyed brown

Intended as a Golden Stonefly nymph and proven effective on streams near Gardiner, Montana, and in Yellowstone National Park, Matt Minch's pattern also has a fine reputation as a dropper. Matt suggests nymphing it in a two-fly rig. Use it as both flies, or with his Bead Brooks Stone or his very popular Minch's Bead, Hare and Copper nymph (see page 11). Walter Weise also suggests using this pattern under a Turk's Tarantula or other such large attractor. That this pattern is easily tied adds to its popularity.

MONDO BITCH CREEK NYMPH

Hook:	#4-10 Dai-Riki 700B
Thread:	Black 6/0 UNI-Thread
Tails:	Medium orange and black barred Centipede Legs
Abdomen:	Parallel weave of black over orange chenille
Hackle:	Dyed bright orange grizzly saddle palmered over thorax
Legs:	Two pair medium orange and black barred Centipede Legs
Thorax:	Black chenille

The Mondo Bitch Creek Nymph is a fly of legend in the Greater Yellowstone Area. Jimmy Gabettas's status in the area as an educator, retailer, fly fisher, and fly tier is supreme, so any fly he produces becomes popular. This pattern has proved itself during regional stonefly activity. To the experienced fly fisher it is also an effective dragonfly nymph imitation, particularly productive on stillwaters during the early season.

RIVERSIDE STONEFLY

Hook:	#4-6 TMC 200R
Bead:	Black tungsten
Weight:	0.020-inch-diameter lead-free wire

Thread:	Orange 3/0 UNI-Thread
Tail:	Copper Wonder Wrap
Abdomen:	Amber/black Vinyl Rib
Thorax:	Black peacock Ice Dub
Wing case:	Black Furry Foam
Legs:	Copper Wonder Wrap
Antennae:	Copper Wonder Wrap

The Riverside Campground to Hatchery Ford reach of the Henry's Fork is one of the most productive parts of the river to fish during the Giant and Golden Stonefly emergences. Both floating and wading are effective here during these times, and the number of anglers present is fewer than in Box Canyon or other parts of the river. Dan Gates presents this pattern on the bottom and frequently in a two-fly rig. He also ties it without weighting wire and suspends it from a large, dry Salmonfly pattern. Through changing size and materials color, he converts this pattern to an effective Golden Stonefly nymph.

SHARPIE

Hook:	#12-16 Daiichi 1100
Thread:	Orange or amber 8/0 UNI-Thread
Rib:	Olive 8/0 UNI-Thread
Body:	Tying thread
Thorax:	Spirit River #Glas-165, ginger clear glass bead,
Hackle:	Sharp-tailed grouse neck in front of Whiting Farms dyed golden yellow hen

The author created this pattern to simulate a Yellow Sally emerger and fished it just under the surface with a twitch when it reached rising fish. It has been successful whenever used for this purpose. Sharp-tailed grouse are common in the region, but not as plentiful as ruffed grouse and Hungarian partridge, so neck hackles from these two can be used. The golden yellow hen hackle behind any of these adds living color.

TAN NORTH FORK SPECIAL

Hook:	#8-14 TMC 2457
Bead:	Silver
Weight:	Ten to fifteen wraps of 0.020-inch-diameter lead or lead-free wire
Thread:	Tan 140-denier
Tail:	Natural goose biots
Rib:	Fine red copper wire
Body:	Yellow Frog's Hair Dubbing
Legs:	Natural goose biots
Wing case:	Three natural goose biots cut to shape

The North Fork of the Shoshone River between Yellowstone National Park and Buffalo Bill Reservoir west of Cody, Wyoming, is a gradient stream that hosts stoneflies in abundance, including smaller *Isoperla* species. The same is true for most of the gradient streams in the Greater Yellowstone Area and results in production of superbly effective stonefly nymph imitations by their anglers. Tim Wade's pattern, meant to simulate smaller stonefly nymphs, has roots in his classic Black North Fork Special and the Terminator. Mount the legs at mid-body and wing case in three sections along the front half top of the body.

TIGER STONEFLY NYMPH

Hook:	#6 Mustad 9674
Weight:	0.015-inch-diameter lead or lead-free wire
Thread:	Black 3/0 Danville Monocord
Tail:	Two barbs from leading edge of a goose quill
Body:	Five 6/0 topaz/black center glass seed beads
Thorax:	Strip of opaque brown 5-mm wide Razor Foam
Hackle:	Burnt brown rooster saddle
Antennae:	Two barbs from leading edge of goose quill

The nymph of the Tiger Stonefly is a predatory creature, instead of a grazer like other stoneflies. In addition, the adult male is flightless, having vestigial wings. He inseminates the nymphal female as she exits the water on her way to molting into a fully functional female. Those characteristics are, indeed, rare among stoneflies. Yet the Tiger Stonefly, also known as the Mutant Stonefly, is widespread and common throughout streams and rivers of the Yellowstone uplift. Fly fishers should add this pattern by Harley Reno to their arsenals of wet flies. You will be surprised how effective it is throughout the year.

TUBE FLY STONE

Stinger hook:	#10 Daiichi 1120
Thread:	Black 6/0 UNI-Thread
Tube:	HMH $^3/_{32}$-inch outside diameter poly tube, inch and a half long
Rib:	Black monofilament
Tails:	Dyed black goose biots
Body:	Black wool dubbing
Shellback:	Strip of black bicycle tire inner tube
Legs:	Black and yellow barred Sili Legs
Carapace:	Three pieces of black bicycle tire inner tube cut to shape
Antennae:	Dyed black goose biots

Don Bishop uses his Tube Fly Stone with great success on the Gallatin and Madison Rivers. When tying in the carapace, cut the front segment long enough to form a head. Pick out the dubbed body to create a "buggy" appearance. Use a black marking pen to color exposed end of the tube, if necessary.

WARBIRD

Hook:	#4-10 Daiichi 1720
Thread:	Black 6/0 Danville
Tail:	Black marabou fibers

Hackle:	Black saddle
Body:	Black chenille
Legs:	Black round rubber legs
Antennae:	Black round rubber legs

What better place is there to prove a stonefly nymph than the middle Madison River? This part of the river is Kelly Galloup's "home water" and he uses it to develop and prove many of his patterns. This is the case with the Warbird, which has become the top stonefly nymph pattern for the Madison River and for other area rivers. It can be tied in other body colors including olive, brown, and with variegated chenille.

WILLARD FLY

Hook:	#2-4 Mustad 79580
Weight:	Thirty turns of 0.030-inch-diameter lead or lead-free wire
Thread:	Black 6/0 Danville Flymaster
Body:	Large black chenille
Hackle:	Black saddle
Collar:	Brown saddle hackle
Head:	Tying thread

To finish this fly by Will Godfrey, place your thumb under the shank at midpoint and bend it. The result looks more like a wiggling Giant Stonefly nymph. Dead-drift this pattern near the bottom on a heavy leader and sinking-tip line. When Giant Stonefly nymphs are moving toward shorelines in such places as the Henry's Fork Box Canyon and Cardiac Canyon reaches, the Madison River between Quake and Hebgen Lakes, the middle Madison River and the Yellowstone River in Paradise Valley and canyon reaches in Yellowstone Park, dead-drifting this pattern can be deadly.

WOVEN GOLDEN STONEFLY NYMPH

Hook:	#10-12 TMC 200R
Bead:	Gold
Weight:	0.015- or 0.030-inch-diameter lead-free wire
Thread:	Olive 6/0
Tails:	Natural goose biot pair
Body:	Half-hitch weave of light olive DMC embroidery floss (top) and midge Diamond Braid (bottom)
Thorax:	Dubbed Whitlock SLF scud shrimp blend
Wing case:	Black Scud Back strip

After placing the bead behind the hook eye, Logan Cutts ties in lead-free wire strips parallel to the rear two-thirds of the shank. He attaches embroidery and Diamond Braid strips, working amounts to the rear along the wire, and covers the wraps with tying thread. He weaves the body over the covered wire wraps. Next he ties in the butt end of the Scud Back wing case strip and dubs the thorax between the body and bead. He combs out the dubbing, trims the thorax bottom, and brings the Scud Back strip over top of the thorax to be tied down behind the bead, completing the fly.

WOVEN STONEFLY

Hook:	#2-8 TMC 200R
Bead:	Black brass, nickel, or tungsten
Weight:	0.025- or 0.030-inch-diameter lead-free wire
Thread:	Black 6/0
Tails:	Black goose biot pair

Body:	Half-hitch weave of black (top) and olive (bottom) DMC embroidery floss
Thorax:	Amber Ice Dub
Hackle:	Four or five turns of black or brown saddle
Wing case:	Black Scud Back strip
Legs:	Black fine rubber legs or Spandex
Antennae:	Same material as legs

After tying on antennae and placing the bead behind the hook eye, Logan Cutts ties in lead-free wire strips parallel to the front two-thirds of the shank. He attaches embroidery strips, working amounts to the rear along the wire, and covers the wraps with tying thread. He weaves the body over the covered wire wraps. Next he ties in the butt end of the Scud Back strip wing case, legs, and butt end of the hackle before dubbing the thorax between the body and the bead. He wraps the hackle and brings the Scud Back strip over top of the thorax to be tied down behind the bead to complete the fly.

ADULT PATTERNS

ARF HUMPULATOR

Hook:	#6-10 TMC 101
Thread:	Yellow 6/0 UNI-Thread
Tail:	Tan calf tail

Back:	Tan 2-mm closed-cell foam
Abdomen:	Yellow poly yarn
Rib:	Brown dry-fly saddle
Underwing:	Opal Mirage Flashabou
Wing:	Tan calf tail
Hi-Vis spot:	Fluorescent orange Para Post
Thorax:	Golden brown Ice Dub
Hackle:	Grizzly saddle dyed golden brown

This is Al Ritt's all-purpose adult stonefly pattern. Depending on size, this pattern can be used to simulate a Golden Stonefly adult or a smaller *Isoperla* stonefly adult such as a Yellow Sally. The brown hackle ribbing should have fiber length one-half to two-thirds the hook gap. The wing and underwing should extend to the rear no farther than the end of the tail.

ARF TRAILING BUBBLE HAREY YELLOW STONE

Hook:	#14-18 TMC 101
Thread:	Yellow 6/0 UNI-Thread
Trailing bubbles:	Opal Mirage Flashabou
Egg sac:	Red closed-cell foam
Rib:	Grizzly dyed yellow hackle
Abdomen:	Yellow Superfine Dubbing
Underwing:	Opal Mirage Flashabou
Wing:	Natural off-white snowshoe hare
Indicator spot:	Red closed-cell foam
Thorax:	Yellow Superfine Dubbing
Hackle:	Barred light ginger

Trim the grizzly hackle rib to shorten the fibers if very short hackle is not available. Winter phase snowshoe hare is an off-white color. If this is not available, use cream color bleached snowshoe hare. Al Ritt recommends cutting a "V" in the bottom of the wound hackle to allow this fly to ride lower in the water. With a yellow body and red egg sac, this pattern is in the Mormon Girl style for an egg-laying Yellow Sally.

BITCHIN' SALMONFLY

Hook:	#2-6 Daiichi 2220
Thread:	Fluorescent fire orange 6/0
Tail:	Moose hair and black rubber hackle

Body:	Woven black (top) and orange (bottom) poly yarn
Wing:	Two layers of plastic screen door material cut to shape under several strands of pearlescent Krystal Flash under elk mane
Legs:	Black rubber hackle
Head and collar:	Bullet style from dyed gray deer hair

Arrick Swanson's use of plastic screening material in the wing of this pattern is unique. This pattern is a blend of synthetic and natural materials that is common in contemporary fly-tying circles. The result is another effective pattern.

BITTERROOT STONE

Hook:	#8-20 Mustad 94831
Thread:	Camel 8/0 UNI-Thread
Tail ball:	Brownish orange Nature's Spirit dubbing with a small amount of orange Antron
Tails:	Dyed brown goose biots
Abdomen:	Brownish orange Nature's Spirit dubbing with a small amount of orange Antron
Underwing:	Brown Wapsi Sparkle Yarn
Overwing:	Mottled oak turkey-wing quill segment cut to shape
Hackle:	Brown barred dun saddle
Head and top wing:	Flared brown deer hair with butts clipped to form head

Michael Snody designed this fly to meet the variety of stoneflies that emerge from streams throughout the Greater Yellowstone Area. Thus he offers versions in black and yellow for Skwalas and Yellow Sallies. Change the hook size, tail, abdomen, underwing, hackle, head and top wing accordingly. Skate it, jiggle it while it drifts, or bob it under the surface. You will find it to be effective for trout keying on floating stoneflies. Tie the tail ball in at the top of the bend before tying in the biots to ensure that they stay apart.

BURKHOLDER SKWALA

Hook:	#10 Daiichi 1850
Thread:	Pale olive Pearsall's Gossamer silk
Tails:	Siberian stallion tail hair
Rib:	Doubled and twisted fine copper wire
Egg sac:	Black Evazote Sheet Foam
Wings:	Brown bear body hair
Abdomen:	Light olive silk floss over brown silk floss, superglued and brushed with Flexament
Thorax:	Golden brown Ice Dub
Pronotum:	Olive Razor Foam marked with a dark claret Sharpie and Fly-Rite golden olive extra fine poly
Legs:	Gray Super Floss
Head:	Brown 3-mm craft foam

Although it is specifically a Skwala pattern, it can be used for any darker stonefly in the ⅞-inch range. Being a musician, Ken Burkholder has a chance to evaluate stringed instrument components. He saw that Siberian stallion tail hair used for cello and bass violin bows could be used for tails and antennae on fly patterns. Brown bear hair is superb material for stonefly wings because of fineness, toughness, and ability to hold shape. The dubbing between and in front of the pronotum is Golden Brown Ice Dub and behind head is Fly-Rite golden olive extra fine poly, which gives a hot spot effect.

FAT BOY CHERNOBYL

Hook:	#8-10 Daiichi 1730
Thread:	Tan 140-denier UTC Ultra Thread
Body:	Hare's ear dubbing
Overbody:	Tan under brown under dark brown closed-cell foam cut to shape
Wing:	Gray Antron
Legs:	Tan round rubber legs striped with a marking pen
Head:	Closed-cell foam used to form body
Eyes:	Black marking pen

Dub the body, then tie in the tan foam overbody piece. Tie in the rear wing and legs above the hook point. Tie in the brown foam overbody piece at the same location and superglue it to the tan foam piece. Tie in the front of the two foam pieces, the front wing, and the front legs behind the hook eye. Superglue the dark brown foam piece to the top of the brown foam piece and tie it in. Doug McKnight recommends this highly buoyant pattern for Mutant Stoneflies on such streams as the Yellowstone River.

FEMALE GOLDEN STONE

Hook:	#4 Gamakatsu 09108
Thread:	Wood duck 70-denier UTC Ultra Thread

Tail separator:	Amber Nature's Spirit dubbing ball
Tail:	Natural goose biots
Rib:	Thin brown Micro Tron strip
Body:	Gold Poly Tron strip
Wing:	Tan EP Fibers in two layers
Thorax:	Amber Nature's Spirit dubbing
Head:	Brown 2-mm closed-cell foam strip trimmed to shape
Legs:	Medium barred rubber leg pair on either side
Indicator:	White closed-cell foam strip

This pattern by Ed Matney has scored very well in the Jackson Hole One Fly contest in addition to being a superb producer on the South Fork reach of the Snake River when trout target Golden Stonefly adults. Elden Berrett builds the wing with two layers of EP Fibers to add volume. The thorax, formed in front of the wing, is the base for the head, legs, and strike indicator.

FIN AND PINK

Hook:	#6-12 Dai-Riki 710
Thread:	Peach 6/0 UNI-Thread
Tails:	Gray/black barred Sili Legs
Underbody:	Peach closed-cell foam strip
Overbody:	Chocolate brown closed-cell foam strip
Wings:	Gray Widow's Web behind flesh Widow's Web
Legs:	Black/pink barred round rubber; gray/pink round rubber
Head:	Foam used to form underbody and overbody
Indicator:	Yellow closed-cell foam

John Way begins the stonefly season with this fly. It has proven effective along the length of the Madison River when large stoneflies emerge. It has three abdomen sections and one large thorax section. John ties in a pair of round rubber legs on each side at the front and rear of the abdomen. The gray Widow's Web wing is tied in on top at the rear of the abdomen, and the pink Widow's Web wing is tied in on top at its front.

FOAM GOLDEN STONE

Hook:	#6-8 TMC 5263
Thread:	Tan 8/0 UNI-Thread
Underbody:	Amber Wapsi Life Cycle dubbing
Egg sac:	Chocolate Razor Foam
Overbody:	Tan closed-cell foam
Wings:	Tan EP Fibers
Legs:	Amber speckled Sili Legs
Head:	Tan Razor Foam used to form egg sac

Mike Lawson extends the Razor Foam strip used to form the egg sac along the shank under the dubbed body. He folds over and ties down the protruding front end to form a distinct head. The Golden Stonefly emergence is usually more reliable than that of the Giant Stonefly emergence on many area rivers, and when the two emerge simultaneously, salmonids tend to prefer Golden Stonefly adults to Giant Stonefly adults. Mike recommends this highly visible Golden Stonefly adult pattern, particularly for float trips. Cut back the wing length if a lower profile is desired.

GIB'S GOLDEN STONE

Hook:	#8-10 Dai-Riki 710
Thread:	Olive 8/0 UNI-Thread
Tail:	Orange hackle fibers
Rib:	Grizzly hackle
Body:	Golden yellow yarn
Underwing:	Three Canadian goose CDC feathers
Wing:	Tan calf tail
Legs:	Black and olive banded Sili Legs
Hackle:	Dyed olive and natural grizzly

Emerging Golden Stoneflies are a favorite for regional salmonids. This pattern has proven itself on the Henry's Fork, the Madison River, the South Fork reach of the Snake River, Fall River, and Doug Gibson's favorite, the Teton River. He maintains a slender body for better flotation and two pair of legs tied in on either side—one just in front of the wing, the other about midway where hackle will be tied in. His dyed olive and natural grizzly hackle are undersized (size 14 for a size 10 hook) to give a more natural silhouette.

GIB'S SALLY

Hook:	#12-14 Dai-Riki 300
Thread:	Olive 8/0 UNI-Thread
Butt:	Red dubbing
Body:	Yellow dubbing
Hackle:	Light dun
Underwing:	Natural mallard CDC curving downward
Wing:	Light elk hair
Head:	Clipped elk hair butts

Tying in hackle before the wing compresses hackle to sides, giving better floatation qualities. Tying in a CDC underwing curving downward gives this pattern better lateral stability. Doug Gibson ties it with the red egg sac to represent an egg-laying female. Throughout the region, a red egg sac with a yellow body is referred to as Mormon Girl style. Doug also ties this pattern without the egg sac to represent a drifting insect.

HALF HEAD

Hook:	#10-14 Dai-Riki 270
Thread:	Orange 8/0 UNI-Thread
Rib:	Brown saddle hackle
Body:	Golden Superfine Dubbing

Underwing:	Orange Montana Fly Company Z-Yarn
Head:	Deer hair
Wing:	Tips of deer hair bunch used to form head

Tie this pattern to the point of finishing the underwing, the tips of which extend to the hook bend. At the base of the underwing tie in, with tips facing forward, the butts of the deer hair bunch used to form the head and wing. Dub over the butts to the hook eye with golden Superfine Dubbing. Fold the deer-hair bunch back to the rear, forming a half head (deer hair in the top 180 degrees of the vertical radius around the hook). Tie off the head at the tie-in point of the underwing. This is Marty Howard's favorite pattern for adult Yellow Sallies and other small stoneflies. He originally tied it for fishing the Firehole River and the South Fork reach of the Snake River, but it is effective anywhere small stonefly adults are present.

HIGH/LOW CDC YELLOW SALLY

Hook:	#14-16 Daiichi 1180
Thread:	Yellow 8/0
Butt:	Orange dry-fly dubbing tied slightly down on bend of hook
Body:	Pale yellow Fine and Dry Dubbing
Wing:	Two yellow CDC feathers
Overwing:	Six to eight dark partridge feather fibers
Hackle:	Cree rooster neck feather
Antennae/legs:	Mirage Accent Flash

Wing and body make up 60 percent of the length of this fly, and the thorax area with hackle and legs make up the remaining 40 percent. When tying a size 12 fly, use a size 14 hook because the wing extends past the

hook bend. For this pattern by Ben Byng, tie your CDC feathers concave side down, laying one feather over the other. The waste from the wing and overwing are extended over the hook eye to represent the head. Trim this material once whipped-finished. Trim the underside of the cree hackle so the fly lays flat on the water. A CDC wing always gives a fly a more lifelike appearance because of the manner of light reflecting through it.

JEANNE'S CATCH-ALL SALMON FLY

Hook:	#4-6 Dai-Riki 710
Thread:	Black 6/0 UNI-Thread
Body:	Salmon closed-cell foam
Rib:	Tying thread
Underwing:	Orange marabou fibers with pearlescent Flashabou
Overwing:	Segment cut from sheet packing foam or from white plastic shopping bag
Bullet head:	Deer hair
Collar:	Tips of deer hair used to form bullet head
Legs:	Black/orange or brown Sili Legs

During the large Salmonfly emergence on the Madison River, Jeanne Williams's fly is in demand from the Odell Creek Fly Shop. From Ennis to Hebgen Dam, it is used because of high visibility and durability. The two materials she suggests for forming the overwing are readily available. For this purpose, she is also considering using weedguard for the overwing, a material sold in thin sheets at lawn and garden shops for eliminating weeds around flowers and vegetable plants.

MYSTERY MEAT GOLDEN STONE

Hook:	#6-10 Dai-Riki 285
Thread:	Yellow 3/0
Tail:	Two medium brown rubber legs
Rib:	Grizzly dyed yellow saddle hackle
Belly:	Tan 2-mm closed-cell foam
Back:	Brown 2-mm closed-cell foam
Wing:	Dark elk
Overwing:	Pearl Krystal Flash
Legs:	Medium brown rubber legs
Head:	Gold dyed elk
Indicator:	Yellow 2-mm closed-cell foam

This pattern is based on the oldest of Scott Sanchez's Mystery Meat series. Tying steps are the same, but colors and size are changed to better imitate the Golden Stonefly adult. Scott prefers large dry flies tied with a combination of foam and natural materials. Natural materials (hair, hackle, etc.) simulate motion and give a "fuzzyness" that better simulates naturals. Natural materials also impart less rigid profiles. Golden Stoneflies emerge from all the famed streams of the Greater Yellowstone Area, and Scott has fished most of these streams and prefers natural materials for forming adult Golden Stonefly patterns.

MYSTERY MEAT SKWALA

Hook:	#10-12 Dai-Riki 710
Thread:	Olive 3/0
Tail:	Two medium gray rubber legs
Rib:	Medium dun saddle hackle
Belly:	Olive 2-mm closed-cell foam
Back:	Brown 2-mm closed-cell foam
Wing:	Dark elk
Overwing:	Pearl Krystal Flash
Legs:	Medium gray rubber legs
Head:	Dark elk
Indicator:	Lime 2-mm closed-cell foam

Rubber legs and tails add to the appearance of motion in this pattern, and as with others in Scott Sanchez's Mystery Meat series, the use of Krystal Flash in the wing imparts the sheen of a natural wing as well as apparent motion. Closed foam has better buoyancy than natural materials, so this pattern includes the best that natural materials and foam offer the fly tier. As with others in the series, this pattern is effective when fished dead-drift, twitched, or stripped underwater. It is also an effective indicator when fished over a sunken pattern.

PINK POOKIE

Hook:	#6-10 Dai-Riki 280
Thread:	Red 6/0 UNI-Thread
Body:	Pink closed-cell foam
Underwing:	Elk body hair
Overwing:	Tan closed-cell foam
Legs:	Yellow/black barred Montana Fly Company Centipede Legs
Head:	Closed-cell foam used to form over-wing and body
Indicator:	Orange closed-cell foam

To create this pattern by Dean Reiner, begin by poking the hook point and barb through the pink foam body piece and running it up the thread-wrapped shank. Secure it to the bottom of the shank with thread wraps, resulting in three body segments and a head. Add super-glue to the head top surface. Place the tan foam wing piece butt on the head with remainder facing forward. Tie this piece in at the eye and wrap thread to rear of head. Tie in the stacked elk-hair underwing, then bend remainder of tan foam piece back, forming the wing. Tie it in at the rear of the head. Tie in legs at each side and an orange foam indicator at the same location. Whip-finish and trim legs and indicator to size. Use the Montana Fly Company Chernobyl Tapered Punch Set to form the body and wing.

PROM QUEEN SALMON FLY

Hook:	#4-6 Daiichi 1270
Thread:	Black flat-waxed nylon for body, fluorescent orange 6/0 for head and legs
Body:	Furled orange and brown Red Heart acrylic yarn
Underwing:	Pearl Krystal Flash
Wing:	Elk mane
Head:	Bullet head formed from 2-mm dark brown closed-cell foam
Legs:	Brown barred Centipede Legs
Indicator:	Salmon 2-mm closed-cell foam

Walter Weise's fly rides low in the water to simulate a drowning or egg-laying adult. Only the head and indicator are on the surface. The fluorescent orange thread for securing the head and legs simulates the orange band behind the head of a natural adult. Walter prefers the furled yarn body because it is more flexible than a foam body, resulting in more action. This pattern is his go-to fly for Yellowstone River float trips during the summer Salmonfly hatch, often trailing a smaller stonefly, caddis, or attractor dry.

ROLLING STONE

Hook:	#14-16 TMC 300R
Thread:	Tan 6/0 Danville
Butt:	Red dubbing
Body:	Whitlock red fox SLF blend dubbing
Head:	Tan 2-mm closed-cell foam
Wing:	White Montana Fly Company Z-Yarn
Legs:	Speckled Montana Fly Company round rubber legs

Although deer hair or CDC feathers can be used for the wing of this pattern, Tim Woodard prefers using Z-Yarn because of its superior durability and sustained buoyancy. For the same reasons he offers that Blue Ribbon Flies Zelon can also be used for the wing of this pattern. Quickly and easily tied, this pattern has proven effective during Yellow Sally activity on waters from the Madison River to the South Fork reach of the Snake River. Tim has Golden Stone and Giant Stonefly adult patterns tied in the same manner as his Rolling Stone.

ROYAL TRUDE SKWALA (FEMALE)

Hook:	#10-14 Dai-Riki 310
Thread:	Black 8/0
Egg sac:	Black closed-cell foam
Body:	Peacock herl and red floss

Wing:	White EP Fibers
Hackle:	Grizzly saddle dyed brown
Legs:	Fine white and black variegated rubber legs
Indicator:	Stub of EP Fibers used to form wings

Here is a fly with a pedigree: the Trude and the Royal Wulff influence its construction. Skwalas, early season stoneflies, emerge from such streams as the Snake, Yellowstone, Gallatin, and Madison Rivers. Rowan Nyman's version of the male Skwala is without an egg sac and uses brown saddle hackle in place of grizzly dyed brown.

SNAKE RIVER SKWALA

Hook:	#8-12 Dai-Riki 730
Thread:	Camel 8/0 UNI-Thread
Egg sac:	Black open-celled foam
Body:	Olive-brown dubbing
Underwing:	Two webby dark dun saddle hackles tied in reversed
Overwing:	Dyed yellow calf tail
Hackle:	One grizzly and one furnace brown saddle
Legs:	Medium brown flat rubber legs

Form reversed hackled wings by pulling hackle fibers on either side of the stem back toward butt end of the hackle and holding them in place with thumb and forefinger. Next, tying thread is used to secure these fibers and stem to the hook shank, forming a wing. Repeat this operation to form the other wing. Adjust length of the wings by gently pulling the secured reversed fibers and stem to the rear, then trimming away the hackle tips. Howard Cole prefers using open-celled foam to form the egg sac because of its light weight, low density, and buoyancy.

SOB

Hook:	#6-10 Mustad 94831
Thread:	Black 6/0
Tail:	Elk body hair
Rib:	Small black saddle hackle
Abdomen:	Orange floss or floating yarn
Underwing:	Dyed black deer hair
Wing:	Elk body hair
Legs:	Medium brown rubber
Hackle:	Small orange, #14 for #6 hook
Thorax:	Amber dubbing

Merrill Tea lives as near as anyone to the lower end of South Fork reach of the Snake River, perhaps the most visited reach of water in the Greater Yellowstone Area. Its Giant Stonefly emergence signals the beginning of its superb fly-fishing season. Merrill's SOB is one of the most popular adult patterns, especially on the lower part of the reach.

TAK'S STONEFLY

Hook:	#4-10 Daiichi 1180
Thread:	Black 120-denier UTC Ultra Thread
Body:	Orange closed-cell foam cut from River Roads Chernobyl Ant cutter

Rib:	Tying thread
Wing:	White Montana Fly Company Lucent Wing Material
Thorax:	Underbody extension
Overwing:	Dyed black deer body hair
Head:	Black closed-cell foam
Legs:	Medium round black rubber legs

To create Rick Takahashi's fly pattern, pierce the underbody foam piece with the hook point and slide along the hook shank underside to just behind the eye. Coat its top surface with cement. Cement the underside of the overbody piece and place it on top of the shank, ends matching the underbody piece. Tie these together, forming four body segments, the rear one extended. Anchor a pair of legs with thread wraps between the second and third body segments. Secure them with the other legs in front of the first body segment. Tie in the wing, overwing, and black foam piece butt end at this location. Advance the tying thread forward to secure black foam piece front and return thread to the foam piece butt end. Fold the piece back and tie it in place, forming the head. Whip-finish.

TODD'S YELLOW SALLY

Hook:	#16 TMC 200RL
Thread:	Red 8/0
Body:	Tan Targus Sparkle Dubbing
Wing:	White Z-Lon
Hackle:	Furnace saddle
Head:	Orange Targus Sparkle Dubbing

Overseeing the guide staffs at South Fork Outfitters gave Todd Lanning plenty of opportunity to evaluate fly patterns. That's an important action when you are working on probably the most popular river in the region: the South Fork reach of the Snake River. Yellow Sallies emerge from the river from June through September, making them an important food form. This pattern, with its visible wing and body having the subtle sparkle of minute air bubbles, has proven itself throughout the season

TWO TONE FOAM STONE

Hook:	#4-6 TMC 200R
Thread:	Orange 3/0 Danville
Rib:	Brown saddle hackle
Body:	Black over orange foam
Underwing:	Sparkle Organza cut to shape
Wing:	Moose body hair
Legs:	Black/orange barred rubber legs
Head:	Black over orange foam
Indicator:	Orange McFly Foam

The body of this pattern by Marty Howard is created by securing the two colors of foam to the shank of the hook in segments. The hackle rib is wound into the segments. The underwing of Sparkle Organza is cut to shape and edges are slightly melted for durability. The moose hair is splayed over the top of the organza. The head is created by tying in the black foam on top of the hook and the orange on the bottom to the eye and then pulled back, creating a bullet-type head. Marty tied this pattern for the LeHardy Rapids stretch of the Yellowstone River in the park but found it to be equally effective in the Box Canyon of the Henry's Fork.

TWO TONE GOLDEN

Hook:	#8-10 Daiichi 1260
Thread:	Tan 6/0 UTC Ultra Thread
Body:	Golden 2-mm craft foam over chocolate 2-mm craft foam
Underwing:	Packing foam trimmed to shape by hand underneath Etha-Wing cut to shape with caddis wing cutter
Overwing:	Smoke Widow's Web
Legs:	Black/pink barred Sexi Legs
Thorax:	Tan dubbing
Antennae:	Black/pink barred Sexi Legs
Head:	Extension of chocolate foam used to form body
Indicator:	Fluorescent pink foam strip

To form the body/extended body of this fly, Clayton Paddie places a piece of golden craft foam over a piece of chocolate craft foam. He folds them together so that the golden craft foam is on top, then uses this combination to form the body/extended body of this fly. These foams are available in craft stores. He superglues the foam strip used to form the indicator to add durability.

CHAPTER 8

STREAMER PATTERNS

merican fly tiers in the late nineteenth century were the first to create streamer patterns for freshwater fishing. Their purpose, of course, was to simulate baitfish. Beginning on northeastern states waters, they were frequently used as trolling flies patterns and gained fame not only for effectiveness but also for beauty. Typically these patterns were formed with wings of bucktail or of feathers, and as such eventually became quite sophisticated in areas like Maine's Rangeley Lake Region.

By the third decade of the twentieth century, streamer patterns began to appear from the vises of Western tiers. Western tiers introduced the use of native materials such as elk hair, squirrel tail, and wolf fur to form wings. Western streamers also acquired fame as trolling flies on such waters as Henry's Lake, Hebgen Reservoir, and southwestern Montana's graben lakes (Cliff, Elk, Hidden, and Wade). Visiting fly tiers from Eastern states were inspired to create streamer patterns based on their trolling experiences on these and other Western lakes. But in the West, streamers increasingly became casting flies where rivers are rich with large trout. West Yellowstone pioneering fly fishers including Pat Barnes and Vint Johnson touted such patterns as the Peacock Doctor and Squirrel Tail Streamer. In Jackson Hole, Roy Donnelly's Mormon Girl streamer gained early casting advocates on the Snake, Lewis, and Gros Ventre Rivers as well as trolling advocates on Jackson, Jenny, and Moran Lakes.

A global expansion in streamer patterns came with the introduction of synthetic fibers, which can be used alone or mixed with natural materials. These man-made fibers have added durability and color selection not available in natural materials. Among the most popular are various types of Mylar fibers, employed because of their superb reflectivity, delicacy, and variety of color. A bit of caution on using Mylar fibers is in order, however. It is best to use Mylar fiber sparingly to produce a subtle effect in the clear waters when regional streams are at base levels.

The use of streamer patterns in Greater Yellowstone waters seems most effective early and late in the season. Early in the season, postspawning cutthroat and rainbows key on baitfish to more efficiently replace energy reserves reduced during spawning. Likewise, late in the season, brown and brook trout strike streamer patterns out of sheer aggression brought on by the spawning urge. In the early season they, too, seek baitfish to more efficiently replace energy reserves.

Remember that in the early and late seasons, availability of both aquatic and terrestrial insects is reduced. But throughout the season, streamers can be effective when presented during low-light conditions. Salmonids are opportunists when seeking food items. When the opportunity comes to take a food item in a perceived safe, energy-conserving manner, they will strike. Arguably the best way to encounter really large salmonids is through presenting streamer patterns that simulate the baitfish on which they prey. Presentation is more important than choice of pattern here. Presentation includes stalking the fish and knowing where they hold the water. But note appearance, size, and color when selecting patterns. By appearance I mean lifelike in movement; size, that the chosen pattern should be roughly the size of available baitfish; and color, close to those of available baitfish.

B-52

Hook:	#1 Daiichi 4660
Thread:	Red 6/0 Danville
Head:	Molded lead jig head
Body:	Gold variant rabbit strip
Belly:	Two white palmered marabou plumes
Flash:	Pearl ice fibers
Wing:	White marabou
Collar:	Hen grizzly saddle hackle

Orange is Doug Kinney's favorite color to paint the head on this pattern. That color seems to bring the most attention from trout residing in the South Fork reach of the Snake River, the Henry's Fork, and the Madison River. Marabou plumes wound soft-hackle style (palmered) around the hook shank provide superb action. When tying this pattern for fishing in Yellowstone Park waters, Doug places a tungsten bead on a pin to replace the molded lead jig head and secures it bead first to the hook shank to provide up-front weight required for jigging action.

BABY MACK

Hook:	#2-6 Dai-Riki 710
Thread:	Black 6/0 Danville Flymaster
Tail:	Olive-tinged yellow marabou

Body:	Braided pearlescent Mylar Tinsel
Beard:	Soft webby red saddle hackle
Underwing:	Sparse brown marabou
Wing:	Canvasback duck covert

This is a flatwing streamer, meaning the covert feather is tied in perpendicular to the hook. According to Chuck Collins, a teal or pintail covert can be substituted in the wing for the more difficult to find canvasback covert. He also ties this pattern with a few strands of pearl or dark green Krystal Flash in the marabou underwing. This pattern represents a lake trout (mackinaw) fingerling. These inhabit some of the shallow portions of some deep lakes in the Greater Yellowstone Area. they can also be found in the meadow reach of the Lewis River between Shoshone and Lewis Lakes in Yellowstone National Park.

BABY SEAL

Hook:	#2 Gamakatsu Glo-Bug Hook
Thread:	Black 6/0 UNI-Thread
Tube:	HMH ^{3}/$_{32}$-inch outside diameter poly tube, 1 inch long
Tail:	Black rabbit strip
Tube body:	Brown Estaz Chenille
Wing:	Green arctic fox hair with a few green Flashbou strands
Facing:	Partridge flank feather

This is Paul Lauchle's favorite searching fly for salmonids prowling for baitfish in the likes of the Snake River, the South Fork reach of the Snake River, and the Henry's Fork. In addition to the colors given for the example above, he recommends tail colors of black, brown, olive, tan, or chartreuse and the same colors for the wing, which he also ties with marabou wrapped soft-hackle style. Paul will try various combinations of these colors, making this a convertible pattern. He also uses guinea flank feather for the facing and green Estaz chenille for the body. He notes that tube flies, which are becoming more popular in the area, seem to be less damaging on hooking, especially to smaller fish. Try fishing this fly unweighted just under the surface. The result can be explosive strikes!

BAD BUTT SCULPIN

Hook:	#4 Daiichi X560
Thread:	Olive 70-denier UTC Ultra Thread
Head:	Large Sculpin Helmet
Tube:	Black HMH $^3/_{32}$-inch outside diameter aluminum tube, $1^1/_2$ inches long
Tube extension:	HMH $^3/_{32}$-inch outside diameter poly tube, 1 inch long
Body:	Peacock Sparkle Chenille
Wing:	Olive sculpin marabou over red Whiting Farms spey hackle
Collar:	Olive EP Streamer Brush

Gary Barnes uses the high-wing technique to tie in marabou segments along the top of the body. At the front of the body, he ties in spey hackle then marabou using the soft-hackle technique. With its compound wing and Streamer Brush collar, this pattern has ample action. The heavy Sculpin Helmet keeps the head of the fly near the stream bottom. A stout rod and heavy leader are a must to cast this pattern. Wearing a hard hat isn't a bad idea either!

BADGER MUDDLER

Hook:	#2-6 Mustad 79580
Thread:	Mono thread
Tail:	Badger body hair
Body:	Dubbed badger body hair
Collar:	Flared deer hair
Head:	Spun deer body hair

Del Canty begins the body of this fly by placing a clump of deer hair at the bend of the hook after the tail is tied in. The remainder of the body is badger hair spun in a dubbing loop, then wrapped forward around the hook shank. The result is a fluffy body that gives this pattern lifelike motion. A deer-hair collar is flared in place with tips pointing outward, then a loosely spun head is tied in place with a separate bunch of deer hair. Del uses a dab of fluorescent yellow T-shirt paint for head cement to give a hot spot. He fishes this pattern on a floating line with a split-shot on the leader about 16 inches above the fly. On the retrieve, this pattern bobs up and down in the water column, simulating an injured minnow. Del finds it to be especially effective under low-light conditions when large trout are in a foraging mood.

BAKER'S HOLE SOFT HACKLE

Hook:	#8 Daiichi 1550
Thread:	Tan 6/0
Rib:	UTC gold wire
Body:	Hydropsyche tan dubbing with small amount of tan hare's ear
Hackle:	Two or three Hungarian partridge or ruffed grouse feathers tied in tip first

The idea of this pattern by Bucky McCormick is to imply some reflected light, motion, and to instill durability. The Z-Lon-based hydropsyche dubbing has good reflective properties, and using a dubbing loop to form the body results in a robust form, especially when shagged out with a brush or dubbing rake. The wire rib ensures durability, and the soft grouse hackle gives motion. This fly can get down deep enough in the Madison River above Hebgen Reservoir to where shy run-up fish are holding. Not being particularly large, its chances of startling these fish are next to nothing.

BARELY LEGAL

Thread:	White 100-denier GSP
Back hook:	#4 Daiichi 1750
Tail:	Two stacked olive marabou plumes over one white marabou plume

Body:	Pearl Cactus Chenille
Wings:	Two stacked olive marabou plumes over two white marabou plumes
Connection:	0.038-inch 19-strand braided stainless-steel wire (Beadalon)
Front hook:	#1/0 Mustad 3366
Beads:	Two red glass
Weight:	Medium Fish-Skull
Body:	Pearl Cactus Chenille
Wings:	Two dyed olive marabou plumes over two white marabou plumes; a few strands of pearl Flashabou on sides
Collar:	Stacked dyed olive marabou plumes over stacked white marabou plumes; a few strands of pearl Flashabou on sides
Topping:	Pair of dyed olive grizzly saddle hackles

Wings on the rear hook are tied in at midshank and at front. Front wing has a few strands of pearl Flashabou. Wings on front hook are tied in at end of shank and at midshank. The collar is tied in just behind the Fish-Skull. Strands of Flashabou are added to the sides of the rear wing and the collar. Tie this pattern by Kelly Galloup without the Fish-Skull for shallow-water presentation.

BIGHORN GONGA

Hook:	#2 Dai-Riki 710
Thread:	Brown 3/0 Danville Monocord
Eyes:	Medium lead or lead-free dumbbell
Tail:	Brown marabou over yellow marabou fibers
Rib:	Brown schlappen
Body:	Yellow Ice Dub
Legs:	Speckled yellow Sili Legs
Collar:	Brown Craft Fur
Head:	Brown EP Fibers spun in dubbing loop

Tie in eyes on bottom of shank. Tie in tail with butts covering shank up to the eye to add body bulk. Twist Ice Dub into rope before wrapping it to form body. After wrapping the schlappen rib, tie in the Craft Fur collar in three clumps: center, left, and right. Wrap the EP Fibers in the dubbing loop to form a head. Brush it, then variegate the collar and head with a black marker. Kit Seaton recommends this pattern for brown trout because of his experiences using it to simulate carp minnows on the Yellowstone River.

BITCHIN' BUGGER

Hook:	#4-8 TMC 5263
Thread:	Black 6/0
Tail:	Black marabou with pearl Krystal Flash and white rubber hackle
Body:	Overhand weave of black and orange chenille
Thorax:	Black chenille
Hackle:	Brown saddle palmered over thorax
Legs:	White rubber hackle

It is common practice to combine past and contemporary tying concepts these days. An example of this practice is Arrick Swanson's effective pattern that combines Toni Sivey's revered Bitch Creek Nymph with the Woolly Bugger concept. The result doubles as a Woolly Bugger and a streamer pattern. What would Toni have thought on seeing this!

BOOGIE MAN

Thread:	White 100-denier GSP
Back hook:	#6 Daiichi 1750
Tail:	Two white marabou plumes with four pearl Flashabou strands between
Hackle:	White schlappen or 5- to 7-inch strung saddle
Body:	White medium Cactus Chenille
Wing:	Mallard flank feather
Connection:	0.038-inch 19-strand nylon-coated braided stainless-steel wire (Beadalon)
Beads:	Red glass
Connection cover:	Same material as tail
Front hook:	#4 Daiichi 1750
Hackle:	White schlappen
Body:	White medium Cactus Chenille
Wing:	Mallard flank feather
Head/Collar:	White rams wool trimmed to shape
Eyes:	Large lead dumbbell eyes painted red

Kelly Galloup's creativity really comes through on this articulated sculpin pattern. With motion like few other streamers, it is making its mark on large trout throughout the area. Besides the white version discussed here, Kelly offers Boogie Man in black, gray, olive, tan, and root beer.

BOOTY'S QUAD BUNNY LEECH

Hook:	#2-6 TMC 5263
Lead hook:	#4 Dai-Riki 710
Stinger:	#4 Gamakatsu straight shank hook
Weight:	Red dumbbell eyes
Thread:	Black 3/0 UNI-Thread
Leech string:	20-pound monofilament
Rear body:	White crosscut rabbit fur
Lower body (belly):	White Magnum Rabbit Strip
Upper body (back):	White Magnum Rabbit Strip
Lateral line (sides):	Natural and black barred Zonker Strip
Collar:	Pearl Ice Chenille
Eyes:	Red dumbbell eyes
Head and Collar:	Spun white deer hair
Adhesive:	Latex contact cement

Boots Allen's Quad Bunny Leech is similar in some ways to Scott Sanchez's Double Bunny, but it is tied with two hooks. Two Magnum Rabbit Strips and two medium-sized rabbit strips form the body. This fly has very lifelike movement when submerged and stripped. It is a favorite for Boots on any stream that holds big brown trout.

BOTTOMS UP

Thread:	Red 100-denier GSP
Back hook:	#4-6 Daiichi 1750
Tail:	Two olive marabou plumes with 4 orange Flashabou strands on either side
Hackle:	Olive schlappen between Pee-Wee Pops
Body:	Two olive Pee-Wee Pops
Connection:	0.038-inch 19-strand nylon-coated braided stainless-steel wire (Beadalon)
Beads:	Red glass
Connection cover:	Same materials as tail
Front hook:	#4-6 Daiichi 1750
Hackle:	Dark olive schlappen
Body:	Light olive Cactus Chenille
Legs:	Olive/black Sili Legs
Head:	Light olive Cactus Chenille
Eyes:	Large painted yellow lead dumbbell eyes

Here is another of Kelly Galloup's unique articulated streamers. He places two closed-cell foam Pee-Wee Pops on the trailing hook shank of this fly. The result on retrieving is a jigging action that takes the fly toward the surface of the water column, rather than to depth. It's a unique action that produces for big browns. Todd Lanning promotes it for use on the big South Fork reach of the Snake River browns, paralleling Kelly's success with Madison River browns.

BOX CANYON DOUBLE BUNNY

Hook:	#1 Gamakatsu J-90
Cone:	Medium tungsten
Thread:	100-denier GSP
Body:	Polar pearl, UV pearl Lite Brite blended and wrapped in a dubbing loop
Overwing:	Olive Zonker Strip
Underwing:	White Zonker Strip
Flash strips:	Rainbow Krystal Flash
Collar:	Red Lite Brite
Adhesive:	Pliobond or Tear Mender

As the season progresses, underwater grasses grow in many rivers of the Greater Yellowstone Area. These grasses make excellent shelter for large salmonids. The Box Canyon reach of the Henry's Fork is a good example of this phenomenon, and Pat Gaffney created this pattern to ride hook point up for fishing around these grasses and the porous, fly-grabbing lava rock in the Box. All season long this is the first streamer out of Pat's box. He uses Pliobond to cement the hide sides of the Zonker Strips that make up the fly's tail. He suggests stripping the fly erratically for best results, but it is also effective when dead-drifting under an indicator in heavy or deep water.

CROSS-EYED RAINBOW

Hook:	#2-6 TMC 777SP
Cone:	Cross-eyed brass
Thread:	Black 6/0 UNI-Thread
Rib:	Medium copper wire
Belly:	White barred Zonker Strip
Body:	Pearl Ice Dub
Wing:	Barred olive Zonker Strip
Throat:	Red dubbing

Nick English developed this pattern. After a few wraps of thread by the eye, slide cone forward on hook shank to the eye and secure in place with superglue. Tie in copper wire. Dub a consistent body, leaving about one-eighth inch behind the cone. Zonker Strips should be twice the length of the body. Use Tear Mender on skin sides to help the rabbit strips bond. Apply the white strip underneath first, sliding hook point through the strip to rest it on the underside of the shank. Tie down by the cone. Apply Tear Mender to the skin side of the olive Zonker Strip, tie it in by the cone, lay flat, and join with the white strip past the hook bend. Spiral the wire forward evenly to secure the rabbit strips together. Tie off wire, then dub a small red throat. Whip-finish. Use a needle or fine-point scissors to pull any rabbit fibers out from under the wire.

CROSS-EYED ZONKER

Hook:	#2-4 Daiichi 2220
Thread:	White A and red A
Underbody:	Lead tape
Body:	Gold or silver Mylar tubing
Head:	Gold or silver X-Eyed cone
Wing:	Dyed olive rabbit strip
Gills:	Red Estaz

Every West Yellowstone fly-fishing retail business offers streamer patterns for early and late season fishing. Many of these patterns, such as the Black Ugly, Blue Ribbon Sculpin, South Branch Chub, Vint's Special, Woolhead Sculpin, as well as this pattern by Arrick Swanson, are in-house patterns—those originating through tying activities of each business.

CW'S BROWN TROUT MINNOW

Hook:	#1/0 Gamakstsu jig hook
Weight/head:	Large gold cone followed by $^3/_{16}$-inch brass bead
Thread:	Red 140-denier UTC Ultra Thread

Body:	Orange Flashabou strands, variegated black/yellow bunny strip tied in at bead, and two variegated blood marabou feathers (black barred white and black barred brown)
Collar:	Variegated brown and black bunny strip
Gills:	Black/red barred marabou fibers.
Eyes:	Yellow doll eyes

To create this pattern by Chris Williams, tie in 8 to 10 strands of orange Flashabou. Wrap Flashabou back to bend, then forward to bead. Tie off and pull remaining strands back over body. Lock in place with thread wraps. Clip Flashabou about one hook length past the bend. Tie in three pieces of black Flashabou on either side, same length as orange piece. Tie in a variegated black barred yellow bunny strip at bead, same length as Flashabou. On underside tie in black barred white marabou quill, same length as Flashabou, then a black barred brown quill, same length as bunny strip. Just behind and covering the bead, wrap collar from variegated black/brown bunny strip. Tie in gills and glue eyes to cone.

CW'S RAINBOW MINNOW

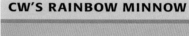

Hook:	#1/0 Gamakstsu jig hook
Weight/head:	Large gold cone followed by $^3/_{16}$-inch bead
Thread:	Red 140-denier UTC Ultra Thread
Body:	Pink, red, and purple Flashabou strands, variegated black/white bunny strip, and two variegated blood marabou feathers (black barred white and black barred olive)

Collar:	Chinchilla bunny strip
Gills:	Black/red barred marabou fibers.
Eyes:	White doll eyes

For this pattern by Chris Williams, tie in 8 to 10 strands of pink Flashabou. Wrap back to bend, then forward to bead. Tie off, and secure back over the body with tying thread. Clip Flashabou to about one hook length past bend. Tie in a piece each of red and purple Flashabou. Cut off same length as pink piece. Tie in variegated black/white bunny strip at bead and two variegated blood marabou feathers (black barred white and black barred olive) on the barbed side of the hook. Tie in on underside black barred white marabou quill, clipped same length as Flashabou, then black barred olive quill, lengths same as bunny strip. Just behind and covering the bead, wrap collar from a chinchilla bunny strip. Tie in gills and cement eyes onto cone.

THE FRANKENSTREAMER

Hook:	#4-8 Daiichi 2546
Thread:	Black 6/0
Tail:	Black marabou
Lower body:	Olive speckled Crystal Chenille
Upper body:	Green/black GlissenGloss chenille
Legs:	White/black barred Centipede Legs
Head:	Large Fish-Skull

Dennie Edwards used this fly late in the season for migrating brown trout. The Fish-Skull head, fairly new in fly-tying materials, ensures that this pattern gets down deep to brown trout migrating to spawning areas. Dennie proved this fly on the South Fork reach of the Snake River, but it is effective on all rivers hosting late season migrating browns. The Greater Yellowstone Area has as many rivers hosting fall migrations of brown trout as any part of our country. Included here are Yellowstone, the Henry's Fork, Madison, Snake, Gibbon, Gardner, Lewis, Gallatin, Salt, and Portneuf, to name a few.

FUR BURGER STREAMER

Hook:	#2 Daiichi 2461
Thread:	6/0, color to match natural
Tail and body:	Whiting Farms Bird Fur
Flash:	Sparse pearl Angel Hair
Collar:	Schlappen, color contrasting to that of body

Tie in along shank, flat-wing style, two feathers 1 to 1½ the shank length. Tie in a few strands of Angel Hair. Tie in by tip and tapered toward rear of hook a Bird Fur feather. Palmer remainder of feather forward while folding fibers toward rear. Repeat with another feather and tie in a few strands of Angel Hair. Repeat until shank is covered. Tie in schlappen by tip and make a few turns to form collar. Whip-finish and varnish head. Rob Parkins, an advocate of Bird Fur, considers Jack Gartside a mentor, thus his creation of this very lifelike fly. His favorite color schemes for this fly include golden olive, tan, coachman brown, white, yellow, or black.

GALLOUP'S OLIVE PEANUT ENVY

Thread:	Olive 100-denier GSP
Back hook:	#6-8 Daiichi 1750
Tail:	Two olive marabou plumes with four copper Flashabou strands between
Hackle:	Olive schlappen or 5- to 7-inch strung saddle
Body:	Olive Ice Dub
Legs:	A pair golden yellow pearl flake Sili Legs each side of shank
Connection:	0.038-inch,19-strand braided stainless-steel wire (Beadalon)
Beads:	Two red glass
Connection cover:	Two olive marabou plumes
Front hook:	#4 Daiichi 1750
Weight:	Large black brass cone
Hackle:	Olive schlappen or 5- to 7-inch strung saddle
Body:	Olive Ice Dub
Legs:	Golden yellow pearl flake Sili Legs
Wing:	Marabou, color to match tails
Collar:	Olive Ice Dub

This pattern by Kelly Galloup is a knockoff of Russ Madden's Circus Peanut. With all parts in motion, it is proving to be one of the most deadly patterns Kelly has developed to date.

GIB'S RABBIT STREAMER

Hook:	#4-12 Dai-Riki 700
Bead:	Black tungsten
Thread:	Tan 6/0 Danville
Underwing:	Gold holographic Mylar, $^1/_{64}$-inch width for small flies, $^1/_{32}$-inch width for larger
Wing:	Tan crosscut rabbit strip, $^1/_{16}$-inch wide

Fly fishers tend to think of spring-creek fishing as requiring very fine leaders and small, delicate flies. This belief may be true for most situations, but those large, wary salmonids inhabiting spring creeks will not refuse a properly presented streamer pattern. Doug Gibson intended this pattern for these super wary inhabitants of spring creeks. He uses a narrow crosscut rabbit strip tightly wrapped around the hook shank to form the wing of this fly. He prefers smaller sizes on such waters to be able to use more delicate rods, lines, and leaders. He also uses this pattern in larger sizes on major waters such as the South Fork reach of the Snake River, the Teton River, and the Madison River.

GOOGLE EYE

Hook:	#4-8 Daiichi #1850
Thread:	140-denier UTC Ultra Thread, color to match body

Eyes:	Medium-sized dumbbell eyes
Body:	Flat Diamond Braid
Inner wing:	Marabou matching body color and a few strands of Krystal Flash
Outer wing:	Grizzly dry-fly saddle tips
Head:	Polar Dub

To create this pattern by Gary Barnes, attach dumbbell eyes ⅛-inch behind hook eye. Glue in place. Attach braid just behind eyes, and wrap back along shank to the barb. Wrap braid forward and tie off just behind the eye. Strip fibers from one side of marabou plume, and tie in by the tip behind the eyes. Wrap plume soft-hackle style, leaving about ⅛-inch behind the eyes. Tie in a few strands of Krystal Flash on top of marabou and tie in hackle tips on sides. The tips create movement and lateral lines. Dub head and whip-finish. Choose colors to simulate those of baitfish present in the waters fished.

ITTY BITTY

Hook:	#6 Daiichi 5108
Cone:	Medium brass Master Cone
Thread:	Tan 70-denier UTC Ultra Thread
Tube:	Black HMH ³⁄₃₂-inch outside diameter tube, 1½ inches long
Body:	Peacock Midge Diamond Braid
Throat:	White Icelandic sheep hair
Underwing:	Black Icelandic sheep hair
Wing:	Yellow saddle under dark pardo Whiting Coq de Leon saddle
Head:	Brown EP Streamer Brush

Gary Barnes enjoys fishing this pattern on an intermediate sinking line, but suggests that to get it into deeper waters weighted or metal tubes should be used. He also suggests changing body component colors to match that of the baitfish present in waters being fished. His favorite version is pictured and described above.

JACKLIN'S BIG EYED BAITFISH

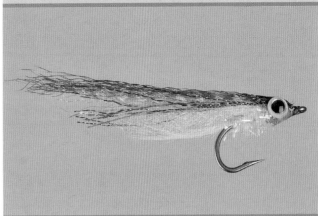

Hook:	#2/0-6 TMC 800S
Thread:	White 140-denier Flymaster
Tail:	White bucktail
Wing:	White CCT Fiber Hair under several strains of silver and pearl Lateral Scale under green Unique Hair under peacock Unique Hair
Body:	Pearl Grande Estaz
Eyes:	Yellow holographic

Bob Jacklin ties in the wing first just behind the hook eye, components pointing forward, and reversed (peacock Unique Hair tied in first, next green Unique Hair, then silver and pearl Lateral Scale, and last white CCT Fiber Hair). He ties in the tail slightly shorter than the body. He ties in the body and brings the wing over the body to form a large head with thread wraps secured in Krazy Glue, then coated with five-minute epoxy. The white CCT fibers and white bucktail simulate a baitfish body. The silver and pearl Lateral Scale simulate the lateral line, and the large head is a base for securing the all-important eyes. Bob originally created this pattern for saltwater fishing but observes that in smaller versions it is deadly for brown trout.

JACKLIN'S YELLOW MUDDLER

Hook:	#8 Dai-Riki 710
Thread:	Black 3/0 Monocord
Tail:	Opposing dyed yellow turkey quill segments
Rib:	Small copper wire
Body:	Flat gold tinsel
Underwing:	Gray squirrel tail hairs
Wing:	Opposing dyed yellow turkey quill segments
Collar:	Tips of spun dyed yellow deer hair
Head:	Trimmed butts of dyed yellow deer hair spun to form collar

This is one of Bob Jacklin's favorite flies for brook trout. Waters hosting brook trout to trophy sizes surround his West Yellowstone home. Perhaps Henry's Lake is the most famed, with individuals ranging as much as eight pounds. Duck Creek and Centennial Valley Streams also host trophy-sized individuals. The upper reaches of the Henry's Fork, Blacktail Ponds, the Firehole River, Nez Perce Creek, and the Gibbon River host large individuals.

JAPALA

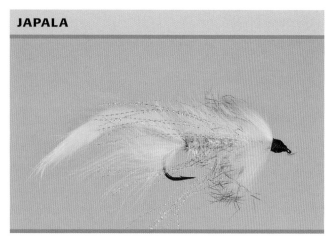

Hook:	#2-4 Mustad 79580
Thread:	Black 6/0 UNI-Thread
Tail:	White marabou fibers

Body:	White Ice Dub
Wing:	Yellow rabbit strip
Collar:	Barred rabbit fur

This is a standard Star Valley pattern for brown trout where the Salt River is famed for hosting very large specimens. During the autumn months there are two distinct runs of spawning brown trout in the Salt River drainage. The earliest, usually peaking around the end of September, is of Salt River fish moving into tributaries such as Crow, Jackknife, and Stump Creeks. The later run, peaking in late October to early November, is of fish moving up from Palisades Reservoir into the Salt River. With its action and predominant yellow color, Josh Peavler's pattern has proven very effective for encountering these brown trout in either spawning run.

LOT LIZARD

Hooks:	#4-8 Daiichi 1850
Thread:	140-denier UTC Ultra Thread, color to match body
Tails:	Marabou fibers
Bodies:	UV Crystal Chenille
Collars:	Whiting hen neck feathers
Wire:	American vinyl coated wire, 11-pound test, 8-inch piece for #4 hook
Eyes:	Medium dumbbell eyes
Head:	UV Polar Dub or mohair

Gary Barnes creates effective patterns for heavy water such as the Madison and Snake Rivers. Wire attaches hooks in this tandem streamer and beads cover the wire in between to significantly reduce fowling. To attach hooks, Gary threads the wire through the completed trailing fly hook eye and slips three to four beads onto the folded wire. He ties the remaining wire up the top of the shank of the lead hook, over the tied-in dumbbell eyes, folds it back on top of the hook shank, and wraps it back to the bend of the hook. He then cements the eyes in place and finishes the lead fly. He ties this mostly with olive materials, but other colors he has found effective include black, brown, yellow, or chartreuse.

LOVE BUNNY

Trailer hook:	#4 Dai-Riki 810
Front hook:	#2 Dai-Riki 810
Thread:	Black 6/0 UNI-Thread
Rear wing:	Black rabbit strip
Rear body:	Black Ice Dub or Cactus Chenille
Joint:	Nylon-coated stainless-steel wire with one black bead
Front wing:	Black rabbit strip
Front body:	Black Ice Dub or Cactus Chenille
Hackle:	Black saddle palmered over front body
Throat:	Red Flashabou strands
Legs:	Black Sili Legs
Collar:	Black saddle hackle
Eyes:	Black I-Balz

This pattern is Walter Weise's articulated streamer for big fish. It is meant for big rivers like the Yellowstone, the Madison, or the South Fork of the Snake River. Use a 7-weight rod and a stout leader. For the joint material in this articulated streamer, Walter prefers Accu-Flex 49-strand nylon-coated stainless-steel bead stringing wire. This item can be found in most craft shops. Walter also ties this pattern in olive, white, or tan.

LUCAS DARK SPRUCE

Hook:	#4 Mustad 79580
Thread:	Black 6/0 UNI-Thread
Tail:	Peacock sword tips
Body:	Rear half red floss, front half peacock herl, looped and twisted to form second half of body
Wing:	Two dyed medium brown grizzly saddle hackles, featherwing quality
Collar:	Saddle hackle used to form wing

The feather-wing streamer has been around for nearly a century, but has become obscured because of the introduction of less expensive synthetic winging materials. Clark Lucas is one of those keeping the featherwing going with this variation of earlier patterns. He recommends using it as a trolling fly from a float tube on Island Park Reservoir in the west end area. Use a slow troll on a full sinking Intermediate Wet Cel II line at any depth it will reach. It proves very effective near springs swelling into the reservoir in late summer.

LUCAS GRIZZLY STREAMER

Hook:	#2 Mustad 79580
Thread:	Black 6/0 UNI-Thread
Tail:	Peacock sword tips
Rib:	Oval silver tinsel
Body:	Flat silver tinsel
Wing:	Two grizzly saddle hackles
Topping:	Peacock swords
Gills:	Red wool yarn
Collar:	Saddle hackle used to form wing

Although one can use separate feathers to wrap the collar of Clark Lucas's pattern after tying in the wing and trimming excess, he suggests that because featherwing quality hackles are in use to form the wing, use the butts of these to wrap the collar after tying in the topping and gills. Again, he suggests using a slow troll on a full sinking Intermediate Wet Cel II line at any depth it will reach in stillwaters.

MARABOU MINNOW

Hook:	#6 Dai-Riki 700
Bead:	Gold
Thread:	Pale yellow Kevlar

Tail:	Six Krystal Flash strands in colors of marabou (black, yellow, pearl)
Body/wing:	Mixed black and yellow blood marabou plumes
Hackle:	Krystal Flash fibers in colors of marabou (black, yellow, pearl)

Jay Buchner ties in the two marabou plumes by the tips at the rear of the hook, twists the plumes around the tying thread, and wraps the result forward in an open spiral to fill the hook shank. He ties in pearl Krystal Flash by cutting retail length fibers in quarters, placing them in split thread that is twisted, folded, and wrapped at the head. This fly is designed to withstand rigors of the Jackson Hole One Fly contest in which it won, in 2009, first and second places. In this renowned event, contestants choose a single fly each day to be fished during the two-day contest. Proceeds from this renowned event go to preserve the native cutthroat trout fishery in the Snake River watershed.

MINCH'S PERCH CANDY

Hook:	#10-12 Dai-Riki 710
Bead:	Gold
Thread:	Chartreuse 6/0 Flymaster
Tail:	Chartreuse marabou fibers with three strands of green Krystal Flash on each side
Body:	Dan Bailey's chartreuse short flash chenille
Hackle:	Grizzly dyed olive or yellow saddle

Montana's part of the Greater Yellowstone Area has only a few warmwater fisheries, of which Dailey and Cutler Lakes are among the most productive. Matt Minch's pattern was intended for yellow perch and other warmwater species in these and other Montana lakes, but to his surprise, a 27-inch rainbow took this fly in Dailey

Lake. Pike and bass in these lakes seem to prefer this pattern in larger sizes.

MINI BUNNY

Hook:	#6 Dai-Riki 710
Cone:	Medium silver
Weight:	0.030-inch-diameter lead-free wire
Thread:	Gray 3/0
Body:	Clump of dubbed white rabbit fur, pearl Ice Dub mixture
Wing:	Pine squirrel strip
Eyes:	Molded eyes, $^7/_{32}$-inch diameter
Adhesive:	Latex contact cement (Val-A Tear Mender) and GOOP

After placing a cone behind the eye of a hook, wrap lead wire around the shank and push the wire into the cone recess. This holds the cone in place. Wrap bunches of the dubbing mixture up the shank beginning at the bend and ending behind the cone. Comb out the dubbed body with scissors or bodkin, and trim the top surface just above the shank. Tie in the squirrel strip at the cone and apply Val-A Tear Mender adhesive to its hide and the trimmed top of the body. Press the two surfaces together to bond. GOOP could also be used for the squirrel strip. Use GOOP to cement the eyes in place with leading edge just under the cone. Scott Sanchez recommends this pattern as a small, mobile streamer. He prefers a 2X long, size 6 streamer hook to achieve more hook bite.

MISS NAURINE

Hook:	#2-6 Mustad 33903 (kink shank)
Thread:	3/0 Danville
Head:	Balsa wood carved to shape, primed, airbrushed orange ventral surface with olive dorsal surface, and finish coating applied
Eyes:	Enamel paints, white iris, black pupils
Underwing:	Marabou fibers white, orange, red, bottom to top, with 10–12 pearl Krystal Flash strands between white and orange marabou
Wing:	Dyed orange cape hackle pair
Overwing:	Light olive marabou fibers
Collar:	Teal flank feather fibers
Cement:	Fast-drying epoxy
Finish:	Twenty-minute epoxy or shellac

LeRoy Cook makes this streamer in rainbow, brown, brook trout, and whitefish themes. His generic theme is described above. The finished head is cemented to the hook first, and the wing and collar components tied on. LeRoy presents this fly using a sinking-tip line. Buoyancy of its balsa head imparts a jigging action that attracts large trout.

NEW FORK KILLER

Hook:	#2 TMC 8089
Weight:	0.030-inch-diameter lead-free wire, optional conehead
Thread:	Olive 6/0 Gudebrod
Front shank:	Stamina Tackle open-loop wire shaft
Tail:	Black marabou
Rib:	Medium red wire
Bodies:	Olive chenille
Hackle:	Dyed yellow grizzly saddle
Legs:	Barred olive and black Sili Legs

Tie in tail and form body on hook first. Remove hook from vise, and insert eye into open end of wire shaft. Place hook at looped end and use needle-nosed pliers to form loop in front end of shaft. Place rear loop of shaft in vise and cover its shank with tying thread. Form chenille body with legs, hackle, and rib on shank of shaft. This is another of Bruce James's go-to flies for big browns.

PINE SQUIRREL STREAMER

Hook:	#4-8 Daiichi #1850
Thread:	GSP 75, color to match body
Head:	Cone

Wing:	Strip of pine squirrel hide, $\frac{1}{8}$-inch-wide dyed olive
Body:	Strip of pine squirrel hide, $\frac{1}{8}$-inch-wide dyed olive close wrapped from above hook bend to behind head

Gary Barnes's pattern is one of the first in the region to use pine squirrel for both wing and body. In tying it, Gary first ties on the strip to form the wing, leaving part extending to the rear about the length of the hook shank. Then he forms the body with wraps of another pine squirrel strip. As an option for more weight to sink deeper, he places a bead into the recess of the rear of the cone before tying in the wing and forming the body. This fly was the official logo for the 2010 East Idaho Fly Tying/Fly Fishing Expo.

RUBBER RABBIT STRIP

Hook:	#2-6 Dai-Riki 710
Eyes:	Medium gold dumbbell eyes
Thread:	Olive 3/0
Rib:	Fine gold wire
Body:	Olive Estaz
Throat:	Red Krystal Flash
Wing:	Olive rabbit strip
Legs:	Montana Fly Company fine rubber legs

When tying this fly, Vic Loiselle first ties on and then secures the dumbbell eyes. He next ties in the rabbit strip at the bend of the hook, leaving about half an inch of hide trailing behind for a size 4 hook and enough in front to cover the top of the shank to the eyes. Bending back the strip, he ties in the wire rib and the Estaz body material. He then wraps the body (leaving enough to figure-eight around the eyes). Then he places the rabbit strip over the body and secures each to the other using turns of wire. The throat material ties next, then the rubber legs, then the head by figure-eight wraps of Estaz. Other color schemes Vic suggests include black, white, or brown.

SCLEECH

Trailer hook:	#6 Dai-Riki 135
Front hook:	#4 Dai-Riki 810
Thread:	Black 6/0 UNI-Thread
Joint:	30-pound Power Pro with 6/0 silver-lined black glass beads
Wing:	Black rabbit strip
Collar:	Black rabbit strip wrapped forward 2–3 turns.
Throat:	Red holographic Flashabou strands
Back:	Black Widow's Web tied on the bottom of the hook shank (top of completed fly) only
Head:	Black Widow's Web applied from a dubbing loop and trimmed to shape
Eyes:	Black I-Balz

This is Walter Weise's articulated streamer when looking for quantity and quality trout. The front hook takes arger individuals, which attack at the head, while the stinger hook takes the tail nippers, especially cutthroat. Not securing the rear part of the Zonker Strip wing and the swinging beads add action. Walter also offers this pattern in olive, white, tan, and a brown/yellow combination.

SEX DUNGEON

Thread:	Black 100-denier GSP
Back hook:	#6 Daiichi 1750
Tail:	Two black marabou plumes with four copper Flashabou strands between
Hackle:	Black schlappen
Body:	Black Ice Dub
Legs:	Three pair olive/black Sili Legs
Connection:	0.038-inch 19-strand braided stainless-steel wire (Beadalon)
Beads:	Two red glass
Front hook:	#4 Daiichi 1750
Hackle:	Black schlappen
Body:	Black Ice Dub
Legs:	Three pair olive/black Sili Legs
Collar and head:	Trimmed black deer hair
Eyes:	Large painted dumbbell eyes

The black Sex Dungeon is described and pictured above. Kelly Galloup also ties a rust, an olive, and a white version. In fact, this fly tied in any color is deadly for large trout. It has superb movement in three dimensions and therefore is more likely to trigger responses from foraging trout. Kelly ties the dumbbell eyes on the underside of the front hook shank, and glass beads are meant to stiffen the connection between hooks. The Sex Dungeon has become a popular streamer pattern.

SHINER MINNOW

Hook:	#10 TMC 8089
Weight:	Gold tungsten cone ahead of $^5/_{32}$-inch-diameter silver tungsten bead
Thread:	Red 6/0 UNI-Thread
Gillplate:	Red 6/0 UNI-Thread
Belly:	Six pearl Flashabou strands, cream marabou, golden brown marabou
Sides:	Three strands orange marabou
Topping:	Four gold Krystal Flash strands
Eyes:	3D eyes

Elden Berrett builds a thread base and adds a drop of glue to firmly seat the cone and bead. The wide gap hook used improves hooking potential of his pattern. He uses Hard As Nails Strengthening Topcoat to set the eyes on the gill plate formed from tying thread wraps. The colors of the version pictured above simulate a shiner minnow, but by changing the top-side color to sculpin olive, this pattern simulates a rainbow trout minnow. Another favorite color combination for Elden is black marabou on top of yellow marabou. Elden proved this pattern on the main stem of the Snake River below Idaho Falls. He recommends a sinking-tip line for presenting this pattern.

SIMPLE ZONKER

Hook:	#4-8 Daiichi 2220
Thread:	White Monocord to tie on rabbit strip, black for remainder of fly, both 6/0
Tail/wing:	White rabbit strip
Body:	Rainbow Crystal Chenille
Gills:	Red saddle hackle fibers or rabbit body fur

Tightly tie in a three-inch rabbit strip at the top of the hook bend. Tie in chenille with the white thread at the same place as the rabbit strip, and form the body. Tie off the white thread behind the hook eye, and tie in black thread to finish the fly. Coat the bottom of the strip with a liberal amount of superglue, and pull it forward and down onto the body. Press down on the strip to secure to the body, and tie off at the head. The fly discussed above is a White Simple Zonker, but try this fly by Buddy Knight in any color combination.

SNIPER

Hook:	#4-6 Daiichi 1750
Thread:	Black 6/0 UNI-Thread
Tail:	Black marabou with a few orange-dyed guinea feather fibers on either side

Body: Orange/black variegated Krystal Chenille

Hackle: Orange-dyed guinea feather tied soft-hackle style

Tim Blount has several versions of this Woolly Bugger-like streamer pattern. This is the Halloween-style version because of the predominant orange and black colors. Others versions are black, brown, chartreuse, olive, and purple. He also has a version for fishing steelhead. Fish this pattern as you would any other streamer pattern. Tim particularly likes this pattern for fooling brown trout.

SOFT HACKLE STREAMER

Hook: #2-6 Mustad 3406

Thread: Red 6/0

Body: None

Hackle: White blood marabou wound as hackle with a few strands of silver Mylar

Collar: Mallard flank feather folded and wound on as hackle

This is the original Jack Gartside classic, an ultimately effective streamer for any season. We present it here, as with the original Chernobyl Ant, to show how variations have been made to this ever-popular pattern. Jack first used it for taking autumn brown and rainbow trout ascending the Madison River from Hebgen Lake. He also gave the tying instructions given above. As with any popular pattern, this one has undergone several variations. Mylar of various colors and multiple marabou colors now make up the wing, and some tiers add a brass bead to run the fly deeper. Even the facing has been altered—peacock body feathers, various pheasant feathers, and schlappen dyed various colors are now used.

SQUONKER

Hook: #2-10 Partridge Barbless Ideal Nymph

Thread: Black 12/0 Benecchi

Rib: Fine copper wire

Body: Chestnut-dyed pine squirrel underfur

Wing: Olive-brown dyed pine squirrel Zonker Strip

Collar: Chestnut-dyed pine squirrel guard hairs

"Squ" is for squirrel; "onker" is for zonker. Hans Weilenmann offers this unique but generic "Zonker-style" pattern and suggests that colors can be changed to conform to those of baitfish in any particular water. Olive themes would also be suitable for simulating baitfish in Greater Yellowstone Area waters. Hans uses the split thread dubbing technique to form the collar of this pattern.

STREAMLINER II

Hook:	#4-6 Mustad 32756
Thread:	Black 3/0 Monocord
Weight:	Brass Dazl Eyes, $^5/_{32}$-inch diameter or $^7/_{32}$-inch diameter
Body:	Gold variant rabbit strip
Venter:	Silver marabou
Throat:	Red marabou
Flash:	Two strands of pearl Krystal Flash folded twice

According to Harley Reno, this is an ideal streamer pattern for all species of trout in all waters of the area. Harley first proved it in waters on the Beartooth Plateau and surrounding mountains. Harley lives adjacent to the South Fork reach of the Snake River, and this pattern has proven deadly there. It is tied on a jig hook to ride with hook point up. It and its antecedent, Streamliner, are his number-one flies for all seasons and all reasons.

SUMI'S SOLDIER PALMER STREAMER

Hook:	#8 Dai-Riki 270
Thread:	Pink 6/0
Tail:	Yellow poly yarn and pearl Krystal Flash strands

Rib:	Fine gold wire
Body:	Yellow or orange Cactus Chenille
Hackle:	Dry badger saddle
Head:	Orange dubbing

The allure of the Henry's Fork has brought many fly fishers to transfer to eastern Idaho, including Sumi Saka-maki. A Golden West Women Flyfishers original member and Andy Puyans's student, Sumi specializes in patterns for the Harriman State Park reach and the lower Henry's Fork near her home. When fished near the surface over shallow water, this pattern takes large browns foraging on baitfish. Sumi named it from the venerable Soldier Palmer pattern in which the hackle is palmered over the body.

SWAMPMAN

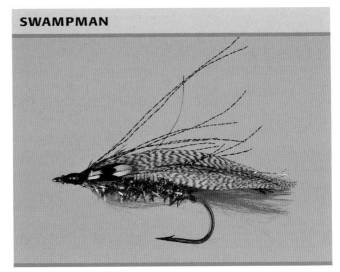

Hook:	#2-6 Partridge D7A
Thread:	Black 70-denier UTC Ultra Thread
Tail:	Red over orange marabou fibers
Body:	Green Crystal Chenille
Beard:	Orange marabou
Underwing:	Black, red, and white Krystal Flash in mixed strands
Wing:	Pair of dyed green mallard, widgeon, or teel flank
Topping:	Black Krystal Flash and red Flashabou
Cheeks:	Jungle cock nail

LeRoy Cook strips away fibers from one side of each feather he uses to form the wing of this pattern. He then mounts them tent-style in the fashion of a roof on a classic Atlantic salmon fly. This is a good streamer pattern for fishing discolored waters early in the season, as well as an effective pattern for fall spawning brook and brown trout.

TLF BLEEDING MINNOW

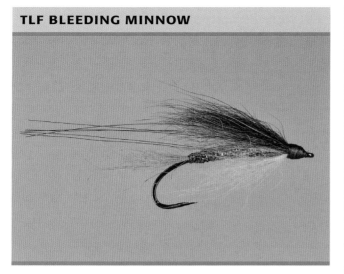

Hook:	#2-10 TMC 200R
Weight:	Flat or round lead-free wire wrapped on entire shank to near hook eye
Thread:	Gray 6/0 to 8/0 UNI-Thread
Tail:	Gray Arctic fox tail guard hairs
Underbody:	Arctic fox tail guard hairs butts covered with tying thread
Body:	Flat multicolored tinsel color to match natural lateral line
Belly:	White arctic fox tail guard hairs
Underwing:	Gray Arctic fox tail guard hairs
Wing:	Arctic fox guard hairs color to match natural
Blood Trails:	Three fibers per side of Marc Petitjean Ice Fiber Red Max

A wounded minnow trailing blood is sure to attract foraging trout, but Jerry Criss couldn't find a streamer designed to imitate such a situation. He went to his tying bench and created this pattern. Immediately on presenting it, slamming takes happened. Now Jerry advocates adding materials simulating a delicate blood trail to any streamer pattern. He suggests Marc Petitjean Ice Fiber Red Max because of its delicate nature, but a few red floss fibers or very fine Mylar work as well.

UGLY SCULPY

Hook:	#1 Gamakatsu worm-rigging hook
Conehead:	$^{7}/_{32}$-inch-diameter tungsten or brass
Bead:	Red glass
Thread:	Olive 6/0 Danville Flymaster
Tail:	Olive-dyed barred rabbit strip topped with dark olive Flashabou strands
Wing:	Gray/black barred marabou behind olive barred marabou
Collar:	Dyed olive grizzly schlappen

With the bulk of this fly toward the front, it is ideal for simulating the triangular shape of a sculpin. Ron Hicks obtains bulk and motion through winding a dense marabou wing soft-hackle style. Weight gets it to the bottom of the deepest holds in rivers. The glass bead holds the cone firmly against the jig hook bend. One of his favorite locations to present this fly is in the Yellowstone River below Gardiner, Montana, during the autumn brown trout migration,but a fly like this would be great for migrating browns anywhere.

UV GRAY CLOUSER

Hook:	#1 Gamakatsu SS15
Thread:	Gray 3/0 Monocord
Eyes:	Silver dumbbell Real Eyes, $^7/_{32}$-inch diameter
Underwing:	White bucktail
Body:	Butt ends of bucktail underwing overwrapped with UV Krystal Flash, then white bucktail
Rib:	Tying thread
Midwing:	Rainbow Angel Hair
Overwing:	Gray bucktail

Large South Fork reach of Snake River and the lower Henry's Fork browns are the reasons for this Clouser variation. Paul Bowen has had many encounters with these trophies. This pattern gets down deep to them in holes and runs with strong currents. Butt ends of bucktail underwing tied in along shank are overwrapped with UV Krystal Flash, the ends of which secure eyes then form second underwing above white bucktail. Paul finishes the head of this fly with Hard as Hull cement used frequently on saltwater patterns.

WHITEFISH CLOUSER

Hook:	#4 Mustad 1197B
Thread:	Olive 140-denier UTC Ultra Thread
Dumbbell eyes:	Montana Fly Company Sparkle Eyes
Body:	EP Fibers in three equal amounts: shades of gray grading from lightest on bottom to darkest on top
Lateral line:	Blue/gray Angel Hair
Gills:	Red Body Fur tied at rear of eyes as a "V"
Collar:	UV Polar Chenille

Rocky Mountain whitefish inhabit most streams and some stillwaters of the region. In these waters they are numerous and therefore prey for large salmonids. Schools of fingerling whitefish are particularly targeted by these salmonids. Noticing this, Allan Woolley modified the original Clouser Minnow to better simulate small whitefish. An optional tungsten cone placed in front of the eyes sinks this pattern into deep waters.

WEISE'S PT BUGGER

WEISE'S SWIMMING MINNOW

Hook:	#4-6 Dai-Riki 710
Thread:	Black 6/0 UNI-Thread
Tail:	Brown and tan marabou with black Krystal Flash strands
Rib (optional):	Gold wire
Body:	Medium tan and black brindle chenille
Palmered hackle:	Grizzly or natural chinchilla saddle
Collar:	Ring-necked pheasant church window feather
Eyes:	Brass hourglass eyes

Walter Weise uses a ring-necked pheasant church window feather as a collar to push more water. The barbell eyes make it ride hook up. This is his primary sculpin pattern for Yellowstone National Park waters. He sink-strips it or presents it under an indicator with an occaisional twitch. Try it for Lewis River channel brown and lake trout just after ice-out and on the Yellowstone River in the fall and at the tail end of runoff.

Hook:	#2-6 Da-Riki 710 or 810
Thread:	Yellow 6/0 UNI-Thread
Underwing:	Yellow bucktail
Gills/throat:	Red Flashabou
Belly:	Yellow marabou
Lateral line:	Black Krystal Flash
Wing:	Brown bucktail
Eyes:	Brass I-Balz

Walter Weise's Clouser variation is legal for fishing in Yellowstone National Park because he uses brass eyes rather than lead. The red throat, suggesting gills or blood, and yellow marabou belly impart action, particularly when this fly is fished dead drift under an indicator. The marabou belly also gives the thicker cross section that trout seem to prefer. Strip it or fish it dead drift under an indicator. Walter recommends this fly for lake trout in lakes such as Heart, Lewis, Shoshone, and Yellowstone, as well as on Yellowstone River floats shortly after runoff recedes. Other color schemes include all black, chartreuse and white, brown with a white belly and black flash, and gray and white.

CHAPTER 9

TERRESTRIAL INSECTS

Essentially all of the Greater Yellowstone Area is in excess of four thousand feet in elevation. Therefore abundance of terrestrial insects throughout the area takes time to develop because of cooler air temperatures at higher elevations. It begins in lowlands sometime in May, with ants and beetles making up the vanguard. By July, other types of insects emerge at locations even around six thousand feet in elevation. Almost by design, the increase of hoppers, true flies, and others coincides with the decrease in the early season aquatic insect activity peak, and increasingly they take over the available food forms for salmonids with the declining number of available aquatic insects (mobile nymphs, emerging insects, egg-laying insects, duns, spinners, etc.). As summer advances, other terrestrial insects make appearances, particularly concentrations of true flies. Blow flies, deer flies, and horse flies take over from mosquitoes as designated pests.

But herein lies opportunity, and the reason for the enduring popularity of the Humpy (or Goofus Bug if you are in Montana). Many times on open reaches of regional streams I have swatted inch-long horse flies, then flipped them, squashed to immobility, into the water. I fish with one ear tuned to events downstream, and sure enough, shortly I hear the surging burble of a fish rising to take my squashed offering. Next I stop to be sure a standard Humpy is on my line to drift near the position of the fish that took the squashed offering. Call it chumming if you will, but my success would make an advocate out of any fly fisher!

But as July moves on, hoppers rule the roost established by terrestrial insects. All sizes are present. Their supremacy lasts until killing frosts of early October arrive. Like the popular stoneflies, patterns for hoppers in the region have become more numerous over the decades. In fact, this dual popularity is one reason for the upsurge of closed-cell foam as a popular construction material for both. Coming into popularity during the 1980s in Utah waters, closed-cell foam was first used in Allan Woolley's Chernobyl Ant. Now versions of this fly and spin-offs are also nearly too numerous to count. Hopper and stonefly patterns—as well as beetle, ant, and moth patterns—that are tied using closed-cell foam have become effective and immensely popular on streams of gradient throughout the region. It is no wonder, considering their low cost, ease of use, supreme buoyancy, and high visibility.

On streams of lesser gradient and stillwaters, foam patterns for terrestrial insect forms remain effective but share popularity with patterns tied with traditional materials. The popularity of closed-cell foam is part of the rise in use of a variety of synthetic materials in the construction of fly patterns for salmonids. About three decades ago, West Yellowstone's Blue Ribbon Flies was in the vanguard of evaluating and applying many of these synthetics.

Gaining extreme popularity is another terrestrial insect that pupates in conifers during July and flies in August: the destructive Western Spruce Budworm moth (Spruce fly). It has been only in the last five decades that fly fishers have realized their importance as a food form for salmonids. True, this importance is mostly on streams flowing through conifer forests, but these forests are numerous in the Greater Yellowstone Area. Initially adult caddisfly patterns were used to simulate it (and these remain effective), but innovative tiers began introducing specific patterns. Beginning with Jack Gartside's pattern for these back in the 1970s, patterns are now flowing from tying vises in the region.

Another terrestrial insect peaking in appearance about the same time as the Spruce fly, but without the same extent of attention, is the flying ant. It has been around forever, and can be seen on every water type on which they fall after mating and egg laying. When trout become aware of its appearance, they key on their drifting forms in an obvious expression of preference. I've seen the surfaces of such lakes as Hebgen, Beula, and Hering dappled with enough of them to confound gulper fisherman who did not anticipate their presence.

The importance of terrestrial insects as a salmonid food form fills a midseason void in the region. From the decline of terrestrial insects' early-season aquatic emergence peak to their lesser late season peak when the streamers emerge, these fly patterns are the ticket to much success.

ARKANSAS HOPPER

Hook:	#2-6 Dai-Riki 710
Thread:	Red 6/0 UNI-Thread
Underbody:	Narrow tan closed-cell foam
Overbody:	Brown closed-cell foam
Wing:	Flesh Widow's Web
Kicker legs:	Tan closed-cell foam and black/red Sili Legs
Legs:	Tan/gray barred round rubber legs
Head:	Peacock herl
Bullet head:	Tan closed-cell foam
Indicator:	Yellow closed-cell foam

John Way wraps the hook shank with red tying thread before forming the body of this fly. When tying on the foam strip underbody, he allows the red thread to be visible, giving an important tone to the finished fly. He forms kicker legs by tying in, then supergluing segments of black/red Sili Legs to the end of tan foam strip "thighs." He trims this foam strip–Sili Legs combination to proper length and ties in one of each on either side at front of the body. Before tying in wing, legs, and head,

he ties in the butt end of the foam strip that will become the bullet head. After finishing the wing, head, and legs, he forms the bullet head, the extension of which secures the wing. This is John's go-to hopper pattern for the Madison River drainage.

AUNT STACKER

Hook:	#13-19 TMC 103BL
Thread:	Purple 8/0 UNI-Thread
Rear body:	Purple dubbing ball
Rear hackle:	Cree or grizzly stacker style
Middle body:	Peacock herl
Front body:	Purple dubbing ball
Hackle:	Cree or grizzly stacker style

Here is Tom Harman's favorite ant pattern. Ants are on the water in varying numbers most of the season until frosty days. Thus Tom fishes this pattern most of the season, and he believes it to be as effective as the classic attractors: Bivisible, Renegade, Royal Wulff, all of which have a reputation for being good ant patterns.

BEETLE

Hook:	#14-16 Daiichi 1760
Thread:	Black 6/0 UNI-Thread
Shellback:	Black deer body hair
Body:	Three peacock herls
Legs:	Small black and purple
Hackle:	Black saddle

Steve Potter trims the hackle fibers from top and bottom before he ties the deer-hair shellback in place. This is a great beetle imitation that has fooled some large trout in Slough Creek and other Greater Yellowstone Area waters. Steve relies on it during summer days when no surface activity is seen. Giving it a slight twitch every 15 seconds or so seems to result in a take. Steve also uses this pattern as an Alderfly imitation.

BIBIO MARCI

Hook:	#14 Kamasan B175
Thread:	Black 12/0 Benecchi
Abdomen:	Dubbed black seal fur
Legs:	Pair of two knotted magpie tail barbs

Wing:	Two strands of pearl Gutermann Holoshimmer
Thorax:	Dubbed orange seal fur behind black seal fur
Thorax cover:	Black 2-mm closed-cell foam
Head:	Trimmed butt of thorax cover

Hans Weilenmann intends this pattern to simulate the St. Mark's Fly (*Bibio marci*) that emerges during springtime in many places worldwide. As is typical of so many of Hans's creations, this one is versatile. I see it also as a great cricket imitation, and thus include it here. Hans suggests that any black-wing feather barb in proportion can be substituted for magpie. Pearl Flashabou should be a good substitute for pearl Gutermann Holoshimmer.

BLACK NECTARINE

Hook:	#12-18 TMC 2312
Thread:	Black 8/0 UNI-Thread
Abdomen:	Black HOH CEN dubbing
Rib:	Black hackle, palmered and clipped
Antennae:	Two black hackle stems, stripped
Wings:	Reversed wrapped dyed black mallard flank feathers
Thorax:	Black HOH CEN dubbing

This nectarine variation from Doug Andres is an excellent cricket imitation. Take off the antennae, and it can also be a beetle pattern. See description of the Green Nectarine on page 50 for tying details. Doug notes that on windy days while fishing the Firehole and Madison Rivers this pattern has been effective, especially along grassy banks that shelter both crickets and beetles. If this pattern is tough to see on broken water, a brightly colored indicator can be added at the wing tie-in point.

BOOM HOPPER

Hook:	#10 TMC 2312
Thread:	Tan UTC Ultra Thread, GSP 50 for head
Body:	Bleached cow elk
Rib:	Fine monofilament
Thorax:	Amber Superfine Dubbing
Legs:	Grizzly hackle stems dyed orange, clipped to shape and bent using hot needle
Underwing:	Badger fur
Wing:	Mottled oak turkey segment
Head:	Deer hair dyed golden brown, spun and clipped to shape

The abundance of grasshoppers in season throughout the region and their importance as food for salmonids is the basis for the rich variety of hopper patterns originating here. Every accomplished tier has a hopper pattern to offer. This is Shawn Bostic's offering. It is very new but has a great future.

BUMBLE

Hook:	#2-6 Mustad 33903 (kink shank)
Body:	Balsa wood carved to shape, primed, yellow marking pen for body and green stippled back, and finish coating applied
Eyes:	Black enamel
Front legs:	Fine black rubber legs
Kicker legs:	Top segments carved into balsa body, bottom segments medium black and orange barred rubber legs
Cement:	Fast-drying epoxy
Finish:	Twenty-minute epoxy or shellac

LeRoy Cook's method of carving top ends of kicker legs from the balsa stock used for the body is unique. He uses Epoxy wood filler to fill the slot in the balsa body where the hook is fitted. Small holes are drilled in the body before painting for inserting and cementing all legs. This fly is a superb floater, but because of its hard body, response to a strike must be without hesitation.

BURKADA

Hook:	#6 Daiichi 1850
Thread:	Iron gray 6/0 UNI-Thread
Body:	Black 6-mm craft foam
Rib:	Neon orange UNI-Thread and olive/pearl Flashabou strip
Wing:	Burkada cicada wing pair imprinted on 0.10-mm-thick clear plastic sheeting
Legs:	Orange speckled Sexi Legs
Indicator:	White Sharpie

To create this pattern by Ken Burkholder, cut an asymmetrical "football" shaped body from black craft foam. Form a Burkada cicada wing from a clear plastic sheet. Vein it with a marking pen. Tie in ribbing ends, then cover hook shank with tying thread. Bind the short end of the "football" body on top of entire hook shank, forming a well-tapered belly covered with tying thread. Remainder of foam must point forward. Hold foam end perpendicular to shank, and superglue belly thoroughly to prevent twisting. Rib belly with tying thread then with Flashabou between thread wraps. Superglue entire belly and allow to dry. Superglue top of belly and fold remaining foam backward to adhere to belly. Tie in foam at point about one-third shank length behind eye, forming head. Tie in wing pair just behind head. Tie in legs at same location and add superglue to secure wings and legs. Paint indicator on head for visibility.

CHERNOBYL ANT (ORIGINAL PATTERN)

Hook:	#8-10 Dai-Riki 060
Thread:	Black 3/0 waxed Danville Monocord
Body:	Black Evazote Sheet Foam strip trimmed to shape
Legs:	Two pair fine black rubber legs
Indicator:	Doubled-over white Evazote Sheet Foam strip

This is the original Chernobyl Ant pattern as created by Allan Woolley. We include it to compare with the elaborate closed-cell foam patterns of today. Allan created this pattern soon after Ukraine's 1986 Chernobyl nuclear power plant disaster. The pattern was a "guide's fly": very simple, fast, and easy to tie; unsinkable and easy for clients to see. When CDC came in vogue, he replaced the white foam indicator strip with a large CDC tuft that had a "parachute effect," making the fly land upright. He still uses this pattern on the South Fork reach of the Snake River, and the Henry's Fork. It is another example of how effective a simple pattern can be, and is certainly as effective in the hands of a skilled fly fisher as its more elaborate successors in the world of closed-cell foam patterns.

CICADA

Hook:	#8 Daiichi 2220
Thread:	Danville flat-waxed nylon for hollow hair steps, 140-denier UTC Ultra Thread for remainder of fly
Body:	Stacked deer or cow elk hair, rust brown, black, and yellow
Antennae:	Hackle stems
Legs:	Small black and yellow Centipede Legs
Hackle:	Grizzly or grizzly dyed brown saddle

Steve Potter stacks the deer-hair body with the predominant rust brown color going on first. Next, on top of the hook shank, he stacks black, then yellow, before trimming to shape. He added legs after observing the popularity of rubber legs on area patterns. Almost immediately this pattern produced on regional waters that he visited. On a South Fork reach of the Snake River float trip, he used this fly as an indicator with either a Zebra Midge or Copper John Dropper. These were effective combinations until larger browns became more interested in the cicada.

CRAIG'S HOUSE FLY

Hook:	#18-22 TMC 900BL
Thread:	Olive dun 8/0 UNI-Thread
Body:	Dyed black peacock herl fibers

Wing:	Two strands dyed light dun Z-Lon
Thorax:	Dyed black peacock herl fibers
Head:	Trimmed butts of peacock herl

After wrapping body of this fly by Craig Mathews, tie in wings to rest at 45-degree angle to shank. Use remainder of peacock herl to form thorax beginning over wing tie-in point. After tying off fly, clip excess peacock herl to form head in proportion to hook size. House flies, deer flies, horse flies, and blow flies are everywhere by summer. They fall into all waters, and fish key on them. They therefore should have representations in every fly box during this part of the season.

CREETLE

Hook:	#10-16 Daiichi 1180
Thread:	143-denier Gudebrod
Body:	2-mm craft foam
Legs:	Super Floss
Wing:	Early season cow elk
Indicator:	Contrasting 2-mm craft foam

Wayne Luallen's pattern mimics a beetle and/or cricketlike terrestrial and, even when dark in color, is visible in the water. Segment the underbody by "bubbling" sections as tying thread is firmly wound back to the bend prior to pulling the back over toward the hook eye. Lock hair butts in place by tying them behind the hook eye and at the "waist" prior to putting on legs and pulling the foam "head" back over. Though tied in a variety of colors (including yellow foam and black thread to match a bee/wasp), tan with dark brown thread, all black, or black with maroon legs seem most effective. Creetle is useful in summer, and also during a hatch, much like using an ant during a Trico hatch. Foam strips are easily cut with a rotary cutter on a hard plastic surface using a metal ruler guide. Leg material is easily separated like floss for smaller flies by nicking the tip and pealing apart.

DANDY'S RUBBER LEG HOPPER

DAVE'S HOPPER

Hook:	#6-10 Dai-Riki 700
Thread:	Gray 140-denier UTC Ultra Thread
Tail:	Red hackle fibers
Rib:	Trimmed brown hackle stem
Body:	Olive Antron
Wing:	Ozark turkey quill segment trimmed to shape and lacquered
Legs:	Tan/yellow barred rubber legs
Collar/overwing:	Tips of deer head used to form head
Head:	Deer body hair spun and trimmed to shape

Dandy Reiner spins deer body hair to form the collar and head, then ties in the rubber legs at the base of the collar. She cuts the head to shape, being careful to hold legs to the rear during the trimming process. Her pattern has gained a superb reputation for being effective on Slough Creek, the Lamar River, and the Yellowstone River.

Hook:	#6-14 TMC 5263
Thread:	Yellow 3/0 for body, size A for head
Tail:	Dyed red deer hair
Rib:	Clipped light brown or ginger hackle
Body:	Cream or yellow poly yarn
Underwing:	Gray (original) or yellow deer body hair
Wing:	Turkey or peacock wing quill sections
Legs:	Knotted golden pheasant tail segments
Head:	First deer hair clump for collar and rear of head, second for front of head

According to Dave Whitlock, this pattern is a hybrid of Joe's Hopper and Dan Bailey's Muddler Minnow. After Jay Buchner showed Dave a Dick Alf hopper that had ring-necked cock pheasant tail barbules jointed by an overhand knot to create kicker legs, Dave tied some on his hopper and liked their looks. Photography of live adult hoppers from underwater also revealed to Dave the dominance of legs in the hopper silhouette. Thus this version became the best known commercial hopper pattern and remains sought-after today by fly fishers throughout the Greater Yellowstone Area.

DELEKTABLE FLYING ANT CINNAMON

Hook:	#16-18 Daiichi 1170
Thread:	Brown 6/0 Danville waxed
Abdomen:	Cinnamon UV Ice Dub
Wing:	One large white CDC plume
Hackle:	Brown saddle
Thorax:	Cinnamon UV Ice Dub
Legs:	Small brown Spanflex

One of Dan Delekta's variations when tying this pattern is to color the cinnamon Ice Dub with a red Sharpie after the fly is completed, adding depth. In forming the wing, he layers the CDC plume in three pieces: tip in the middle and lower sections on either side, resulting in a tent effect. He prefers Spanflex for the legs because it doesn't degrade as fast as rubber legs. He adds the legs, one piece per side, over the first dubbed layer of thorax, and dubs a second layer that helps separate the legs. For finishing the fly, Dan uses a drop of superglue on the end of the dubbing; then he makes one turn around the hook shank. When the dubbing with the glue comes in contact with the dubbing on the hook shank, the fly is completed.

DFH HOPPER

Hook:	#8-12 Dai-Riki 730
Thread:	Yellow 6/0 UNI-Thread
Tails:	Two strands of red Wonder Wrap (Spandex)
Body:	Amber UV Frog's Hair Dubbing
Overbody:	2-mm gold foam folded into a bullet head in front
Wing:	Caddis tan Widow's Web
Legs:	Barred gold/yellow Sexi-Floss

Walter Weise's pattern also doubles as a Golden Stonefly adult. It combines the profile of Doug Korn's Wrapped Foam Hopper (page 192) with the synthetic wing and fuzzy dubbed body of the Chubby Chernobyl. Try it on the Yellowstone River in August. Walter also recommends this pattern in these foam/body combinations: tan over yellow, black over purple, and tan over pink. DFH stands for "dubbed foam hopper."

DINGBAT

Hook:	#14 Gamakatsu P10
Thread:	Black 6/0
Body:	Overhand knot weave using blue and green Sparkle Braid, blue over green
Wing:	Chartreuse Antron yarn
Hackle:	Black dry fly
Head:	Blue Sparkle Braid

Rainy Riding distributes Lori Burchinal's Dingbat into the Greater Yellowstone Area. Lori, a creative tier living in Vernal, Utah, owned the Bigfoot Fly Shop in Vernal for about two decades. Her innovative use of Sparkle Braid to form a woven body pattern is unique and deserves notice because through using different colors of Sparkle Braid, bodies of other life-forms can be simulated. The Dingbat can be a beetle or blue bottle fly. Switch the weaving sequence to green over blue and it becomes a green bottle fly.

EASY FOAM HOPPER

Hook:	#8 Daiichi 1270
Thread:	Yellow 6/0 UNI-Thread
Tail:	Red saddle hackle fibers
Body:	Yellow Float Foam
Legs:	Yellow rubber legs
Wing:	Turkey quill segment
Hackle:	Brown saddle

You are burning the midnight oil getting ready for the crack of dawn in August for departure to Slough Creek where cuttthoat trout are taking hoppers with gusto. Tackle and gear are packed, but it is late and you need to whip out half a dozen or so hopper patterns to enjoy those cutthroat. You are tired and those eyelids are getting heavier. Greg Messel has experienced this scenario, and this is his answer to quickly turning out that number of hopper patterns.

EVIL EYE CRICKET

Hook:	#10-14 Dai-Riki 280
Thread:	Black 8/0 UNI-Thread
Body:	Black medium closed-cell foam
Underwing:	Brystal Flash fibers

Wing:	Clear Scud Back trimmed to shape
Overwing:	White EP Fibers
Kicker legs:	Knotted and trimmed small black rubber legs
Thorax:	Black Superfine Dubbing
Legs:	Small black rubber legs
Head:	Extension of body foam
Eyes:	Dumbbell eyes from melted Amnesia shooting line

To create this pattern by Callan Wink, cover shank with a thread base and position thread about an eighth-inch behind the eye. Split an inch and a half long foam cylinder piece lengthwise and glue to hook shank with front and rear ends extending. Secure with thread wraps in place and trim angle in rear. Tie in underwing, wing, and overwing components, all extending to end of body. Tie in on either side of thorax the kicker legs of three knotted black Sili Legs strips with two strips cut away below knot, forming the lower leg. Tie in legs at same location, cover tie-in point with dubbed thorax, and tie off. Penetrate head with bodkin and insert eyes. Trim head to proportion.

EXCITOR

Hook:	#10-12 Daiichi 1180
Thread:	Black 8/0
Tail:	Deer body hair with two strands of orange Krystal Flash on either side
Rib:	Undersized brown saddle hackle palmered over rear of body
Body:	Black poly yarn or color to match natural
Underwing:	Four strands of orange Krystal Flash
Overwing:	Deer body hair
Hackle:	Same as rib

LeRoy Hyatt's many years of fly fishing in the Greater Yellowstone and northern Idaho regions provided experience to inspire this pattern. He uses this pattern primarily to simulate flying ants, which in both regions attract salmonids to feed excitedly. However, this pattern has proven versatile enough to simulate adult stoneflies in a manner similar to the famed Stimulator. LeRoy prefers using the shorter shank Daiichi 1180 rather than the longer shank Daiichi 1280 for this fly in order to minimize any flexing of the shank.

FLYING ANT

Hook:	#12-18 TMC 100
Thread:	Red 6/0
Body:	Three segments; chestnut Antron, red tying thread, rust Antron
Wing:	White Para Post
Hackle:	Grizzly saddle dyed brown

During the latter part of each summer in the region, flying ants emerge on a broad regional basis. Trout key on their swarms, and at times feed on them almost to the exclusion of other available foods. Thus it is not surprising that flying ant patterns have been in the fly bins of past shops, remain in the fly bins of current West Yellowstone fly shops, and are created anew each year. Arrick Swanson created the Flying Ant pattern described above.

GORILLA GLUE BEE

Hook:	#10-16 Dai-Riki 320
Thread:	Yellow 3/0
Body:	Yellow-tinted white Gorilla Glue drizzled with black acrylic paint
Wing:	Gray Z-Lon, Antron, or Polar Dub
Hackle:	Grizzly saddle dyed yellow

Scott Sanchez recommends that white Gorilla Glue is most convenient because it cures in about 45 seconds. Place a drop of water on a plastic surface (plastic causes water to bead) and a drop of Gorilla Glue beside it. Use a toothpick to color glue with acrylic paints. Mix colored glue and water with toothpick. The mixture quadruples in volume while curing. Before it cures, dab it onto the hook shank to make two separated body segments. Turn by hand to distribute into symmetrical body segments. Allow segments to cure, place hook in vise, and tie in wing material between body segments. Divide material into left and right wing, both forming a 45-degree angle over rear body segment. Tie in hackle between segments and in front of wing. Trim hackle fibers from bottom of fly. Flies formed with Gorilla Glue float very well, and they are durable. Use any paint colors desired.

HENRY'S FORK FOAM HOPPER

Hook:	#14-16 TMC 100
Thread:	Tan 8/0 UNI-Thread
Underbody:	Tan Razor Foam
Body and extension:	Olive/cream two-tone closed-cell foam trimmed to shape
Underwing:	Tan EP Fibers
Wing:	Speckled hen saddle feather backed with waterproof tape
Kicker legs:	Three tan round rubber legs on either side of thorax knotted to form a joint, two strips cut away below joint forming lower leg
Legs:	Round rubber legs
Head:	Extension of tan Razor Foam used to form underbody

"Grasshopper patterns are one thing we have plenty of in the fly-fishing world!" says Mike Lawson. But new ones are in demand, so this is the foam version of his famed Henry's Fork Foam Hopper. For the underbody, he chose Razor Foam because of its inherent friction against closed-cell foam. This friction holds the body in place better than a dubbed underbody. Mike extends the Razor Foam underbody strip forward to be folded over the foam body to give a sizeable head. He stripes the legs with a black marking pen.

HONEY ANT

Hook:	#14-16 TMC 100
Thread:	Pale orange 8/0 UNI-Thread
Body:	Amber Superfine Dubbing
Legs:	Rusty brown Krystal Flash strands
Wing:	Slate EP Fibers
Thorax:	Mahogany Superfine Dubbing

Mike Lawson observes that most ant patterns with hackle tied at the waist do not float in a manner like a natural insect. He offers this pattern tied to land on the surface in the "blown-over" manner typical of drifting ants. Ant swarms are sporadic late summer events on the Harriman State Park reach of the Henry's Fork and other waters such as Slough Creek and Fall River in Yellowstone National Park. They can also occur over stillwaters, including Beula and Hering Lakes at the head of Fall River in the park. When ants from these swarms are on the water, salmonids feed on them ravenously and almost to the exclusion of other food forms. Therefore it is prudent for the late summer fly fisher to have ant patterns available.

HORMIGA

Hook:	#10-16 TMC 100
Thread:	Brown 6/0 UNI-Thread
Shellback:	Dyed black deer hair

Abdomen:	Black Superfine Dubbing
Wing post:	Butt ends from shellback
Legs:	Butt ends from shellback
Hackle:	Parachute-style brown saddle
Thorax/head:	Black Superfine Dubbing

Federico Prato's Hormiga (Spanish for ant) works in the Greater Yellowstone Area as well as any domestic ant pattern. Federico places a deer-hair shellback over the abdomen, then uses most of its butts to form a wing post at midshank. The remaining butts are tied in flat on either side to form legs. According to Federico, the Hormiga is just as effective when tied with brown deer hair to simulate a cinnamon ant.

HUDGENS FLYING ANT

Hook:	#14-16 TMC 206BL
Thread:	Black 6/0 UNI-Thread
Body:	Amber Superfine Dubbing
Hackle:	Black or tan saddle
Wing:	Blond deer hair
Head:	Black Superfine Dubbing

John Hudgens offers this pattern tied to land on the surface in the "blown-over" manner typical of drifting ants. Thus he ties in the hackle just behind the head and before he ties in the wing. Through guiding on the Henry's Fork and several Montana waters, he observes that examples of his pattern tied in this manner more closely resemble the drifting insect. When midsummer arrives, he recommends that this pattern should be in all fly boxes.

JACKLIN'S BULLET HEAD HOPPER

Hook:	#6-10 Dai-Riki 700
Thread:	Yellow 140-denier Danville or 6/0
Egg sac:	Dyed red deer hair
Rib:	Brown saddle hackle
Body:	Yellow closed-cell foam
Wing:	Turkey quill segment
Bullet head:	Bleached elk or blond elk rump

This pattern succeeds Bob Jacklin's original Bullet Head Hopper conceived in the 1990s. Durable and effective, this pattern is proving itself on the abundance of meadow streams in the Greater Yellowstone Area. After the end of July on through September, this is a pattern any fly fisher visiting Slough Creek, Lamar River, the Madison River's famous Grasshopper Bank, Duck Creek, the Harriman State Park reach of the Henry's Fork, or Gibbon River meadows should have in the fly box to dead-drift or skitter for waiting trophy brookies, browns, cutthroats, or rainbows.

JOE'S FOAM HOPPER

Hook:	#12-16 Dai-Riki 700B
Thread:	Red 3/0 Danville Monocord
Body:	Red UV Ice Dub
Overbody:	Black closed-cell foam
Wing:	Cream silky EP Fibers
Legs:	Small dark brown Spanflex legs,
Head:	Extension of overbody foam strip

Joe Burke uses the UV Ice Dub to secure legs and overbody to the middle of the body as well as at the front to secure front pair of legs, wing, and overbody. His pattern has done quite well in recent Jackson Hole One Fly contests. The same is true for a version tied with a pale yellow Polar Dub body and pale yellow tying thread. He suggests twitching this pattern, in either color, on the surface with a tight line as an effective way to entice cutthroat trout to hit.

KLOD HOPPER

Hook:	#6-12 Mustad 9671
Thread:	Dark brown 3/0
Body:	Tan closed-cell foam strip, 2-mm thick for #10-12, 3-mm for #6-8
Hackle:	Brown saddle

Overbody:	Tan Antron dubbing
Wing:	Elk hair
Legs:	Red and black banded rubber legs

Paul Stimpson claims not to be an enthusiast in tying hopper patterns, but he enjoys fishing them. Living in Ogden, Utah, he worked summers in the West Yellowstone fly-fishing industry. Having a hopper pattern here is almost a must when August rolls around because the places where they are effective nearby are almost boundless. So Paul adapted this pattern from an earlier cicada pattern. He recommends fishing this pattern any time hoppers are present.

KORN'S WRAPPED FOAM HOPPER

Hook:	#8-10 Montana Fly Company 7026
Thread:	Red 6/0 UNI-Thread
Legs:	Montana Fly Company yellow speckled legs, medium for #8 and small for #10
Underbody:	Pink 2-mm craft foam
Overbody:	Tan 2-mm craft foam
Wing:	Natural deer hair
Indicator:	Orange for #8 hook, yellow craft foam for #10 hook

Doug Korn designed this fly to have a segmented foam wrapped body and a foam overbody. Its flat-fanned wing of deer hair allows it to ride low in the water to help represent a desperate hopper. Pink, light yellow, and peach-colored bodies make these patterns highly visible to fish and trigger their aggressive strikes. They have quickly become favorites wherever hoppers are present throughout the Yellowstone area.

LINDA'S ES HOPPER (GREEN)

MICRO HOPPER

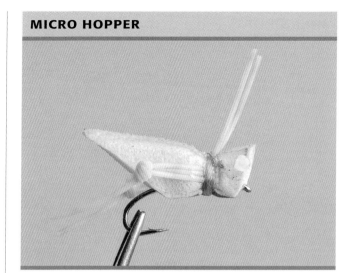

Hook:	#8-10 Dai-Riki 710
Thread:	Olive 6/0 UNI-Thread
Body:	Yellow Rainy's Float Foam
Sharpie permanent	
markers:	Olive and bright green
Post:	Fluorescent orange Orvis Para Post
Hackle:	Grizzly saddle, oversized for stability
Legs:	Small, speckled white Centipede Legs

Prepare body from one-inch foam piece. Use an X-Acto knife to make a flat bottom and slot for the hook in foam piece. Color foam with markers: bright green body and olive across top. Allow to dry, then diagonally cut each end, so top is longer than bottom. Use a black marker to make eyes. Cover shank with thread, attach foam body to rear three-quarters of the hook, and divide body into four even segments. A small embroidery needle brings legs through middle of second foam segment. Attach post at front segment. Wrap hackle concave side up and tie off. Attach thread between second and third segments, tie down legs, and tie off. Apply superglue on bottom slot and base of hopper legs. This pattern by Linda Windels imitates early season hoppers, thus "ES" for early season. It works especially well on spring creeks and small streams.

Hook:	#12-16 Dai-Riki 280
Thread:	Tan 70-denier UTC Ultra Thread
Body:	Formed from two light green 4-mm-thick closed-cell foam sheets cemented and trimmed to shape
Kicker legs:	Knotted and trimmed speckled tan Montana Fly Company Centipede Legs
Antennae:	Speckled tan Montana Fly Company Centipede Legs
Head:	Extension of foam sheets used to form body
Eyes:	Dumbbell eyes from melted Amnesia shooting line

To form the body, Callan Wink cuts right and left sides out of foam sheet, trims them to shape, cements top and bottom surfaces to each other, seals their top joint with a butane lighter, and slides the result onto the hook shank. He secures this body to the shank with thread wraps on the shank about a third of its length behind the eye. On either side of thorax he ties in kicker legs of two knotted Centipede Legs with one strip cut away below joint, forming the lower leg. He ties in antennae and ties off at the same location, penetrates the head with bodkin, inserts the eyes, and trims head to proportion. This is a superb pattern for young grasshoppers.

MIKE'S HOPPER

Hook:	#4-10 TMC 200R
Thread:	Olive 8/0 UNI-Thread
Body:	Chartreuse closed-cell foam
Rib:	Sparkle green DMC yarn
Underbody:	Olive hare's ear dubbing
Underwing:	Peacock black Crystal Mirror Flash
Overwing:	Dyed olive deer body hair
Legs:	Orange barred and brown barred round Sili Legs
Eyes:	Black foam 1/8-inch-diameter cylinder

Yellowstone country has plenty of windy days in mid to late summer. These days are Mike Lawson's favorite times to present his hopper pattern close to streamside banks. Trout lying in wait there will hit a hopper as soon as it comes in their sight, so he covers all likely holds with short drifts. This technique allows him to cover many holds in a day of fishing.

OLIVE FOAM PARACHUTE HOPPER

Hook:	#6-14 Dai-Riki 285
Thread:	Olive 6/0 UNI-Thread
Rib:	Doubled 3/0 tying thread
Underbody:	Golden olive Antron dubbing

Wing:	Blue dun hackle tip or olive fabric coated with Flexament
Overwing:	Olive EP Fibers or Widow's Web
Wing post:	Light lime EP Fibers
Legs:	Single strand of chartreuse rubber legs superglued to doubled olive rubber legs barred with a brown marker
Body:	Olive 2-mm closed-cell foam strip
Wing:	Blue dun hen hackle tip or olive fabric coated with Flexament
Hackle:	Grizzly dyed olive saddle
Head:	Olive 2-mm closed-cell foam strip over golden olive Antron dubbing

Scott Sanchez's method for making foam hopper legs follows: Separate two sections of rubber legs together. Bar with a marking pen. Dip an end of a single piece of rubber leg into superglue, and set it perpendicularly on one end of the doubled pieces. Do the same with another single piece of rubber leg, and set it on the other end of the doubled piece. Trim joints formed on either end of doubled piece and cut it in half to make a pair.

PURPLE SHEILA HOPPER

Hook:	#6-12 TMC 300
Thread:	Purple 6/0 UNI-Thread
Underbody:	Red and purple Ice Dub on remainder
Overbody:	Brown Furry Foam cemented to brown 4-mm closed-cell foam
Thorax:	Closed-cell foam used to form body
Wing:	Tan Antron
Legs:	Black and silver Sili Legs
Indicator:	Orange closed-cell foam
Head:	Closed-cell foam used to form body and thorax

Cement the Furry Foam strip to the bottom of the formed closed-cell foam and trim it to the same shape. Tie this combination to the hook shank just in front of the midpoint. Tie in a set of legs on either side the wing and the rear of the indicator at this location. Between the thorax and head, tie in another set of legs at either side and in the front of the indicator. This pattern by Will Dornan is seeing increased popularity on Jackson Hole and eastern Idaho waters.

RAZOR HOPPER

Hook:	#12-14 Klinkhamer 15BN
Thread:	Yellow Pearsall's silk
Rib:	Yellow Pearsall's silk
Body:	Layer of tan Razor Foam under hook, one piece of tan craft foam doubled and segmented up hook shank
Wing:	Translucent dun Razor Foam
Legs:	Tan/black rubber legs
Kicker legs:	Knotted and trimmed tan/black rubber legs
Head/Collar:	Bullet style of deer hair with tips forming collar

To create this pattern by Chris Williams, thread Razor Foam onto hook and tie in under hook at bend. Segment forward to just behind eye. Return thread to bend and superglue top surface. Tie in craft foam piece at bend and form an extended body. Double foam forward and segment to point behind hook eye where head begins. Trim body materials. Tie in Razor Foam wing and trim to shape. Form bullet head and collar. Tie in kicker legs and legs at collar, whip-finish, and trim legs to correct length.

RAZORBACK HOPPER

Hook:	#10-14 Daiichi 1260
Thread:	Tan 6/0 UTC Ultra Thread
Body:	Pink 2-mm craft foam over tan 2-mm craft foam
Kicker legs:	Pink closed-cell foam and black/red barred Sili Legs
Legs:	Copper/brown barred Sexi Legs
Underwing:	Packing foam underneath Etha-Wing, both trimmed to shape by hand
Overwing:	Tan Widow's Web
Head:	Extension of pink and tan foam pieces used to form body

Clayton Paddie forms kicker legs by tying in, then supergluing segments of black/red Sili Legs to the end of tan foam strip "thighs." He trims this foam strip–Sili Leg combination to proper length and ties in one of each on either side at front of the body. He cuts both underwing pieces together to ensure consistent shape. He superglues the foam strip used to form the indicator to add durability. The foams Clayton uses to form the body are available at craft stores.

SPENT SPRUCE MOTH

Hook:	#12-14 TMC 100
Thread:	Primrose 8/0
Body:	Light Cahill Antron dubbing
Underwing:	Amber Z-Lon
Wing:	Bleached deer body hair

Nowhere else in the world will you find as many Western Spruce Bugworm (spruce fly) patterns as in West Yellowstone. Mistaken in the past for caddisflies or even overlooked, they are now recognized as a major midsummer emergence. Flying insects deposit eggs in conifers in August. Immature larvae hatch and spend winter cased. When spring arrives, they escape their cases to feed on newly formed conifer buds. By July they pupate, then by August they fly to mate and deposit eggs, completing their life cycle. Available in huge numbers, they are an important food form for salmonids, so every fly-fishing shop in the region will feature patterns for them, like the pattern by Patrick Daigle pictured above.

SPIDER

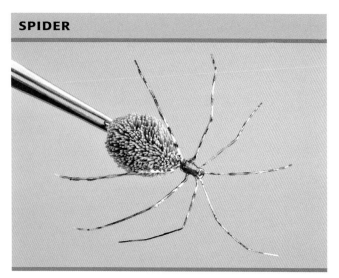

Hook:	#10-12 Dai-Riki 320
Thread:	140-denier UTC Ultra Thread, color to match

Body:	Spun deer hair clipped to shape
Legs:	Tips of stripped saddle hackle stems bent to shape using heated needle, colored with marker, then coated with varnish
Thorax:	Built up with thread wraps over butts of tied-in hackle stems
Head:	GSP thread, color to match body

Spiders in all their forms seem to be relatively overlooked by fly tiers when creating terrestrial insect patterns for salmonids. Not as numerous of a food form for salmonids as ants, beetles, or hoppers, they are available around the edges of waters. Shawn Bostic's use of stripped hackle stems is the key for making this pattern realistic, but monofilament or round rubber can be substituted for durability.

SPRUCE MOTH (HUDGENS)

Hook:	#14 TMC 100
Thread:	Cream 6/0 UNI-Thread
Body:	Cream Antron dubbing
Underwing:	Orange CDC feathers
Hackle:	Light ginger
Wing:	Blond deer hair

In the Greater Yellowstone Area Spruce fly patterns are a major item in filling the dry-fly void after the spring–early summer peak of mayfly activity. These patterns are particularly effective on streams going through Douglas fir stands Here they may be as important as ant and beetle patterns. Spent egg-laying females can fall into streams, and their numbers are cyclical. Mornings are usually when the moth activity is greatest, so it's the best time to present patterns such as John Hudgens's version of the Western Spruce Budworm.

SPRUCE MOTH (ISHIYAMA)

Hook: #14 Daiichi 1170
Thread: Tan 6/0 Flymaster waxed
Body: Light tan Superfine Dubbing
Underwing: Deer body hair
Top wing: Tan hen-back feather, backed with Scotch Tape, reinforced with Flexament, and cut to triangular shape

For this pattern by Nelson Ishiyama, prepare wing first by laying the feather, dull side down, onto the sticky side of Scotch Tape. Ensure stem is straight and the feather is in its full shape. Coat wing with generous amount of Flexament and allow to dry. Dub medium fat body to a point three-quarters of shank from bend to eye. Tie in underwing on top of hook, just in front of body, and extending just past hook bend. Squash flat with fingers. Cut dried wing into triangular shape, leaving some stem and tape to tie in. Tie in wing, lying flat, and extending just past underwing. A thin dubbing bed here can help wing and underwing lie flat. The triangular wing gives the natural silhouette for this insect.

SPRUCE MOTH (JACKLIN)

Hook: #12 TMC 9300
Thread: Cream 140-denier
Wing: Natural or dyed ginger elk hair

Rib: Ginger saddle hackle trimmed flat on top and bottom
Body: Underbody of elk hair and creamy-tan Australian opossum dubbing

Tie on the elk-hair wing first with tips pointing forward and butts toward rear along the shank. Tie in the butt end of the saddle hackle. Use the butts and thread wraps to form a pontoonlike underbody. Beginning at the top of the bend and leaving the elk-hair butt tips exposed at the bend, dub the body. Rib and trim the hackle. Tie down the wing flat over the body so that a small bullet head forms. The wing should have the flat wedge shape of the natural Spruce moth. Bob Jacklin designed this fly for the regional Spruce moth emergence. Although diminishing recently, the adult form of this insect remains an important terrestrial food form for salmonids in regional rivers and alpine lakes.

SPRUCE MOTH (KORN)

Hook: #14-18 Daiichi #1550
Thread: Tan 200-denier Serafil
Rib: Tag end of tying thread
Abdomen: Parks' Fly Shop DK#14 Sandy Spruce Moth dubbing
Hackle: Honey or light ginger rooster neck
Wing: Two buff hen pheasant feathers or light ginger hen saddle

Fish key on Spruce moths in season in favor of other available food forms. Thus, having a good imitation available is essential when fishing sections of streams near evergreens. Many commercial patterns float high, but Spruce moths quickly waterlog and sink or float low in the surface film, especially in the fast water. Doug Korn's version imitates this behavior perfectly. Palmer hackle front to back, securing with tag end of thread ribbed back to eye. Clip hackle fibers short on top and bottom. Tie in stacked wings at eye and facing forward.

Fold stems over, forming a head with wing facing rear and extending one gap-length past hook. When this pattern lands on water, it floats briefly then absorbs water to ride lower. Fish it without floatant as a dropper behind a visible dry such as a hopper.

SPRUCE MOTH (NYMAN)

Hook:	#14 TMC 100
Thread:	Fire orange 8/0
Body:	Hare's ear dubbing
Hackle:	Brown saddle palmered over body, then fibers on top clipped away
Wing:	Tan EP Fibers doubled to form half bullet head
Legs:	Tan and black fine rubber legs

The West Gallatin River, the Taylor's Fork of the Gallatin, the West Fork of the Madison River, the upper Yellowstone River, and portions of the Madison River are prime locations for enjoying trout greedily responding to the later summer Western Spruce moth emergence. Rowan Nyman, of the Firehole Ranch on the west shoreline of Hebgen Lake, creates effective flies for the region, whether for terrestrial forms like this, or for all aquatic insects.

TAKAHOPPER

Hook:	#10-14 Daiichi 1180
Thread:	Hopper yellow 70-denier UTC Ultra Thread
Body:	Golden yellow Fly-Rite dubbing
Wing:	Pellon #808 craft backing
Overwing:	Deer body hair
Head:	Trimmed deer-hair butts

As midsummer approaches, small grasshopper patterns are always productive around Greater Yellowstone Area waters. As the weather warms, and depending on elevation, they begin populating grassy banks and fall into waters, particularly under breezy conditions. Foraging trout take them with gusto, so the media is full of stories on how hoppers have "made the day" for so many fly fishers. Patterns range from complex renditions requiring a wealth of material and considerable time and tying ability to complete, to simpler yet effective patterns like the Takahopper by Rick Takahashi.

TAK'S HOPPER

Hook:	#6-12 Daiichi 1180
Thread:	Yellow 120-denier UTC Ultra Thread
Body:	Tan closed-cell foam cut from River Roads Chernobyl Ant cutter

Rib:	Tying thread
Underwing:	Orange Krystal Flash
Wing:	Yellowish tan Montana Fly Company Lucent Wing Material
Thorax:	Underbody extension
Overwing:	Dyed yellow deer body hair
Head:	Tan closed-cell foam
Legs:	Medium round black rubber legs

To create this Rick Takahashi pattern, pierce the underbody foam piece with the hook point and slide along the hook shank underside to just behind the eye. Coat its top surface with cement. Cement the underside of the overbody piece and place it on top of the shank, ends matching the underbody piece. Tie these together, forming four body segments, the rear one extended. Anchor a pair of legs with thread wraps between the second and third body segments. Secure them with the other legs in front of the first body segment. Tie in the underwing, overwing, and tan foam piece butt end at this location. Advance the tying thread forward to secure tan foam piece front and return thread to the foam piece butt end. Fold the piece back and tie it in place, forming the head. Whip-finish.

THINGAMA ANT

Hook:	#12 TMC 100
Thread:	Black 8/0 UNI-Thread
Body:	Small black ant Thingamabody
Wing:	White poly yarn
Legs:	Black barred rubber legs
Hackle:	Cree saddle

Stefanie Jones ties the ant body to the hook shank at the two waist locations. She ties in the legs and wing behind the head, then wraps the hackle at the same location. Thingamabobbers have been popular strike indicators for years. Now this concept is applied to fly tying as

a "Thingamabody." Cinnamon, white, and clear versions are available. The white and clear versions can be colored with a marking pen. Buoyancy is never an issue when a fly is tied with a Thingamabody!

3D HOPPER

Hook:	#8-10 TMC 2312
Thread:	Yellow 8/0
Tail:	Red golden pheasant breast feather fibers
Body:	Yellow and orange SLF dubbings blended in two-thirds to one-third proportions
Underwing:	Yellow closed-cell foam strip ($^{3}/_{8}$-inch wide by $^{1}/_{16}$-inch thick) to form wing, then folded back toward rear, forming head and thorax
Overwing:	Brown or blond bear or deer hair
Legs:	Three Sili Legs strips tied in below thorax
Kicker legs:	Three Fire Tip chartreuse/fire orange Sili Leg strips on either side of thorax, knotted to form a joint, two strips cut away below joint to form lower leg

This fabulously visible hopper pattern is designed for fishing on broken water or during low-light conditions. Ken Bitton's multidecade fishing and guiding experience on the South Fork reach of the Snake River and the lower Henry's Fork combined with his skills at the tying vise produced this pattern.

TIGER BEETLE

Hook:	#12-16 Dai-Riki 320
Thread:	Black 6/0
Shellback:	Black/orange/black closed-cell tiger beetle foam strip
Body:	Black Z-Lon tiger dubbing
Legs:	Small black Bug Legz or Spandex legs

Easy to tie, highly visible, and consistent of form, this pattern by Rowan Nyman has become a favorite in the region from June through September, when terrestrial insects are active. Fished on a long delicate leader, it produces along grassy banks of still and moving waters. Some newer variations use peacock herl to form the body. In smaller sizes (18-20), it is known as the Mini Tiger Beetle. Tiger beetle foam strips are available in several color combinations and are the basis for other multicolor terrestrial patterns.

TWO TONE HOPPER

Hook:	#4-6 TMC 5263
Thread:	Brown 3/0 Danville
Rib:	Brown saddle hackle
Body:	Tan over yellow closed-cell foam

Wing:	Ring-necked pheasant church window feather
Overwing:	Elk body hair
Kicker legs:	Knotted peacock wing secondary feather segments
Legs:	Black barred tan rubber legs
Head:	Tan over yellow closed-cell foam

Create the body by securing the two colors of foam cemented together to the hook shank in segments. Wind the hackle rib between the segments. Coat the church window feather wing with nail polish and dry before tied in. Splay the elk hair overwing above the tied-in church window feather. Tie in both wing components, the kicker legs, and legs just behind the head. Create the head by tying in the tan foam extension on top of the hook and the yellow foam extension on the bottom to the eye. Pull back each extension to the wing and leg component tie-in point to be tied in creating a bullet head. Marty Howard suggests foam combinations of tan over green and black over red for the body.

WIDOW MOTH

Hook:	#12-14 Montana Fly Company 7004 KBL
Thread:	Tan 8/0 UNI-Thread
Body:	Sandy Spruce moth DK Dubbing blend; overall scheme is light tan with some darker fibers
Underwing:	Beige Widow's Web fibers
Wing:	Caddis tan Widow's Web fibers
Hackle:	Light or barred ginger saddle

Walter Weise suggests clipping hackle fibers from the bottom and leaving the dubbed body undressed, allowing it to go into the surface film simulating the low-riding adult Spruce fly. These suggestions and tying the fly without a palmered hackle make this one of the lowest-riding adult Spruce fly patterns available. Use it during Spruce fly appearances, most likely in August, on streams flowing through evergreen stands.

WINGED ANT

Hook:	#12-18 Partridge SUD
Thread:	Black 12/0 Benecchi
Abdomen:	Black Wapsi SLF dubbing
Legs:	Black crinkled moose body hair
Thorax:	Black Wapsi SLF dubbing
Wing/sighter:	Light silver Z-Lon

Hans Weilenmann usually uses black Yorkshire Fly-Body Fur to fashion the abdomen and thorax of this pattern, but he offers that black Wapsi SLF is a suitable substitute for these components. It is also more easily obtained on this side of "The Pond." This is a proven pattern that is not seen much in the Greater Yellowstone Area.

WINGED BEETLE

Hook:	#4-6 Dai-Riki 700
Thread:	Gray 70-denier UTC Ultra Thread
Body:	Spun black deer hair trimmed to shape
Underwing:	White and gray CDC feathers
Collar:	Tips of deer head used to form head
Head:	Spun deer body hair trimmed to shape

The underwing of Dean Reiner's fly represents the wings a beetle holds under its wing cases and unfurls to take flight. The white CDC feathers are tied in on the sides and the gray feathers are tied in at the center, all above the body trimmed to shape. The deer-hair collar could be considered the wing cases. This is a great pattern to use during summer days in August and early September. Not only can it imitate a large beetle, it can be a cicada or a Mormon cricket, both of which are a mouthful for foraging trout.

CHAPTER 10

TRUE FLIES

This is the most diverse of the food forms available for salmonids that we will discuss. Crane flies, midges, house flies, and mosquitoes: all belong to the order Diptera, the true flies. They can originate on land or from water. House flies, deer flies, and horse flies originate totally on land. Almost by design, it seems, deer flies and horse flies take over as pests when mosquitoes diminish. All true flies have complete metamorphosis: a progression from egg, larva, pupa, and on to adult stage.

All anglers encounter mosquitoes, especially in June and July. We consider them to be pests in the extreme, but their larvae and pupae hanging in the surface film of stillwaters are an important food form. This holds true only in swampy, vegetated stillwaters, which are not the best salmonid habitat. But anyone who has fished Duck Creek in the meadows or side channels of the river in Bechler Meadows will find that presenting mosquito larva imitations will bring surprising results.

Crane flies emerge from spring through the fall season. Some are terrestrial, living in moist margins of water bodies. In streams, gravelly or sandy bottoms are favored habitat, but crane flies populate coarser stream bottoms if the substrate is loose. Larvae are the most important food form of their life cycle where runoff and spates resulting from heavy rainstorms scour them from stream bottoms to make them available to salmonids. Leech patterns can be used to simulate larvae during and soon after these times. Spider and variant patterns suggest adults that are usually formed on land.

Midges are surely the most important Diptera as a food form for salmonids. They occur in all water types. They emerge throughout the year in moving waters. Like caddisflies, some are free living, some burrow, and some build cases. At times during winter and early spring, they provide the only dry-fly fishing when larvae and pupae of certain species drift on stream currents to emerge. In many waters, moving and still, midges provide the bulk of food for young salmonids, and in certain waters they do the same for adults. In terms of biomass, in many stillwaters they are the bulk food form for all resident fish. Blanket emergences occur from stillwaters and spring creeks having muddy bottoms and abundant vegetation. Early season midge swarms along shorelines of many stillwaters give evidence that they have emerged. When midges coat shoreline features along stillwaters and when they seem to fly into noses, ears, and eyes, these are signals to go elsewhere to fish because trout are filled from feeding on the emerging insects. Trout are present around the clock to intercept emerging midges. Fly fishers during their hour-long visits therefore deal with diminishing interest after round-the-clock availability and day-long feeding.

But being there when salmonids are feeding on midges can be one of the rewarding experiences in fly fishing, whether early in the season on moving waters or on stillwaters when cruising fish pursue rising pupae. In recent years "midging" has become refined on stillwaters to mean placing a midge pupa under an indicator, then finding the depth at which fish are intercepting it. This approach requires knowledge of the bed of the water being fished as well as utmost patience. But when the taking depth is determined, another rewarding fly-fishing experience takes place.

WET PATTERNS

ARF MIDGE PUPA

BLACK MAGIC

Hook:	#16-20 TMC 2487
Bead:	Diamond glass
Thread:	Black 8/0 UNI-Thread
Antennae:	White organza
Underbody:	Tying thread
Rib:	Extra small silver wire
Overbody:	Clear Micro Tubing
Wing:	White organza
Thorax:	Black hare's ear Ice Dub
Hackle (optional):	Starling

Hook:	#10-14 TMC 2487
Thread:	Black 8/0 UNI-Thread
Rib:	Extra fine silver UNI-Wire
Trailing shuck:	Sparse black poly yarn strands
Abdomen:	Tying thread coated with Softex
Wing:	Three or four strands of pearlescent Midge Flash
Thorax:	Black Ice Dub

Observing midge larvae and pupae reveals that their bodies are quite translucent. Midges emerge with a gas bubble formed near the head. Remembering the Larva Lace craze, it occurred to Al Ritt to put the wire rib inside tubing. This technique results in a durable body protected by the tubing and has "depth" as the wire is suspended inside the tubing above the thread body but under the outer surface. Al varies this pattern to imitate life stages from larva through emerger by using or omitting body parts such as the wing, "thorax" (midges have no thorax, but pupae will have a slightly enlarged forward portion where the wings and legs develop), glass bead, and hackle. His pattern is effective in black, red, tan, olive, white, and blue.

Salmonids respond to emerging midges with what the English call "smutting rises." In this case fish are taking emergers no more than an inch or two below the surface. Such rises are common in Yellowstone Area waters, and when they occur, proper presentation is required for success. Michael Snody suggests that dressing the tippet helps to present this pattern at the correct depth. Its sparse poly yarn shuck and Midge Flash wing provide the subtle sparkle that makes this pattern effective.

CRANEFLY LARVA (JONES)

Hook:	#6 TMC 5265
Weight:	0.025-inch-diameter lead or lead-free wire
Thread:	Brown 8/0 UNI-Thread
Rib:	Clear Stretch Flex strip
Body:	Medium bonefish tan Krystal Flash
Head:	Brown Ice Dub

Cranefly larva can inhabit the loose substrate in the swiftest riffles or backwater areas. In any type of bottom, they are always at a depth of several inches. Thus they are not ordinarily available for salmonids until the substrate is disturbed. Cranefly larva imitations such as Nick Jones's are very effective when water is dropping right after a rainstorm. In this case, tumble the pattern along the bottom. When Nick ribs this pattern, he places the Stretch Flex strip under tension, making it thin enough to provide translucence to the finished fly.

CRANEFLY LARVA (URBANSKI)

Hook:	#10 TMC 2488
Thread:	Red 6/0 UNI-Thread
Abdomen:	Light tan 1-mm Ultra Chenille
Wing case and gills:	White Antron
Thorax:	Dark green rabbit fur dubbing

In much of the Greater Yellowstone Area, aquatic craneflies begin emerging in April. Larvae migrate from loose gravel, silty bottoms, or are washed out during high water periods throughout the season. When drifting or moving along the bottom, they are attractive to salmonids as a food form because of their large size. Scott Urbanski's pattern has proven effective at these times. He uses a white Antron strip to form the wing case and the extension of it forms the gills. After he ties the strip down, he uses a dubbing brush to separate the Antron fibers to form gills, then trims them to proportion. On completing the fly, he burns the end of the Ultra Chenille abdomen to ensure durability.

DA MIDGE

Hook:	#16 Da-Riki 075
Thread:	Black 70-denier Flymaster
Tail:	Three pearl Krystal Flash strands
Rib:	Fine silver wire
Body:	Tying thread
Thorax:	Black Superfine Dubbing
Hackle:	Soft black hen
Overwing:	Two pieces Cascade Crest Krinkel Mirror Flash

Taper the body with turns of tying thread before adding the ribbing. Body occupies back two-thirds of the shank. Dub the thorax and tie in the hackle by the butt end. Wind the hackle, pinching barbs to rear. Add the overwing that should extend above and to end of the body. The two different flash components of this fly by Willie Self create an attractive halo. Fish this pattern just under the surface and try presenting two of them at same time, one behind the other.

DY BLOODWORM

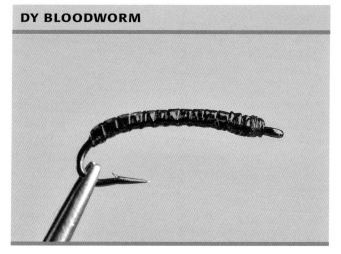

Hook:	#14-22 Daiichi 1273
Thread:	Red 8/0 UNI-Thread
Body:	Red micro Stretch Tubing

The fly-fishing world now realizes the importance of the bloodworm, a midge pupa colored red because it contains a hemoglobin-like substance that retains oxygen needed for survival in near anaerobic aquatic environments. Bloodworms are sought after by salmonids because of their high protein content, and they inhabit all water types. Because of this importance, patterns for bloodworms are becoming numerous. Deward Yocum's pattern is simple and effective. It should be fished at or near the bottom of streams or stillwaters. Deward ties another version of this fly using the same hook and thread, but with clear Stretch Tubing.

DY BUZZER

Hook:	#14-22 Daiichi 1270
Thread:	Black 8/0 UNI-Thread
Tail:	Sparse Antron fibers
Rib:	Fine black UNI-Wire or twisted tying thread

Body:	White floss
Wing case:	Black Thin Skin or pheasant tail fibers
Thorax:	Peacock herl
Gills:	White Antron

Deward Yocum coats the body of this pattern with Hard As Nails polish to add a luster, then spirals the rib, about eight turns, over it. In larger sizes, this pattern appears unusual, but large size 12 midge pupae inhabit many Greater Yellowstone Area stillwaters, including the rich irrigation reservoirs of southeastern Idaho and Henry's and Ennis Lakes. Deward varies size and color of this pattern to match the physical characteristics of midge pupae he encounters wherever he fishes.

EVANS BUZZER

Hook:	#8-20 Mustad C49
Thread:	Black 8/0 UNI-Thread
Rib:	Extra small silver UNI-Wire
Body:	Gun metal gray Flashabou and red Micro Tubing
Thorax:	Tying thread
Wing pads:	Peacock orange UNI-Mylar strips
Gills:	White poly yarn

Everet Evans first covers the hook shank with thread while tying in the rib and body components. He wraps the Flashabou and Micro Tubing and ribs between these two with the UNI-Wire. He anchors the UNI-Mylar strips on either side at the front of the body and builds the tying thread thorax over their ends. He forms right and left UNI-Mylar wing pads on the thorax and ties these off with a tuft of poly yarn for gills on top of the head. He coats the finished fly with Hard As Nails or varnish for added durability to give a superb midge pupa pattern for fishing under an indicator.

FRISKY

Hook:	#12-16 Dai-Riki 300
Bead:	Gold
Thread:	Tan 6/0
Tail:	Small clump of fox squirrel or hare's mask guard hairs with one strand of opal Mirage Flashabou
Rib:	Pearl Flashabou with reverse wrap of 5X monofilament
Body:	Light hare's mask dubbing mixed with a small amount of gray dubbing

Midge pupae are almost always available as a food item for salmonids in moving and stillwaters. Jay Buchner's pattern can be used in either type. Always important in moving waters, midges make up the bulk of insect life in most stillwaters. Pupation can occur at any depth in both water types.

HOMIE MIDGE

Hook:	#12-20 TMC 2312
Bead:	Silver, 3/32-inch for #14-16
Thread:	Light gray 8/0 or 6/0 UNI-Thread
Shuck:	White Fluoro Fibre
Rib:	Fine silver wire

Body:	Black, blue, or red Flexi Floss or Micro Tubing
Thorax:	One peacock herl
Gills:	White ostrich herl

Counterwrap the rib around the body material. Spiral it, also counterwrapped through the peacock herl thorax to give durability. This is one of Buddy Knight's favorite midge patterns. He fishes it below an indicator and adjusts the length below until he determines the taking depth.

IRISH SPRING

Hook:	#12-14 Gamakatsu Red Octopus 02305
Bead:	Copper, 7/64-inch, or tungsten
Thread:	Black 70-denier UTC Ultra Thread
Rib:	Fine copper wire
Body:	Kelly green Flashabou or holographic tinsel
Overwing:	Medium pearl Mylar
Thorax:	Peacock herl
Gills:	White Para Post

This is Joni Tomich's version of a chironomid pattern of Utah fame. She originally used a red tag, but on discovery of Gamakatsu Red Octpus hooks, switched to tying this pattern on them. The results were immediately positive. She prefers the Wulff-style gills because she observes the wiggling motion they give to the fly during a slow stripping retrieve. She usually ties this pattern in size 12, but size 14 is a great choice for rivers and picky fish. She has used it on an intermediate line in Hebgen Lake's Madison Arm with great results. Joni fishes this fly under an indicator in up to 30 feet of water, but with a Type VII line, a 4-foot leader, and a figure-eight retrieve, it also produces.

KG'S CHROMIE BUZZER

Hook:	#14 Dai-Riki 125
Thread:	Black 8/0 UNI-Thread
Rib:	Small hot orange UNI-Wire
Abdomen:	Tying thread ribbed with UNI-Wire
Back:	Opal UTC Mirage Tinsel over wire ribbed abdomen
Wing case:	Pheasant tail fibers
Thorax:	Regular and white peacock herl, one each, wrapped together
Gills:	White peacock herl

After adding bead to hook, tie in tinsel and wire at top of bend. Tie in and rib the body. Wrap tinsel over back and tie off. Tie in wing case fibers, then form the thorax and the wing case. This simple midge pupa by Kelly Glissmeyer has proven effective on such famed stillwaters as Henry's Lake and lesser known, but quality waters of Sand Creek Ponds and Paul Reservoir.

LIL' URBY

Hook:	#18 Dai-Riki 135
Thread:	Black 8/0 UNI-Thread
Body:	Red midge Larva Lace
Head:	Peacock herl

Any water hosting salmonids will hold midges. Midges emerge throughout the year and in all kinds of weather and from all water situations. In many situations their emergence is overshadowed by those of larger aquatic insects, but they are almost always available as a food form. There are times when they are the only aquatic insect emerging. This is Scott Urbanski's pattern for use any time. He finds it to be quite effective during times when waters are discolored.

MACKAY MIDGE

Hook:	#16-18 TMC 200R
Thread:	Black 70-denier UTC Ultra Thread
Body:	Stripped peacock herl
Thorax:	Peacock herl
Hackle:	Starling neck feather

Before wrapping the stripped peacock herl body, Doug Kinney coats the hook shank with Hard As Nails to better secure the stripped herl. Easily tied, very effective, but not overly durable, Doug recommends that a number of these patterns be tied for an outing. The starling neck feather used to hackle this pattern is "iridocytic," meaning that its color comes not from pigment, but from structure. Doug recommends presenting this pattern under a BWO dun pattern in a two-fly rig. He uses this combination throughout the season.

MILLWARD SPECIAL

Hook:	#17-19 TMC 102Y
Weight:	Three wraps of 0.015-inch lead-free wire under thorax
Thread:	Black 8/0 UNI-Thread
Rib:	Fine silver wire
Body:	Black Superfine Dubbing
Thorax:	Peacock herl
Hackle:	Soft hen grizzly or grouse with barbules as long as hook shank

This lifelike midge pupa pattern by Dr. Jim Millward and tied by Buz Roach originated in southern Utah, but through discovery of its excellent attractive properties, it has become a popular pattern on southeastern Idaho. In stillwaters, it is effective when slowly trolled or fished under an indicator. In moving water, it is effective as a dropper behind a parachute-style dry fly and when fished as any soft-hackled pattern.

MUSKRAT MIDGE

Hook:	#20 Dai-Riki 075
Bead:	Silver brass
Thread:	Iron gray 8/0 UNI-Thread

Rib:	Fine silver wire
Body:	Tying thread
Wing:	White Z-Lon
Thorax:	Muskrat dubbing

Bucky McCormick offers this fly not only as an effective pattern for winter fishing, but also for any time midges are emerging. It's a rugged little fly sure to make you notice its durability as well as effectiveness. It is Bucky's favorite on all regional rivers for emerging midges. He also offers it as a dropper pattern behind a dry mayfly or caddis pattern. Another option he suggests is to try it alone under an indicator when fishing stillwaters.

RAINBOW BRITE MIDGE

Hook:	#8-12 TMC 200R
Bead:	White
Thread:	Purple 8/0
Body:	Purple Midge Diamond Braid
Rib:	Lime and red Ultra Wire
Thorax:	Peacock herl and deer hair

Wrap Diamond Braid tightly when forming body, then take several wraps of both wires together to give durability and segmented effect. Spiral the peacock herl around tying thread before wrapping it to form a more durable thorax. Midges make up the bulk of insect life in stillwaters, and Henry's Lake, which inspired this pattern by Dennie Edwards, is no exception. These midges range from micro sizes on up to size 12. Wise fly fishers will always have midge pupa patterns of various sizes in their fly boxes when visiting stillwaters.

RED ROCKET

Hook:	#8-14 Mustad C53
Bead:	Gold
Thread:	Red 8/0 UNI-Thread
Tail:	Red hackle fibers
Rib:	Extra small silver UNI-Wire
Body:	Red Flashabou strand

Everet Evans builds up a small thorax with tying thread behind the bead mainly to keep it in place. He ties the body of his pattern slender to best simulate that of a bloodworm. The Flashabou body gives sparkle to simulate the gasses collected under the shuck in order for the insect to rise to the surface. On completing this fly, Everet coats it with Hard As Nails for added durability. He uses this pattern mostly as an indicator fly fished near the bottom of any stillwater. It seems most effective early and late in the season.

ROD WOUND BRASSIE

Hook:	#16-18 TMC 2457
Thread:	Black 6/0 UNI-Thread
Body:	Fine red UNI-Wire
Head:	Peacock Ice Dub

Mark MacLeod's unique method of using wire significantly improves durability of the traditional Brassie to make it near indestructible. He passes a length of wire through the hook eye and along the bottom surface of the shank past the hook bend. He makes four or five tight turns forward of the wire from the bend, then pulls forward on the end extending from the hook eye. This tightens the four or five turns near the bend. He finishes turning wire in tight spirals around the shank and wire below, leaving room to attach Ice Dub to form a head after trimming excess wire. He attaches tying thread here, dubs the head, and whip-finishes the fly. Mark's experience with this pattern indicates that red wire is more effective in simulating midge larvae than wire of other colors.

SARAH'S RED COPPER MIDGE

Hook:	#16 Dai-Riki 135
Thread:	Red 8/0 or 70-denier UNI-Thread
Bead:	Copper tungsten, $3/32$-inch
Rib:	Copper wire (brassie)
Body:	Red Hareline Midge Diamond Braid

Over the last decade the fly-fishing world has come to realize that red is a very effective color for midge pupae. In many circles, midge pupae of this color are known as bloodworms. Bloodworms inhabit both still and moving waters, and relatively simple patterns can be very effective in imitating them. Roger Thompson's pattern is named after an incident when a fishing friend discovered her waders were coated with bloodworms after leaving a local stream.

STREAMSWEEPER, THE 12:30 FLY

Hook:	#16-18 Daiichi 1130
Bead:	Silver, $^3/_{32}$-inch, or tungsten, 2.3-mm
Thread:	Light gray 8/0 UNI-Thread
Shuck:	White Fluoro Fibre
Rib:	Fine silver wire
Body:	Royal blue Stretch Floss
Collar:	Blue dun Superfine Dubbing

Buddy Knight gave this fly the peculiar name for good reason. He finds it to be most effective as a midge pupa in the afternoon. He fishes it as a dropper under a strike indicator or a dry fly. Wrap the stretch floss body tightly to prevent slippage. Counterwrap the rib around the body material for durability.

TAK'S HOLO BUZZER

Hook:	#16-18 TMC 2302
Thread:	Black 8/0 UNI-Thread
Underbody:	Tying thread
Body:	Silver holographic tinsel
Wing case:	Mirage tinsel
Thorax:	Tying thread
Wing buds:	Tan goose biots
Gills:	Oral-B Ultra Floss

After tying in the holographic tinsel along the hook shank, wrap the entire shank with tying thread from the top of the bend to just behind the eye. Tie in the butt ends of the wing case and wing buds at a point about two-thirds of the way going forward from the top of the bend to the eye. Build the thorax from this point with tying thread, tie in the piece of Ultra Floss. Bring the wing case and wing buds forward and tie off just behind the eye. Trim the Ultra Floss to form gills. Coat the entire fly with Clear Cure Goo Hydro to achieve a glossy finish. Try presenting this pattern by Rick Takahashi dead drift under an indicator, letting wave action impart motion.

$3 DIP

Hook:	#14-18 Dai-Riki 070
Bead:	Gold
Thread:	6/0 Danville no. 47 (burnt red)
Rib:	Fine gold wire
Body:	Tying thread
Wing:	Fine deer hair

The full name of this fly is Three Dollar Bridge Serendipity. This bridge across the Madison River is a few miles downstream of the Reynolds Bridge and gives passage to Cliff Lake, Wade Lake, and the south bank of the Madison River. From Wade Lake came the Montana State record brown trout. This easily tied fly created by Nick Nicklaus and tied by Bucky McCormick is gaining in popularity throughout the region. To the south it is recognized as a producer during the lower Henry's Fork midge activity. Try it with and without a bead, depending on taking depth where you are fishing.

DRY PATTERNS

ARF MIDGE ADULT

Hook: #16-20 TMC 101
Thread: Black 8/0 UNI-Thread
Abdomen: Black quill
Wing: White organza
Post: Fluorescent orange Gator Hair
Hackle: Grizzly saddle, tightly palmered

Many midge patterns are hard to see and often aren't constructed like the natural. Many use tails and upright wings. While these can be effective in many instances, they don't truly imitate an actual midge. In some lakes Al Ritt fishes, a more accurate pattern is needed for success. Like the insect, his ARF Midge Adult pattern has a down wing, about body length, and no tail. Al felt there was no need for a thorax, as a tightly wound palmered hackle with a "V" cut in the bottom supports the body of the fly off the water and results in a more accurate imprint on the water. The small strip of fluorescent orange over the back and stub sticking up add excellent visibility. Al often suspends a small midge larva or pupa off the back of this pattern in still or slow-moving water.

BONDAGE MIDGE

Hook: #16-20 Gamakatsu C12
Thread: Olive 70-denier UTC Ultra Thread
Shuck: Ginger Spandex strip
Body: Tying thread
Shellback: Light dun snowshoe rabbit foot
Thorax: Olive-brown Ice Dub
Wing: Tips of snowshoe rabbit fur

Wade Moulton received his undergraduate and graduate education in eastern Idaho. While doing so, he fell in love with the region and its fly fishing. He now lives in Vernal, Utah, but returns in season to the Greater Yellowstone Area to fly fish. He developed this "stuck in the shuck" midge pupa pattern during visits to the Green River near Vernal. He used it with instant success in the Greater Yellowstone Area when drifting it on moving waters or under an indicator on stillwaters.

BUZ'S FOAM HEAD EMERGER

Hook:	#16 Mustad 94845
Thread:	Black 8/0 UNI-Thread
Tail:	Bright white Antron
Rib:	Fine silver wire
Body:	Black Superfine Dubbing
Thorax:	Peacock herl
Wing/head:	2-mm craft foam, cut into 2-mm-wide strips and folded over to make a bubble

Originally Buz Roach tied this pattern for simulating midge pupae, and it is still used as such. But as is the case with many small, easily tied midge pupa patterns, discovery comes when BWO and midge emergences overlap. Such was the case with this pattern on the lower Henry's Fork and on regional spring creeks Buz enjoys fishing. This pattern is very effective when presented about two feet behind a dry fly such as a #16 Parachute Adams. Try this combination on small streams for superb results.

CABIN FEVER MIDGE

Hook:	#18-22 TMC 100
Thread:	Black Griffiths 14/0 sheer
Tail:	Sparse white Antron or Z-Lon fibers
Body:	Tying thread

Wing:	White CDC
Hackle:	Dry-fly quality grizzly saddle

Simplicity, visibility, and availability of materials help make a pattern popular, and this pattern by Tim Woodard fits the bill. Materials for tying small fly patterns such as this must be both delicate and of high quality. The body should be slender. For such, CDC is more appropriate than any synthetic for forming the wing, and, as Tim Woodard points out, only the highest grade of saddle or cape hackle will be useful. Tim's pattern has seen use on regional rivers, including the Madison, the Henry's Fork, and South Fork reach of the Snake River.

CRANEFLY (BURKHOLDER)

Hook:	#8-10 Daiichi 1850
Thread:	Tan 8/0 UNI-Thread
Body:	Tan Razor Foam strip
Rib:	Palmered barred ginger hackle and 6X monofilament
Wing:	Blond Alaska bear hair
Hackle:	Oversized ginger saddle

Ken Burkholder forms wings for this pattern in a unique manner with bear hair fine enough for use. First he clips away a bunch of hair from the bear hide and cleans it of its undercoat. With the butt section of the bunch exposed through the end of a funnel, he ties a snug triple surgeon's knot around the bunch just above its ends. He trims the ends of the knot and applies superglue to it. He repeats this to form a second wing. Then he ties the pattern up to the point of tying in the wings. He now ties in the wings by the hair tips to lie on either side of the hook shank. In the same plane, he secures each to extend at a 45-degree angle away from the shank, with glued butts extending to just past the hook bend. He finishes the fly by trimming the tips and adding the oversized hackle.

CRANEFLY (DENNIS)

Hook:	#8-16 TMC 2312
Thread:	Orange 6/0 UNI-Thread
Rib:	Tying thread
Abdomen:	Brown 4-mm closed-cell foam
Underwing:	Pearl Krystal Flash
Wing:	Light elk hair
Legs:	Three pair medium Spanflex for flies larger than #10, otherwise small
Thorax:	Brown Antron and brown Arizona crystal rabbit blend with tan closed-cell foam back
Head:	Red Antron dubbing

Shape the brown foam strip to be tapered wider at the rear and tie it in at the shank center. Segment the strip with wraps of thread going back and then forward to tie-in point. Tie in underwing and wing at abdomen tie-in point. Tie in three pair of legs and butt of tan foam piece in thorax area. Dub the thorax and roll tan foam piece to front and tie off behind eye. Dub the head, tie off, and use scissors to round the butt of the brown foam. Use this fly by Jack Dennis in late summer when adult craneflies "dive-bomb" eggs onto the water. Move it along the surface to entice hits.

CRANEFLY ADULT

Hook:	#10-12 Daiichi 1170
Thread:	Orange 6/0 UNI-Thread waxed
Body:	Furled Z-Lon yarn
Wings:	Cree hackle tips
Legs:	Stiff elk mane
Hackle:	Mixed brown and grizzly

To create this pattern by Nelson Ishiyama, furl Z-Lon yarn by twisting tightly into a "rope." Fold the rope in middle while holding ends tightly together and allowing the doubled rope to twist around itself. While holding ends tightly, tie in above hook point, extending half a shank length beyond bend. Tie in wings just in front of body tie-in point, with wings slanted back in swept configuration reaching rear of body. Tie in 8 to 10 hairs per side, just in front of wing tie-in point with hairs also in swept configuration, but slanted downward toward point of hook. It is important to tie legs in this configuration that allows fly to skate on their tips when stripped to simulate the natural buzzing along the surface. Hairs should extend at least as far back as body and wing. Wind hackle fairly heavily over front half of shank and whip-finish at eye. Any stiff hair can be substituted for stiff elk mane in forming the legs of this fly.

CW'S POLY WING CRYSTAL MIDGE

Hook:	#20-26 TMC 2488
Thread:	Black or dun 70-denier UTC Ultra Thread
Shuck:	March brown Antron dubbing
Body:	Single strand of black Krystal Flash
Wing post:	Light dun poly yarn
Hackle:	Grizzly saddle
Thorax:	Black Superfine Dubbing, black thread, or two peacock eye herls

After tying in a thread base and shuck, tie in a black Krystal Flash strand and wrap it forward to cover the rear half of the shank. Tie in 10 to 15 poly yarn fibers at the front end of the body and make a horizontal loop wing. Trim excess and tie in a grizzly hackle. Tie in thorax material. Form a thorax with the chosen material, palmer two turns of hackle through the thorax, and tie off. Cut a "V" in hackle fibers underneath the thorax. This easily tied midge emerger by Chris Williams is effective on still-waters and moving waters alike.

CW'S CDC SPLIT WING MIDGE

Hook:	#20-26 TMC 2488
Thread:	Black or dun 70-denier UTC Ultra Thread
Shuck:	March brown Antron dubbing
Body:	Black thread with extra fine silver wire rib
Wing:	Goose CDC feather
Hackle:	Grizzly saddle
Thorax:	Black thread

After tying in the shuck, body, and its rib, tie in a goose CDC feather at its halfway point. Pull both sides upward and figure-eight the tying thread between them, forming an upright, divided wing. Make a few thread wraps in front of the wing to form a thorax and tie in the stem of a grizzly hackle. Do two wraps of hackle over the thorax and tie off. Trim shuck to length of hook shank, and wing to about half the length of the abdomen. When fishing this fly by Chris Williams dead-drift, try a very short, quick twitch to simulate an escaping midge. This action can stimulate a take from a feeding fish.

HACKLE STEM CRANEFLY

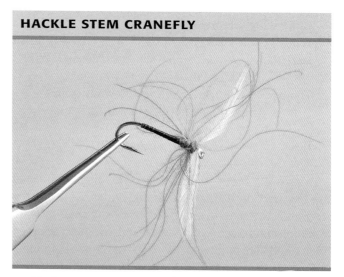

Hook:	#10-12 Dai-Riki 320
Thread:	Dark brown 8/0 UNI-Thread
Body:	Medium brown stripped hackle stem
Wings:	Light dun hen hackle tips
Thorax:	Brown Superfine Dubbing
Legs:	Long, fine black CDC feather fibers

The fly pictured above was created by Dean Reiner and tied by Dandy Reiner. After soaking the stem to minimize splitting during wrapping, tie it in by the tip, natural curve down and dull side facing up. The resulting body should be slender to imitate that of the natural. Coat it with superglue for durability. The wings are tied in spent, concave sides upward. The sparse CDC feathers are tied in just behind the wings, the fibers forming delicate legs. The dubbed thorax covers the base of the wings and the legs, but must be kept small, keeping the slender character that best imitates the natural insect.

HAIR WING VARIANT

Hook:	#6-14 Mustad 94840
Thread:	Black 6/0 Flymaster
Tail:	Calf tail fibers
Wing:	Upright and divided calf tail fibers
Body:	Stripped peacock eye herl
Hackle:	Dark brown saddle

Although this pattern dates back to Merton Parks in the 1950s, it was mostly forgotten until fairly recently and has never been published. Richard Parks has revived it to great success. It features traditional variant wing and hackle sizes, meaning these components are at least one size larger than standard for a given hook size. With its light footprint on the water, it has proven ideal for high-country cutthroat trout. Try it as a cranefly adult pattern on flat water, such as the Henry's Fork in Harriman State Park, the Yellowstone Lake estuary, Nez Perce Ford, and the Lewis River meadow reach above Lewis Lake in Yellowstone National Park.

HOUSEFLY

Hook:	#12-14 Daiichi 1170
Thread:	Black 6/0 UNI-Thread
Body:	Four peacock herls

Legs:	Butt ends of peacock herl trimmed to length
Wings:	Light yellow Fishaus fly sheet

Ward Thompson doubles a piece of fly sheet to cut wings simultaneously using a wing cutter. A caddis wing cutter works well. The length of the wings should be cut parallel with the grain of the sheet. Light yellow wings make this pattern highly visible when used to imitate a house fly, deer fly, or horse fly. Weedguard, found in home and garden shops and plant nurseries, can also be used to form wings for this simple pattern. Weedguard can be colored with a marking pen.

KG'S FULLBACK FOAM MIDGE

Hook:	#14-22 Dai-Riki 125
Thread:	Black 8/0 UNI-Thread
Shuck:	Amber olive Arizona Simi Seal
Foam back:	White packing foam strip, $1/32$-inch wide
Rib:	Extra small silver UTC Ultra Wire
Abdomen:	Tying thread
Thorax:	Canadian black Arizona Simi Seal
Indicator:	Foam strip used to form back

Kelly Glissmeyer designed this pattern to represent a midge pupa crawling out of its exoskeleton. He prefers a Dai-Riki 125 hook for tying these small-sized patterns because of its wide gape. Tied properly, this pattern hangs in the surface film, and fish key on its portion below the film. When tying this pattern, secure the shuck at top of the bend and tie in the ribbing wire and end of foam strip there. Dub and rib the body, dub the thorax, and pull the foam strip over both to simulate wings. After tying off the fly, cut the stub of the foam strip in length proportion to hook size to form an indicator.

KG'S PARASOL MIDGE EMERGER

Hook:	#12-16 Dai-Riki 125
Thread:	Black 8/0 UNI-Thread
Tail:	White Z-Lon fibers
Rib:	Small chartreuse UNI-Wire
Body:	Black tying thread
Thorax:	Black "spectrumized" spiky dubbing
Parasol:	White, yellow, orange, or chartreuse macramé yarn
Parasol connector:	3X tippet clinch knotted to macramé, cemented to shank near eye, and secured with thread wraps

Fran Betters began the parasol concept, and this pattern by Kelly Glissmeyer is based on Jim Schollmeyer's Parasol Emerger. See KG's Cased Caddis on page 39 for a description of black "spectrumized" spiky dubbing. Kelly fishes this pattern dead-drift and limits the length of the monofilament connector to less than an inch because most feeding salmonids will take emergers just below or in the surface film.

THE MIGHTY CREE

Hook:	#20-26 TMC 2487
Thread:	Rust brown 8/0 UNI-Thread
Tails:	Three or four barbs from a rooster neck feather
Rib:	Extra fine copper wire
Abdomen:	Two or three center tail barbs from a cock ring-necked pheasant twisted with one barb from the eye of a peacock herl twisted to form a rope
Thorax:	Gold Hare's Ear Plus dubbing
Wing:	Light gray deer hair
Hackle:	Cree saddle

The shape of this pattern is based on Michael Snody's close observation of adult midges drifting on the surface. The wire rib is necessary to add durability to the fragile barbs twisted into a rope then spiraled around the hook shank to form the abdomen. Michael uses this pattern with great success during autumn midge emergences throughout the Greater Yellowstone Area. Tie it as small as your hackle allows.

POLY PARASOL EMERGER

Hook:	#16 Dai-Riki 075
Thread:	Black 8/0
Body:	Fine red UNI-Wire

Thorax:	Peacock herl
Wing case:	Poly yarn post
Post:	Poly yarn
Hackle:	Ginger saddle

Kent Henderson's method of making a poly yarn post to place an emerger below the surface film follows. Place one end of a 12-inch piece of post yarn under a heat-proof tile, and stretch the strand across the tile. Using a pencil torch, cut the yarn into approximately two-inch sections. Stretch a section between two opposing vises and rotate one to twist strand tightly. Dab some Zap-A-Gap onto the strand and tightly wrap tying thread in about a half-inch section over the glue to form post. Location of hackle on post determines depth of fly. Tie in a hackle and take three to five turns around the post to form parasol. Tie an emerger (Kent's midge emerger is described above), laying butt end of the post along the top of the hook, butt end aft. Tie the post in vertically, then clip butt end to form a wing case. Clip post about 1/4-inch above the parasol wing to form an indicator.

REVERSE HACKLE STACK MIDGE

Hook:	#18-24 Daiichi 1110
Thread:	45-denier Gudebrod, color matching natural
Shuck:	UTC silver Holo Tinsel and body thread
Abdomen:	Tying thread
Rib:	Contrasting twisted 6/0 Flymaster thread
Thorax:	Mole or other natural fur color matching natural
Wing and antennae:	Light dun Float-Viz
Hackle:	Grizzly or dun Whiting Farms rooster saddle one size larger than standard for hook

Wayne Luallen designed this pattern for fishing Madison River midge hatches. Twist tinsel for the shuck and stretch to set the twist. Overlay the contrasting thread, twist both together, then allow to furl. Secure a two-inch piece of wing yarn with three winds near the abdomen. Post a short yarn section extending toward the hook eye. Dub a slender thorax prior to winding hackle. Wind the hackle down (reverse) rather than up the post with two or three winds, creating the "hackle stack," being more of a parachute than is typical. Pull yarn down to the eye, secure with two or three winds, then whip-finish underneath to push up what, when trimmed, will be antennae. If a wider, off-set hook gape is preferred, consider the Daiichi 1640.

SKITTERING MIDGE

Hook:	#18-20 Dai-Riki 125
Thread:	Olive dun 8/0 UNI-Thread
Shuck:	Midge gray Z-Lon
Body:	Tying thread
Wing:	Midge gray Z-Lon tied spent
Hackle:	Oversized grizzly saddle

This pattern by Bucky McCormick simulates a midge cluster. It is a go-to pattern for winter fishing on the Madison River, but is highly effective anytime and anywhere midges are emerging in big numbers. Use of an oversized hackle (size 18 for a size 20 hook, size 16 for a size 18 hook) helps give the impression of a cluster. To further help this impression, the hackle is tied in on top of wing base, then figure-eight-wrapped between wings. Oversized hackle wrapped in this manner also aids visibility of this pattern.

STONE SKIPPER

Hook:	#10 Partridge K3A
Thread:	Black 3/0
Body:	Deer hair
Wings:	Light blue dun or dun grizzly saddle hackle tips
Legs:	Pheasant tail fibers
Hackle:	Sparse grizzly saddle

LeRoy Cook has experienced fish taking adult crane-flies on waters from Fall River Basin to Slough Creek. Looking for a delicate material to form trailing legs, he settled on pheasant tail fibers, although single moose mane hairs or fine hackle stems can be used. The latter two, however, seem a bit coarse for the character of this fly, but are more durable. For the legs, LeRoy suggests putting bends at intervals by using a hot bodkin or needle held as close as possible without touching the chosen material. This operation requires a gentle touch, so be careful!

TLF SPARKLE MIDGE

Hook:	#15-19 TMC 102Y
Thread:	Black 8/0-14/0 UNI-Thread
Shuck/back:	Clear poly Sparkle Emerger Yarn
Body:	Black Superfine Dubbing and tan Ice Dub, mixed
Hackle:	Light to dark dun or grizzly

Jerry Criss offers this fly as a good searching pattern when midge emergence seems slow, but midges are on the water. He suggests that light or dark dun can be substituted for the grizzly hackle and that callibaetis Ice Dub for the body makes an effective variation. He fishes this pattern dry or allows it to sink just below the surface. Fish often seem to prefer the near-surface presentation.

CHAPTER 11

VERTEBRATES

Swimming vertebrates were addressed in our chapter on streamers. But these are not the only vertebrates available to salmonids. We look at patterns for some here, and out of necessity we will jump from life form to life form, warm-blooded and cold-blooded, flying, walking, or crawling.

These life forms are strictly targets for large salmonids, and many experienced fly fishers have observed encounters between a vertebrate and a large salmonid. In my entry years of fly fishing, René Harrop and Mike Lawson suggested I try what was known in those days as the Railroad Ranch waters of the Henry's Fork. This was in the mid-1970s when one would commonly see no more than five or six other anglers there the entire day. Armed with suggestions from the two anglers that remain the most informative for those waters, I walked in from Last Chance about a mile to where the river bends from flowing west to south and braids into channels around a few islands. It was a bright early-July day, and I looked forward to encountering the legendary rainbows.

Sure enough, following recommendations that Mike and René offered for presenting Flavs and PMDs, I had some success. One of those landed was a burly hen of around 20 inches. I do not recall what pattern fooled her, but while reviving her, I felt peculiar lumps along the sides of her belly. Leaving her in the water, I eventually looked into her mouth to observe the tail of a small snake protruding from her gullet. With suppressed glee I wondered why my two friends had not suggested a snake pattern! The hen rainbow I released that July day in the 1970s was only the first I have encountered having ingested a snake. The riparian zone around the river in Harriman State Park is lush with wildlife, invertebrate and vertebrate. It is just another example of the life-rich surroundings common to waters in the Greater Yellowstone Area.

Meadow voles, frogs, toads, fledgling birds, even baby waterfowl can be targeted by very large salmonids. There are the stories of fledgling swallows falling out of cliffside nesting burrows along the Gallatin and Yellowstone Rivers and the South Fork reach of the Snake River only to be gathered by huge brown trout. A hair mouse pattern skittered along the surface of beaver ponds inhabited by huge brown trout has worked wonders for me over the years when invertebrate patterns fail to produce. Again, back on the Harriman reach of the Henry's Fork at twilight sometime during the early 1980s, a hair mouse would have done the same for me except for the parting of an 8-pound-test tippet. We all have considered presenting frog patterns along slow-moving or stillwaters where bankside vegetation provides cover and food for frogs.

Certainly not many salmonids are encountered on presenting patterns representing vertebrates, but when one is done so properly, there is likelihood that it can result in the fish of the year, if not a fish of a lifetime. So yes and by all means, pay attention to that good advice available with respect to which aquatic insect or annelid or streamer pattern to use during visits. Stock up on those patterns because they are what will provide success. But it is the fly fisher with foresight who leaves room for a frog, hair mouse, or the like in his or her fly box if large salmonids inhabit the waters to be visited.

CHEEKY MOUSE

Hook:	#2-6 TMC 5263
Thread:	Black 6/0 UNI-Thread
Tail:	Gray Ultra Chenille
Back:	Gray Evazote Sheet Foam $^3/_{16}$-inch thick
Body:	Natural pine squirrel Zonker Strip
Cheeks:	Gray Rainy's high-density Cross-Link Sheet Foam, 1.5X hook shank width, 2-mm thick

To create this pattern by Nick Jones, cut point at rear of Evazote Foam and bevel edges. Gently buff out bevel with flame from a butane lighter. With thread wraps pinch Cross-Link Foam on either side along rear half of shank. Remainder protrudes forward on either side of hook. Tie in tail. Tie in Evazote shellback strip point, beveled side down, on top of bend and rear portion of shank. Compress wraps, tie in stripped end of pine squirrel strip at top of bend. Spiral strip forward, with touching wraps, to an eighth-inch behind eye. Form shellback tied in forward at same point and trim. Fold Cross-Link Foam back on either side of hook and tie in at hook eye to form cheeks. Singe tail with lighter. Want a mouse pattern that floats forever? Here it is!

CHICK

Hook:	#2-6 Daiichi 1720
Thread:	Black GSP
Tail:	Tip of speckled Brahma hen hackle
Underbody:	Spun and trimmed white deer hair
Back:	Black deer hair
Wings:	Pair of speckled Brahma hen hackle per side
Head:	Spun and trimmed black deer hair
Eyes:	Yellow holographic dome eyes

Swallows nest in high soil banks along certain waters in the area. In the canyon of the South Fork reach of the Snake River, brown trout of legendary size wait for helpless swallow chicks to fall into the water. The same nests can be seen on the cut benches of the Madison River in the Beaver Meadows and on Blackfoot River Reservoir. Casting one of these patterns by the author on the water to simulate a fallen chick struggling in the water may not get you many fish, but it may get you the catch of the season.

GATOR FROG

Hook:	#2-6 Mustad 33903
Thread:	Black 70-denier UTC Ultra Thread

Hind legs:	Two dyed olive grizzly hen hackles on either side
Rear skirt:	Dyed olive grizzly schlappen
Trailing bubbles:	Olive Krystal Flash
Body:	Balsa wood carved to shape, primed, airbrushed gray with black muzzle and finish coating applied
Eyes:	Doll eyes
Cement/filler:	Fast-drying epoxy

This is Gerry "Randy" Randolph's signature fly. Randy forms the body with a mounting slot off the hook and attaches and bonds it to the hook shank with epoxy. Holes are drilled to place the eyes, and the form is sanded, primed, and painted. Lastly, the hind legs, tail, trailing bubbles, and rear skirt are tied on, and the eyes cemented in place and coated with epoxy. Frogs are common inhabitants around the weeded shorelines of stillwaters and beaver ponds. Imitations of frogs properly presented are certain to bring interest from large salmonids.

GRAY BALSA MOUSE

Hook:	#2-6 Mustad 33903
Thread:	Black 70-denier UTC
Tail:	Silver badger saddle pair, Flashabou fibers
Hind legs:	Light dun saddle
Body:	Balsa wood carved to shape, primed, airbrushed gray with black muzzle and finish coating applied
Ears:	Grizzly hackle tips stiffened with nail polish
Eyes:	Doll eyes
Whiskers:	Black saddle

Balsa wood used for making mice has the advantage of durability and consistent buoyancy over hollow hair

versions. Of course, finishing balsa versions is more time-consuming. Randy Randolph forms the body with a mounting slot off the hook and attaches and bonds it to the hook shank with epoxy. Holes are drilled for the ears, and the form is sanded, primed, and painted. Lastly, the tail and whiskers are tied on and the eyes and ears cemented in place. Finally comes a trip to a beaver pond or a meadow stream such as Slough Creek or Bechler River.

RABBIT RAT

Hook:	#4 TMC 9395
Thread:	Gray GSP 75
Tail:	Rabbit strip
Underbody:	6-mm closed-cell foam block
Body:	Rabbit spun in a wire loop
Head:	Deer hair spun and clipped to shape

Rabbit fur may be known for absorbing water, but it sure makes a realistic mouse. So Shawn Bostic trims a closed-cell foam block to shape and cements it to the hook shank as a buoyant base for spinning rabbit fur. No problems with sinking now! Mice are residents of stream banks and shorelines. Big cruising salmonids are opportunistic feeders, and if they are aware of a mouse or vole in the water, they will not pass it up. Particularly in the evenings, a mouse pattern skittered close to a shoreline might bring out a fish of the year.

SNAKE

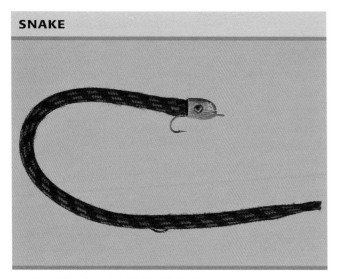

Front hook:	#8-12 Daiichi 1120
Connection:	Fifteen-pound test monofilament tippet material
Rear hook:	#8-12 Daiichi 1120
Head:	Balsa wood carved to shape, primed, airbrushed or marking penned olive, and lacquered to finish
Eyes:	Doll eyes
Body:	Shoelace sheath cut to length

To create this pattern by the author, form the head with a mounting slot along the bottom surface. Attach and bond it with epoxy to the hook shank. Drill holes to place the eyes with epoxy. Sand to shape, prime, then paint the head. Push one end of the tippet through the shoelace sheath near rear end. Knot a hook onto rear end of the monofilament, then knot the other end of tippet to the front hook, holding the snake head. Trim excess tippet. Bond the body to rear of the head using epoxy. Pull the rear portion and saturate with epoxy to form a tapered tail. This is necessarily a big fish fly. Dress the body to help it float, and retrieve it with a wiggly motion to simulate a swimming snake.

Contributing Tiers

The Greater Yellowstone Area is the top destination in this country for the fly-fishing world. Fly tiers worlwide strive to offer patterns for all seasons and all waters here. Note that many reside outside the Greater Yellowstone Area.

Boots Allen, Jackson, Wyoming
Todd Allen, Ashton, Idaho
Mike Andreasen, Bountiful, Utah
Doug Andres, Portland, Oregon
John Arnold, Craig, Montana
Jim Aubrey, Durango, Colorado
Tom Banyas, Pocatello, Idaho
Gary Barnes, Ririe, Idaho
Pat Barnes, West Yellowstone, Montana (deceased)
Al Beatty, Boise, Idaho (1999 Buszek Award recipient)
Gretchen Beatty, Boise, Idaho
Brad Befus, Woodbury, Minnesota
Elden Berrett, Blackfoot, Idaho
Don Bishop, Belgrade, Montana
Ken Bitton, Idaho Falls, Idaho
Phil Blomquist, Irwin, Idaho (deceased)
Tim Blount, Burns, Oregon
Shawn Bostic, Idaho Falls, Idaho
Paul Bowen, Rexburg, Idaho
Dave Brackett Jackson, Wyoming
Charlie Brooks West Yellowstone, Montana (deceased)
Jay Buchner, Jackson, Wyoming
Lori Burchinal, Vernal, Utah
Dr. Joe Burke, Jackson, Wyoming
Ken Burkholder, Boise, Idaho
Ben Byng, Tracy, California
Del Canty, Delta Colorado
Scotty Chapman, Gardiner, Montana (deceased)
Howard Cole, Jackson, Wyoming
Chuck Collins, Pocatello, Idaho

LeRoy Cook, Idaho Falls, Idaho
Jerry Criss, LaPine, Oregon
Tom Cundith, Pleasant Hill, California
Logan Cutts, Roseburg, Oregon
Patrick Daigle, Cameron, Montana
Dan Delekta, Cameron, Montana
Jack Dennis, Jackson, Wyoming
Will Dornan, Kelly, Wyoming
Chuck Echer, Pollock Pines, California (1993 Buszek Award Recipent, deceased)
Dennie Edwards, Idaho Falls, Idaho
Nick English, Bozeman, Montana
Ron English, McAllister, Montana
Everet Evans, Rexburg, Idaho

Brenda's trophy trout. PHOTO COURTESY OF DAVE PACE.

Bill Fenstermaker, Mora, New Mexico
Steven Fernandez, Venice, California (2012 Buszek
    Award Recipent)
Jim Fisher, Jefferson, Oregon
Russ Forney, Beulah, Wyoming
Kieran Frye, Mt. Pleasant, Pennsylvania
Jimmy Gabettas, Idaho Falls, Idaho
Pat Gaffney, Island Park, Idaho
Kelly Galloup, Cameron, Montana
Jack Gartside, Boston, Massachusetts (deceased)
Dan Gates, West Jordan, Utah
Doug Gibson, Newdale, Idaho
Kelly Glissmeyer, Rigby, Idaho
Will Godfrey, Lewiston, Idaho
Buck Goodrich, Shelley, Idaho
Dave Hamilton, Grants Pass, Oregon
Tom Harman, Dillon, Montana (deceased)
René Harrop, St. Anthony, Idaho

Chris Helm, Toledo, Ohio (2004 Buszek Award recipient)
Kent Henderson, Lewiston, Idaho
Don Heyden, Bozeman, Montana
Jim Hickey, Jackson, Wyoming
Ron Hicks, Twin Falls, Idaho
Spencer Higa, Provo, Utah
Marty Howard, Heber City, Utah
John Hudgens, Bozeman, Montana
Hugh Huntley, Billings, Montana
LeRoy Hyatt, Lewiston, Idaho
Misako Ishimura, Lakeview, Arkansas
Nelson Ishiyama, Island Park, Idaho
Bob Jacklin, West Yellowstone, Montana (2000 Buszek
    Award recipient)
Bruce James, Jackson, Wyoming
Charles Jardine, United Kingdom
Frank Johnson, Sheridan, Wyoming
Jim Johnson, Big Fork, Montana

Red Rock Creek in Montana's Centennial Valley. PHOTO COURTESY OF LEROY COOK.

Nick Jones, Hyrum, Utah
Stefanie Jones, Hyrum, Utah
Merne Judson, Gunnison, Colorado
John Kimura, Alturas, California
Tim King, Providence, Utah
Doug Kinney, Idaho Falls, Idaho
Buddy Knight, Sandy, Utah
Doug Korn, Hilton, New York
Todd Lanning, Idaho Falls, Idaho
Paul Lauchle, Jackson, Wyoming
Mike Lawson, St. Anthony, Idaho
Bob Lay, Helena, Montana
Vic Loiselle, Pocatello, Idaho
Wayne Luallen, Visalia, California (1991 Buszek Award
    recipient)
Clark Lucas, New Meadows, Idaho
Mark MacLeod, Bozeman, Montana
Kuni Masuda, Vancouver, Washington
Craig Mathews, West Yellowstone, Montana
Bucky McCormick, West Yellowstone, Montana
Doug McKnight, Livingston, Montana
Marty McLellan, Idaho Falls, Idaho
Greg Messel, Twin Bridges, Montana
Matt Minch, Gardiner, Montana
Wade Moulton, Vernal, Utah
Walt Mueller Jr., Morrison, Colorado
Richard Munoz, Delta, Colorado
Sylvester Nemes, Bozeman, Montana (deceased)
John Newbury, Chewelah, Washington (2009 Buszek
    Award recipient)
Marvin Nolte, Bar Nunn, Wyoming (1995 Buszek Award
    recipient)
Rowan Nyman, West Yellowstone, Montana
Devin Olsen, Fort Collins, Colorado
Clayton Paddie, Ennis, Montana
Rob Parkins, Victor, Idaho
Richard Parks, Gardiner, Montana
Josh Peavler, Afton, Wyoming
Fred Petersen, Idaho Falls, Idaho
Steve Potter, Tracy, California
Federico Prato, Argentina
Gerry "Randy" Randolph, Idaho Falls, Idaho
Dandy Reiner, Livingston, Montana
Dean Reiner, Livingston, Montana
Steven Rendle, Bozeman, Montana

Harley Reno, Idaho Falls, Idaho
Al Ritt, Longmont, Colorado
Buz Roach, Rigby, Idaho
Sumie Sakamaki, Rexburg, Idaho
Scott Sanchez, Jackson, Wyoming (2010 Buszek Award
    recipient)
Bill Schiess, Rexburg, Idaho
Willie Self, Churchill, Montana
Fred Sica, Shelley, Idaho
Kit Seaton, Billings, Montana
Michael Snody, Halifax, Pennsylvania
Bruce Staples, Idaho Falls, Idaho (2001 Buszek Award
    recipient)
Robert Starck, Rigby, Idaho
R. L. "Stew" Stewart, Shingletown, California
Aaron Stich, Heber City, Utah
Paul Stimpson, Ogden, Utah
Arrick Swanson, West Yellowstone, Montana
Rick Takahashi, Fort Collins, Colorado
John Taylor, Pocatello, Idaho
Merrill Tea, Lewisville, Idaho
Ed Thomas, Bozeman, Montana
Roger Thompson, Pocatello, Idaho
Ward Thompson, Ennis, Montana
Jerry Toft, Fruita, Colorado
Tim Tollett, Dillon, Montana
Joni Tomich, Salt Lake City, Utah
Bob Trowbridge, Providence, Utah
Branden Tueller, Spring Creek, Nevada
Guy Turck, Sedona, Arizona
Phil Turck, McAllister, Montana
Scott Urbanski, Lander, Wyoming
Tim Wade, Cody, Wyoming
John Way, Ennis, Montana
Hans Weilenmann, The Netherlands
Walter Weise, Gardiner, Montana
Dave Whitlock, Welling, Oklahoma (1972 Buszek Award
    recipient)
Chris Williams, Boise, Idaho
Jeanne Williams, Ennis, Montana
Linda Windels, Idaho Falls, Idaho
Callan Wink, Livingston, Montana
Tim Woodard, Idaho Falls, Idaho
Allan Woolley, Idaho Falls, Idaho
Deward Yocum, Los Lunas, New Mexico

Bibliography

Beatty, Al and Gretchen. *LaFontaine's Legacy: The Last Flies From an American Master.* Guilford, CT: Lyons Press, 2008. ISBN 978-1-59921-275-3.

Bergman, Ray. *Trout.* New York: Alfred Knopf, 1981. ISBN 0-394-49957-3.

Hafele, Rick, and Dave Hughes. *The Complete Book of Western Hatches.* Portland OR: Frank Amato Publications, 1981. ISBN 0-936608-12-9.

Harrop, René. *Learning from the Water.* Mechanicsburg, PA: Stackpole Books, 2010. ISBN 978-0-8117-0579-0.

LaFontaine, Gary. *Caddisflies.* New York: Nick Lyons Books, 1981. ISBN 0-87691-350-8.

Lawson, Mike. *Spring Creeks.* Mechanicsburg, PA: Stackpole Books, 2003. ISBN 0-8117-0068-2.

Staples, Bruce. *Trout Country Flies.* Portland, OR: Frank Amato Publications, 2002. ISBN 1-57188-248-0.

Swisher, Doug, and Carl Richards. *Selective Trout.* New York: Crown Publishers, 1972. Lib. Of Congress Cat. Card 78-147342.

Madison River and Three Dollar Bridge

Index